Area Activity Analysis

Other McGraw-Hill Books by H. James Harrington

- *The Improvement Process: How America's Leading Companies Improve Quality* (1987)
- *Business Process Improvement: The Breakthrough Strategy for Total Quality, Productivity, and Competitiveness* (1991)
- *Total Improvement Management: The Next Generation in Performance Improvement,* written with James S. Harrington (1995)
- *High Performance Benchmarking: 20 Steps to Success,* written with James S. Harrington (1996)
- *The Complete Benchmarking Implementation Guide—Total Benchmarking Management* (1996)
- *ISO 9000 and Beyond—From Compliance to Performance Improvement* (1997)
- *Business Process Improvement Workbook,* written with Erik K. C. Esseling and Harm van Nimwegen (1997)
- *The Creativity Toolkit—Provoking Creativity in Individuals and Organizations,* written with Glen D. Hoffherr and Robert P. Reid, Jr. (1998)
- *Statistical Analysis Simplified—The Easy-to-Understand Guide to SPC and Data Analysis,* written with Glen D. Hoffherr and Robert P. Reid, Jr. (1998)
- *Reliability Simplified—Going Beyond Quality to Keep Customers for Life,* written with Les Anderson (1998)

Area Activity Analysis

Aligning Work Activities and Measurements to Enhance Business Performance

H. James Harrington

Glen D. Hoffherr

Robert P. Reid, Jr.

McGraw-Hill

New York San Francisco Washington, D.C. Auckland Bogotá
Caracas Lisbon London Madrid Mexico City Milan
Montreal New Delhi San Juan Singapore
Sydney Tokyo Toronto

McGraw-Hill

A Division of The ***McGraw-Hill*** *Companies*

1 2 3 4 5 6 7 8 9 0 DOC/DOC 9 0 1 0 9 8 7 6

P/N 027049-X
PART OF
ISBN: 0-07-134703-8

Library of Congress Cataloging-in-Publication Data

Harrington, H. J. (H. James)
Area activity analysis : aligning work activities and measurements to enhance business performance / H. James Harrington, Glen D. Hoffherr, Robert P. Reid, Jr.
p. cm.—(Harrington's performance improvement series)
Includes index.
ISBN 0-07-027049-X
1. Total quality management. 2. Industrial productivity. I. Hoffherr, Glen D. II. Reid, Robert P. III. Title. IV. Series.
HD62.15.H3694 1998
658.4′013—dc21 98-24214
CIP

The sponsoring editor for this book was Roger Marsh. The editing supervisor was John M. Morriss and the production supervisor was Suzanne W. B. Rapcavage. Production was managed by John Woods, CWL Publishing Enterprises, Madison, WI. It was designed and composed at Impressions Book and Journal Services, Inc., Madison, WI.

Contents

About the Series

Area Activity Analysis is one title in McGraw-Hill's *Harrington's Performance Improvement Series.* Each of the products in this series is a complete communication system that includes a book and a support CD-ROM. The series is designed to meet an organization's need to understand the most useful approaches now available to bring about improvements in organizational performance as measured by

- Return on assets
- Value-added per employee
- Customer satisfaction

Each title in the series is easy to read, view, and listen to. It has a user-friendly style designed to reach employees at all levels of an organization. Our goal is to present complex methodologies in a way that is simple but not simplistic. The following are other subjects covered in the communication systems in this series:

- Statistical process controls
- Process redesign
- Process reengineering
- Establishing a balance scorecard
- Reliability analysis
- Fostering teamwork
- Simulation modeling
- Rewards and recognition
- Managing the change process

Communication systems already released are

- The Creativity Toolkit—Provoking Creativity in Individuals and Organizations

- ▶ Statistical Analysis Simplified—the Easy-to-Understand Guide to SPC and Data Analysis
- ▶ Reliability Simplified

We believe that thc products in this series will provide an effective way to learn about these practices as well as a training tool for use in any type of organization. The series design features a set of icons that are placed in the margins that call your attention to different points. Use these icons to guide your reading and study

It is our hope that you will find this series of Performance Improvement Management books enjoyable and useful.

H. James Harrington
Principal, Ernst & Young LLP
International Quality Advisor
(408) 947-6587

About the Authors

Dr. H. James Harrington is one of the world's quality system gurus with more than 45 years of experience. He has been involved in developing quality management systems in Europe, South America, North America, and Asia. He currently serves as a principal with Ernst & Young LLP and is their international quality advisor. He is also chairman of Emergence Technology Ltd., a high-tech software and hardware manufacturer and developer.

Before joining Ernst & Young LLP, he was president of the consulting firm Harrington, Hurd, and Rieker. He was a senior engineer and project manager for IBM, and for almost 40 years, he worked in quality function. He was chairman and president of the prestigious International Academy for Quality and the American Society for Quality Control. He has released a series of videos and CD ROM programs that cover ISO 9000 and QS-9000. He has also authored a computer program on benchmarking, plus members' video tapes on performance improvement. He has written ten books on performance improvement and hundreds of technical reports.

The Harrington/Ishikawa Medal was named after him in recognition of his support to developing nations in implementing quality systems. The Harrington/Neron Medal was also named after him to recognize his contribution to the quality movement in Canada. China named him their Honorary Quality Advisor, and he was elected into the Singapore Productivity Hall of Fame. He has been elected honorary member of seven quality professional societies and has received numerous awards and medals for his work in the quality field, including the 1996 Lancaster Award from ASQC in recognition of his work to further the quality movement internationally.

Glen D. Hoffherr is a senior consultant for James Martin Government Consulting. He has spent over twenty years in management in the high-technology industry. For the last eight years he has been a consultant and author focusing on strategic planning, organizational design, change management, and creative decision making.

He has authored, co-authored, or been a contributing author to more than fifteen books and numerous magazine articles. He is an animated, interesting, and entertaining speaker who has lectured at national and international conferences on five continents and at numerous colleges and universities around the world.

He has worked with organizations in many fields including local, state, and national government, foreign governments, telecommunications, high technology, service, manufacturing, health care, and software.

Robert P. Reid, Jr., is a dynamic and innovative presenter, with over thirty years experience as an educator, author, speaker, and organizational developer. Reid has written extensively in the areas of organizational change management, creative thinking, and systems design. He has worked with more than one hundred major organizations on six continents and has conducted courses and seminars at seventeen universities. His ability to communicate complex systems issues in a clear nonthreatening fashion is recognized worldwide.

I walk down the street.
There is a deep hole in the sidewalk.
I fall in.

I am lost . . . I am hopeless.
It isn't my fault.
It takes forever to find a way out.

I walk down the same street.
There is a deep hole in the sidewalk.
I pretend I don't see it.
I fall in again.
I can't believe I'm in the same place.
But it isn't my fault.
It still takes a long time to get out.

I walk down the same street.
There is a deep hole in the sidewalk.
I see it is there.
I still fall in . . . it's a habit.
My eyes are open.
I know where I am.
It is my fault.
I get out immediately.

I walk down the same street.
There is a deep hole in the sidewalk.
I walk around it.

I walk down another street.

—*Tibetan Book of the Living and the Dead*

Dedication

My father passed away this past year. His death has heightened my awareness of all the good things that make up our lives: The squirrel that is sitting on a branch just outside of my window eating a walnut; my dog, Angel, who is curled up around my feet so warm and soft; the pink and white geranium that dances in the gentle breeze from the hanging basket, silhouetted against the light blue sky; my son, Jim, and his wife, Leslie, who take the time from their very busy day to stop by and give me a loving hug; the fact that I could get up this morning and go to work with interesting, happy people. For all this and more I am grateful. But most of all, I thank my Lord for providing me with my wife, Marguerite. She makes my joy more joyful and my cares less heavy. She truly is the frosting on my cake. For her love and dedication to making my life the best that it can be, I dedicate this book to her.

Preface

Without Satisfied Employees, You Can't Have Satisfied Customers

As viewed by the employees, the organization chart often looks like everyone above them exists just to generate work for them, and all that management wants from them is their complete discipline.

Since the early 1960s, management has unsuccessfully chased after the elusive pot of gold at the end of the rainbow called "Internal Supplier/Customer Relationships." This concept is a very sound and relatively simple one, but it is extremely difficult to implement and maintain. Theoretically, treating the person who receives your output the same as you would treat an external customer is relatively straightforward. Unfortunately, people are less inclined to react to a person who is not paying for their output than to individuals who show the value they place on their output by paying directly for it.

To find an organization that has effectively implemented the internal customer concept is a lot like looking for the Holy Grail. You know it should exist, but no one has been able to find it. Well, here comes Indiana Jones (in the form of H. James Harrington, not Harrison Ford) to the rescue with a treasure map for you called Area Activity Analysis (**AAA**). Now, at long last, a methodology has been developed to cement these internal customer relationships while also developing effective performance measurement systems that optimize the value-added content of each individual's activities.

Area Activity Analysis is a methodology designed to establish agreed-to, understandable efficiency and effectiveness measurement systems and communication links throughout the organization. The methodology consists of

a seven-phase process. Only the last phase, Continuous Improvement, is a continuous process; the first six phases of the **AAA** process usually have fixed start and end points. These six phases are normally treated as a project and are included in the organization's strategic business plan. This by no means indicates that the measurements and the associated requirements are developed and not updated on a regular basis.

We hear a great deal these days about the importance of developing the internal customer/supplier relationship within our organizations. No matter where you go, people profess to be concerned about satisfying their internal customers. Every quality training program teaches it, every book on quality preaches it, and clearly most people today truly believe internal customer satisfaction is critical to business success. The truth of the matter is that it is very difficult for any organization to have good external customer satisfaction unless it has excellent internal customer satisfaction.

I recently flew from San Francisco to Rio de Janeiro, with a stop in Miami. During the stopover in Miami, we had to leave the plane but were told that we could leave our personal items on board. When I returned 40 minutes later, my business papers and the book I was reading were gone. I notified the flight attendant immediately. She told me that she would contact the ground crew and have them return my papers to me right away. So began my horror story of lack of concern for both the internal and external customer.

After the plane took off, another attendant came to me because he was told I had a problem; he wanted to understand it so he could get it corrected. I explained the problem once again. He indicated it was too late to do anything about it at that time but he would contact the ground crew in Miami to have them send my things on the next plane. He also asked me to contact lost luggage when I got to Rio and fill out the necessary paperwork, which I did. I will relate only a small part of this experience to highlight why internal customer satisfaction is so important to external customer satisfaction, skipping things like the ground crew and the lost luggage people in Rio who did not react, the complete lack of concern by the airline's U.S. headquarters, and so forth. At the hotel where I was staying in Rio, this U.S.-based airline had a ticket office. I contacted a young lady in this office, and she tried to help me with my problem. After trying for three days, she wrote me a letter stating that she had done everything that she could. She had called her manager who had called Miami three times, but Miami had not returned their calls. She had sent two faxes herself, but Miami had not answered her faxes. She had even called Miami, which she was not allowed to do, with no results. She documented in her letter that she tried everything she could, but her company in Miami would not react in any way to the problem, and if I wanted to do anything further I was on my own. She provided me with two phone numbers for lost and found and for lost luggage at her airline in Miami. It is hard for me to believe that any employee would get so upset with the organization that she works for that she would send a letter to a customer explaining that her organization would not react to an external customer problem and to inquiries from one of their own employees.

I am a 2,000,000+ mile flier with this particular airline and, as hard as I tried, I could not get any better reaction. I even had trouble getting my problem addressed when I got back to the United States. After making many unsuccessful calls to the airline's Miami office, their frequent flier 800 number, and their U.S. headquarters, I tried to contact the airline's quality manager by phone, as a last resort, but was unable to get his phone number. I wrote a letter to the airline's vice president of operations in which I asked him what he could do to correct the organization's problems. I specifically requested that they take action to correct their process, not send me free tickets. This resulted in a returned phone call, but I still didn't get a satisfactory answer. When the representative for the vice president of operations contacted me, I asked about the phone system. I was told that the phone system was designed purposely to keep customers from bothering important people within the organization. They wanted to give me a free upgrade on my next flight.

I wanted them to correct their processes so that another customer would not be subjected to the many problems I had experienced. As hard as I tried, they would not commit to changing their processes in any way to prevent the original problem from recurring or to improve their internal customer relationships and responsiveness. And of course, I never did get my papers back. *The airline I am discussing is one of the three biggest airlines in the world.*

Is this a one-of-a-kind story? No, not really. I can give you many more examples, from food chains to the big three auto manufacturers. Everyone talks about internal customers and meeting their needs, but everywhere we go, we find employees that are all but ready to give up on their organization because no one seems to care about what is going on within the organization.

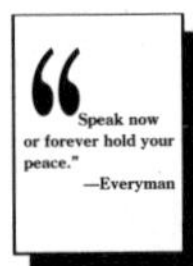

If you don't keep your internal customers enthusiastic about the service they receive, they will not provide adequate service to the external customers.

—KEN LOMAX, LOMAX CONSULTING GROUP

—H. James Harrington

Acknowledgments

I started this book in 1987 and now, 10 years later, it is ready for you. Along the way, many people have worked with me to develop and refine the concept. I know that I will miss a few of these individuals who contributed so much to this concept. So please forgive me if your name is missing.

In the late 1980s, Norm Howery helped me develop a training program and manual for **AAA**. In 1995, Ted Cocheu pitched in to help me upgrade the training manual into a book. In between, many of my colleagues and clients added depth and content to this approach. The experience gained by consultants such as Dave Farrell and Ken Lomax in using **AAA** as they serviced their clients provided a major contribution to the development and improvement of the methodology as it is documented in this book.

I would particularly like to acknowledge the excellent work and effort put in by Loria Kutch, who converted and edited endless hours of dictation into this final product. John Woods and Bob Magnan of CWL Publishing Enterprises have worked closely with me in giving the manuscript one final review and managing the production, turning it into the book you now hold. I would also like to acknowledge the effort put forth by the personnel at SystemCorp in preparing the CD ROM. Mahmoud Afshar, who brought the storyboard to life, and Ari Kugler, who provided the resources to create the CD ROM free of charge. And last, but not least, Jaime Benchimol who managed and followed the process that created the CD ROM.

I would be remiss if, as always, I did not acknowledge the excellent contribution my wife, Marguerite, made to the book by proofreading the manuscript and challenging my thinking.

—H. James Harrington

Area Activity Analysis

Introduction

**Internal Supplier/Customer Relationships:
The Next Frontier of Quality Improvement**

Introduction

Most organizations talk about improving internal customer satisfaction but do little to change the way they function. As soon as you ask people what they are actually doing to understand, plan for, and meet their internal customers' requirements, the conversation gets very quiet. Extending the concept of customers and suppliers to our relationships with one another within our organizations represents the next frontier of quality improvement. We are overdue to stop talking about the concept of internal customers and start doing something about improving this internal supplier/customer relationship.

The Truth about Teams

Another overstated theme, heard everywhere from local government to high-technology firms and from the boardroom to the boiler room, is teamwork. As soon as two people in the company cafeteria sit down to have a cup of coffee and talk about the weekend, they are somehow a team. People say they work on all sorts of teams, from natural work teams to cross-functional project teams. Too often, teams are somehow looked at as a group of people meeting together to solve a problem, but that is only a small part of what a team is. Organizations can have very effective teams that never discuss or solve a problem. As Robert Haas of Levi Strauss put it, "I see us moving toward a team-oriented, multiskilled environment in which the team takes on many of the supervisor's and trainer's tasks. If you combine that with some sort of gain sharing, you probably will have a much more productive plant with higher employee satisfaction and commitment."

The truth about teams, however, is much the same as with internal customer satisfaction. Simply getting people together once a week for a staff meeting, project status review, or to solve problems does not make a group function as a team.

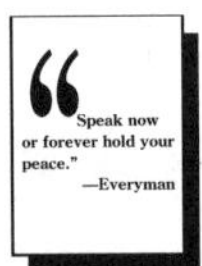

Just putting a bunch of people in a room together does not a team make.
—HOWARD AND SHELLEY GITLOW[1]

Although billions of dollars have been spent on team skills and problem-solving training, and billions of hours of lost productivity have been racked up attending team meetings, the return on investment in many cases has been inadequate to fund the continuation of the programs. Teams were formed, provided with tools, and told to go out and slay the dragon called "waste" without understanding where to look for the dragon or how to recognize it when they saw it. If they are lucky enough to find a dragon, they slay it and then keep going, trying to find another dragon, seldom taking the time to find the dragon's eggs and destroy them also. Is it any wonder, then, that these teams are surprised a year or two later to find out that there are three dragons where there used to be just one? This type of operation results in teams spending their valuable time reshuffling the deck chairs on the Titanic.

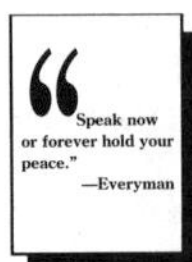

Performance .. is the primary objective while a team remains the means, not the end. Being part of a team or a small group that provides security, acceptance, and a sense of belonging is a basic need for most human beings.
—JOHN KATZENBACH AND DOUGLAS SMITH[2]

CUT R&D SPENDING!
GET BETTER SUPPLIES!
INCREASE IMPORT TAX!
RELEASE AN ERROR-FREE STANDARD!
BUY BUILT IN THE USA!
MOTIVATE THE EMPLOYEES!
PAY OFF EMPLOYEES!
TITANIC LOSS OF MARKET

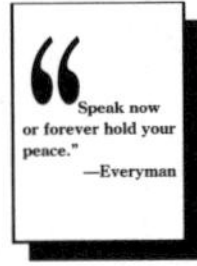

Few incentives are more powerful than membership in a small group engaged in a common task, sharing the risks of defeat and the potential rewards of victory.

—ROBERT B. REICH[3]

There is a big difference between teams and teamwork. You can have a team, but have little teamwork going on among the team members. A bowling team is a good example. On the other hand, you can have teamwork without having a formal team. The chat centers on the Internet are good examples. Let's define three key terms. First we will look at four definitions for the word "team," in the dictionary's preferred order.

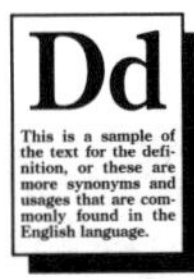

Team (1) Two or more draft animals harnessed to a vehicle or farm implement. (Note: This sounds like the way we worked at the beginning of the 1900s.) (2) A vehicle along with the animal or animals harnessed to it. (Note: People are animals and most of us are harnessed to our work, so we must be a team.) (3) A group of players on the same side in a game. (Note: This is a better definition, but business today is not a game and we cannot afford to have employees playing at being businessmen. To be successful, all the teams within an organization must be on the same side.) (4) Any group organized to work together. (Note: This is a definition we can live with. The key words are "work together" not "meet once in a while to review status or to solve problems.")

A **teamster** is a person who drives a team. (Note: In a team environment, all of our managers should be called "teamsters" instead of "managers" or "coaches.")

Teamwork is the cooperative effort by the members of a team to achieve a common goal. (Note: This is what we are after in business today. The key words are "cooperative effort" and "common goal." Meetings will not result in teamwork. Training and problem solving will not result in teamwork. Teams are not the answer. Teamwork is the key to meeting stakeholders' requirements.)

John Oakland put it this way, "Teamwork throughout any organization is an essential component of the implementation of TQM for it builds up trust, improves communication and develops independence."[4] William R. Hewlett and David Packard in their 1980 book, *The HP Way*, stated, "In the last analysis, [the HP way] is a feeling that everyone is part of a team, and that team is HP."[5] This thought was reinforced by Stephen Murgatroyd and Colin Morgan in their 1993 book, *Total Quality Management and the School,* where they wrote, "No team is an island within an organization."[6]

Teams are an essential part of any organization, not just for the problems they solve but more importantly for how a team-oriented organization evolves.

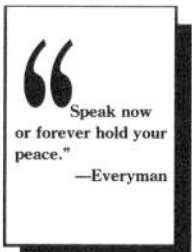

Teams offer greater participation, challenge, and feelings of accomplishment. Organizations with teams will attract and retain the best people. The others will have to do without.

—RICHARD S. WELLINS, WILLIAM C. BYHAM, AND JEANNE M. WILSON[7]

The Two Basic Types of Teams

In business, one of the most important things management can do is to develop an environment in which teamwork flourishes. Of secondary importance is developing an organizational structure that consists of effective and efficient natural work teams. The third is to develop a system that enables project (often cross-functional) teams to operate effectively.

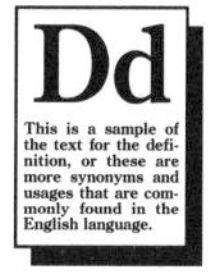

Natural work team (NWT), or natural work group (NWG)—a group of people who are assigned to work together and report to the same manager or supervisor. AAA projects are implemented by natural work teams.

There is often a big difference between a committee and a NWT. The NWT must work together much better because the NWT will spend much more time together for a much longer time. A committee is often a group of unwilling individuals, chosen from the unfit, to do the unnecessary, for self-serving reasons. A NWT, on the other hand, must be a group of people with common interests that benefit from working together by growing their talents and learning from each other, with the objective of increasing their combined value to the organization and their customers.

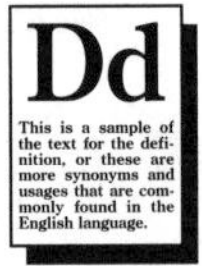

Project teams are groups of people who are temporarily assigned or volunteer to work together to accomplish a short-term objective or to solve a specific problem. These teams may be made up of individuals from different NWTs or from one NWT. Project teams are often called problem-solving teams or cross-functional teams. They have a specific goal to accomplish and are disbanded when this goal is accomplished. (Examples: release a new product, make a sale, solve a problem, install new equipment, complete a study, etc.)

Why Area Activity Analysis (AAA)?

We know that teamwork holds tremendous potential for improving coordination, productivity, quality, and customer satisfaction, but our progress toward realizing that promise has not matched our hopes or our rhetoric. **AAA** is a simple, powerful tool to jump start our progress toward these important but elusive goals—internal customer satisfaction and teamwork. It provides the leverage needed to make the transformation from traditional, hierarchical organizations to empowered NWTs in which people understand where they are going, who their customers are, and how to measure their own performance. It can be effectively used at the NWT or individual employee level.

When most people pick up a book, they wonder if it will help them address a problem they are having. Read the following 13 key operating questions, candidly answering yes or no, to see if you really need to read this book.

	Yes	No
1. Are you sure that everyone in your NWT knows what upper management expects from your NWT?	☐	☐

	Yes	No
2. Are you sure that everyone in your NWT knows what customers expect from your NWT?	☐	☐
3. Are you accomplishing more with less effort?	☐	☐
4. Do you know how much your department improved over the last quarter?	☐	☐
5. Are the other NWTs always satisfied with your NWT's output?	☐	☐
6. Do the other NWTs agree with your NWT's priorities and think it is doing a very good job?	☐	☐
7. Do you have time to do the mountain of minor activities as well as the important things?	☐	☐
8. Do you prevent fires from occurring so that you do not find yourself in a firefighting mode of operation?	☐	☐
9. Do you get what you need from other departments to do your job effectively?	☐	☐
10. Do you get all the resources you need to do your job?	☐	☐
11. Do you know how much of your NWT's efforts are no-value-added?	☐	☐
12. Do all the members of your NWT fully understand the NWT's priorities?	☐	☐
13. Do the members of your NWT fully cooperate with each other?	☐	☐

If you answered no to any of these questions, then the chances are that this really is the book for you. By using the **AAA** methodology, you can design your processes so that you can answer yes to the 13 key operating questions and still have processes that function at peak performance. **AAA** will help you

- ▶ Clarify your NWT's real purpose
- ▶ Identify those time-consuming activities that do and do not support your mission

- Bring better alignment between your mission, activities, and the expectations of your internal and external customers
- Align your employees' activities with the NWT's priorities
- Identify which activities add real value and which can be minimized or eliminated
- Understand how to make the transition from finding and fixing problems to preventing them
- Clarify your requirements for your internal and external suppliers and measure their performance
- Define a comprehensive measurement system for the critical activities that take place within your NWT and set performance standards for each of them
- Put together an implementation plan to make it all happen.

Many of us are frustrated with our inability to accurately put a finger on the source of the problems we are facing every day. We know we work hard, deliver quality output, and drive the people who work for us to do the same. The harder we work and the more we push, the more entrenched the problem seems to get, and employees' morale seems to sink. It is indeed a vicious, negative cycle that can sap the energies of even the most dedicated manager or employee. Here again **AAA** can help.

- **AAA** is a simple but powerful tool that you can begin using immediately to provide clear direction on what may otherwise have become a confusing journey toward improving customer service.
- **AAA** can help you align your energy and resources with your organization's mission in a way that can result in greater effectiveness, efficiency, satisfaction, and teamwork.
- **AAA** serves as a compass to help you find your way through the jungle of overwork that threatens to overtake us all.
- **AAA** helps you sort out the vital few from the trivial many so that you can focus on delivering the value that you, and you alone, can add to your organization and your customers.

We are all under increasing pressures to get things done better and faster with fewer resources. We need to do this in an increasingly complex and confusing work environment. The old work standards no longer apply. Today we operate in an intensely competitive environment. No matter how hard we work, there never seems to be enough time, money, people, or customers. The only thing that there is enough of is competitors.

In response to these pressures, organizations have tried a variety of new programs, tools, and techniques over the last few years. One after another has come and gone, from total quality management and empowered teams, to process reengineering and quality function deployment. The list of potential fixes is as long as our frustrations are many. We have a list of over 420 different improvement tools that have been used in the last 10 years.

All of these approaches can be valid and helpful when applied appropriately in the right situations. The problem has been that large, organization-wide improvement interventions are expensive, take a long time to put in place, and often don't provide much short-term help to most of us who struggle to get the work out every day. We need simple but powerful tools that we can apply within our own work areas to identify opportunities for improvement that are within our immediate abilities to influence.

AAA was designed by busy managers who needed a way to analyze and organize their work areas to get better results from their current resources. As the weeks, months, and years go by, the organizations we manage inevitably take on more and more responsibilities and our jobs get more and more complex. We begin to feel like we're running on a never-ending treadmill while someone keeps turning up the speed.

AAA is unlike any other technique for improving processes, reducing costs, or decreasing turnover. It helps everyone clarify expectations and focus their efforts on the area's mission. **AAA** is the tool that should be used before other interventions such as continuous improvement, total quality management, or reengineering are put into operation.

AAA is an appropriate tool for new or existing areas or departments. It is a tool that will help to ensure that everyone understands their area's mission, customer expectations, what they need to do to succeed, and how to measure their performance.

AAA can be used by managers at any level of the organization to improve the efficiency, effectiveness, and teamwork within their operations. It can be used by an individual unit or as part of a coordinated, organization-wide effort. It can also be used by an individual to improve his or her performance. It can and should be used by every person in the total organization at every level, from the team of employees (vice presidents) who report directly to the president of the organization to the team of maintenance workers who report directly to the maintenance line manager.

We had problems naming this improvement tool. At first in the 1980s we called it Department Activity Analysis, but some managers didn't like that name because they called personnel, engineering, production control, and so forth "departments," while other managers called them "functions." After using the term Department Activity Analysis for about five years, we eliminated the term "department" and the confusion it created, changing the name to Area Activity Analysis (**AAA**), so that it would relate to any organizational NWT at any level within the organization.

The Key Objective

There are many people around the world who think the United States has reached its zenith and is on its way down. For example, Konosuke Matsushita, head of Matsushita Inc., said:

> We are going to win and the industrial West is going to lose out; there's not much you can do about it because the reasons for your failure are within yourselves. Your firms are built on the Taylor Model. Even worse, so are your heads. With your bosses doing the thinking while the workers wield the screwdrivers, you're convinced deep down that this is the right way to run a business. For you, the essence of management is getting the ideas out of the heads of the bosses and into the hands of labor. We are beyond the Taylor Model. Business, we know, is now so complex and difficult, the survival of firms so hazardous in an environment increasingly unpredictable, competitive and fraught with danger, that their continued existence depends on the day-to-day mobilization of every ounce of intelligence.[8]

Will we believe he is wrong if we really get serious about wanting to improve our performance? This can best be accomplished by aligning each group and each individual within the organization with the organization, then providing each person with a means to improve the total performance of the group they work with. That's what **AAA** is all about.

Putting the Puzzle of AAA Together

The biggest single mistake an organization can make in its improvement process is not starting the process with well-defined, documented objectives and measurement systems in place that will quantify the progress made as a result of the improvement activities. **AAA** is a systematic approach to establishing meaningful efficiency and effectiveness measurement systems for all levels of the organization, allowing the organization to calculate the return on investment related to the improvement activities.

At the end of each chapter, we will put together the **AAA** puzzle. Why a puzzle? Is **AAA** so difficult that understanding it is like solving a puzzle? **AAA** is not difficult. It is very straightforward and can be understood quite easily. The words on the puzzle pieces may be familiar to some people, but for many they will be just words. Though they are shown as random parts of a puzzle, they really have a well-defined relationship with each other. As you will see, each piece of the puzzle is explained and then progressively assembled into a completed jigsaw puzzle ("The Solution") that puts everything in the proper perspective. At the end of each chapter is a page showing the puzzle with the appropriate pieces highlighted and put into its proper relationship.

Notes

1. Howard Gitlow and Shelly Gitlow, *The Deming Guide to Quality and Competitive Position* (Englewood Cliffs, NJ: Prentice Hall, 1987).
2. John R. Katzenbach and Douglas K. Smith, *The Wisdom of Teams: Creating the High-Performance Organization* (New York: Harper Business, 1994).
3. Robert B. Reich, *The Work of Nations: Preparing Ourselves for Twenty-First-Century Capitalism* (New York: Vintage Books, 1992).
4. Helio Gomez, *Quality Quotes* (Milwaukee, WI: American Society for Quality Control (ASQC)-Quality Press, 1996), 174.

5. William R. Hewlett and David Packard, *The HP Way* (Palo Alto, CA: Hewlett-Packard, 1980).
6. Stephen Murgatroyd and Colin Morgan, *Total Quality Mangement and the School* (Buckingham: Open University Press, 1993).
7. Richard S. Wellins, William C. Byham, and Jeanne M. Wilson, *Empowered Teams: Creating Self-Directed Work Groups That Improve Quality, Productivity, and Participation* (San Francisco, CA: Jossey Bass, 1991.
8. Helio Gomez, *Quality Quotes* (Milwaukee, WI: American Society for Quality Control (ASQC)-Quality Press, 1996), 34.

Overview of Area Activity Analysis

You Can't Measure Improvement If You Don't Know Where You Started From

What Is Area Activity Analysis?

Usually, our employees have an excellent understanding of what they do, and as a result, they are normally the experts in their specific assignments. But are they doing the right thing? Too often employees waste resources because they do not understand how they fit into the total organization. They often view the organization as a complex puzzle that has never been put together.

Area Activity Analysis (**AAA**) is the first performance improvement tool that a manager should use to help his or her area get started on a sound footing. **AAA** helps the organization accomplish the most basic of all management tasks, defining

- The purpose of each area
- What activities must be done to satisfy the area's mission
- The area's internal and external customers' requirements
- How the area's performance should be measured
- What is acceptable performance

AAA is not another technique for improving processes, lowering cycle time, or reducing costs. Simply stated, it helps managers clarify what is expected of their groups, define key measurements, set performance standards, and focus people's efforts like a laser beam on the organization's mission. It defines whether the area needs to improve and where the improvement opportunities exist. It helps the employees understand what is important for their customers and managers. It also helps the employees understand how they fit into the organization and contribute to the organization's goals. It is a people-building approach that helps them stand on their own feet with a high degree of confidence in themselves and helps them understand that they are doing something worthwhile. Dr. Kaoru Ishikawa, the leader who made quality a way of life in Japan, explains,

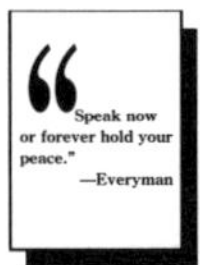

A people-building philosophy will make the program successful; a people-using philosophy will cause the program to fail.

—DR. KAORU ISHIKAWA[1]

AAA Applied to the Government

AAA not only applies to businesses but also to all government departments. Our top government officials have been talking about quality and productivity improvement for the last 30 years with no measurable results. On February 25, 1986, President Ronald Reagan issued Executive Order #12552 that stated, "The goal of the program shall be to improve the quality and timeliness of service to the public, and to achieve a 20% productivity increase in appropriate functions by 1992. Each executive department and agency will be responsible for contributing to the achievement of their goal."[2]

The words stated in the executive order were good words, but they did not include a measurement system to support the order. As a result, quality and productivity did not get better. In 1950 the average person had to work for 93 days to pay his or her federal income taxes. Today we need to work for more than 130 days to pay our income taxes. If the government lived within its income, we would have to spend more of our lives working to pay taxes than to support our families. Our accumulated national debt has jumped from $4 trillion to $10 trillion in 10 years, and it is getting bigger each day without a plan to pay for it. Now that is real negative productivity.

Past President Reagan put it well when he wrote, "The need for and importance of improving the efficiency with which the federal government delivers goods and services to the American public cannot be overstated. The federal government now accounts for 24.6% of the GNP."[3] **AAA** provides an excellent starting point for a government performance improvement process directed at reducing the federal government expenses to the sum percentage of the GNP as it was in 1980 within five years. Let's start with the definition of area.

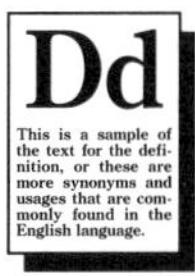

An **area** is any natural work team (NWT) that is organized to work together for an extended period. For example, it can be the organization's president and all the vice presidents and staff reporting to him or her. It can also be the maintenance foreperson and all the maintenance workers reporting to him or her.

AAA is the foundation tool that should be used before other, more complex interventions are begun, such as Total Quality Management (TQM), Process Reengineering, or Team Problem Solving. Whether an area is being newly created, combined, or has existed for a number of years, **AAA** is the tool for ensuring that everyone understands their area's overall mission, what their customers expect, what they need to do to succeed, and how to measure their performance. **AAA** can be used effectively at all management levels, from the chief operating officer (COO) area that includes all the vice presidents to a production area that is made up of a line supervisor and the employees doing assembly work. It is about the sound management of processes. Getting to the task level requires analysis.

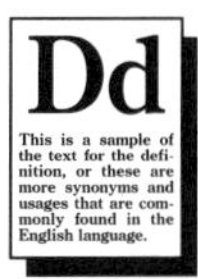

A **process** is an activity or interrelated series of activities that takes an input, adds value to it, and produces an output. A process can be as small as a single activity or it can include many activities and subprocesses. A process usually involves more than one NWT. Processes are usually subdivided into activities (see Figure 1).

Activities are subsets of a process or subprocess. Activities that are connected together are often referred to as a process. An activity will

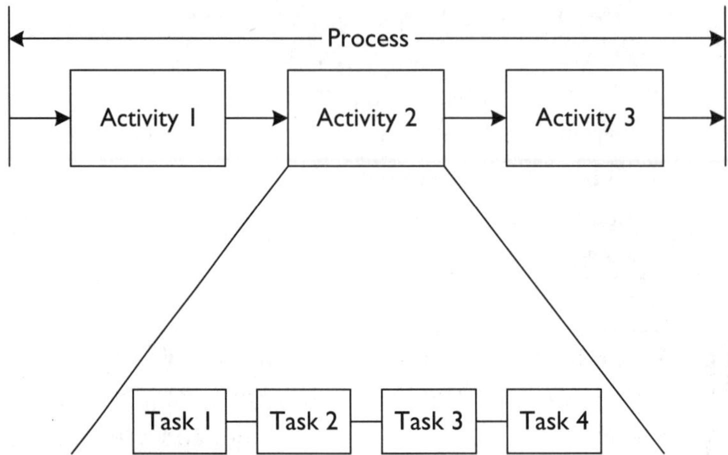

FIGURE 1. **Process Breakdown**

normally take place in a single area. Each activity can be further divided into tasks that are performed by individuals.

A **task** is an individual element that is a subset of an activity. Normally, tasks relate to how an individual performs a specific assignment.

Analysis is a way to look at a situation and remove the irrelevant factors so that the true situation can be clearly defined. As used in **AAA**, this analysis means that the members of the **AAA** team are able to clarify what is expected of their area, define key measurements, set performance standards, and focus their efforts on the area's mission.

An **AAA** team is made up of the members of a NWT who have undertaken the project of applying the **AAA** methodology to their area.

Customer/Supplier Relationships

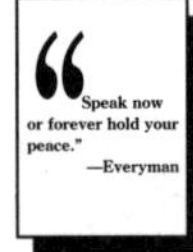

Everyone in IBM has customers, either inside or outside the company, who use the output of his or her job; only if each person strives for and achieves defect-free work can we reach our objective of superior quality.

—JOHN R. OPEL, PAST CHAIRMAN OF THE BOARD, IBM[4]

Before we go any further, let's discuss what we mean by customer/supplier relationships as they relate to internal and external customers. Basically, a customer/supplier relationship can develop in two different ways:

- An individual or organization can determine that it needs something that it does not want to create itself. As a result, it looks for some other source (supplier) that will supply the item or service at a quality level, cost, and delivery schedule that represents value to the individual or organization (customer).
- An individual or organization (supplier) develops an output that it believes will be of value to others. Then the individual or organization looks for customers that will consider the supplier's output as being valuable to them (for example, the Internet, VCRs, etc.).

Although both these situations reflect real life, we will use the first one to discuss how customer/supplier relationships develop. We feel that after reading this explanation, the reader will be able to apply the concept to the second situation.

The customer defines a need for an input and begins looking for some source that can fulfill this need (see Figure 2). To find a source for this input, the customer needs to define the performance parameters related to the required input, when the input needs to be delivered, how well the input needs to perform, and how much the individual or organization is willing to pay for the item or service. Usually all of these data are communicated to potential sources of the item or service with the exception of how much the customer is willing to pay for the item or service. Once the potential source of the input receives the potential customer's information, it is evaluated to determine whether the source is capable of providing the input to the customer in keeping with the customer's performance, quality, and delivery requirements.

If there is a near match, the potential source will contact the customer and discuss how their differences can be resolved. Once these requirement is-

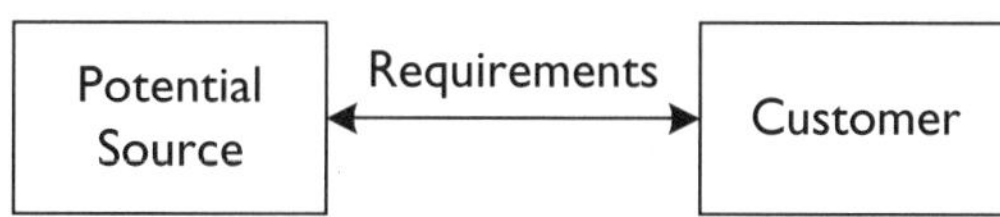

FIGURE 2. Search for a Potential Source

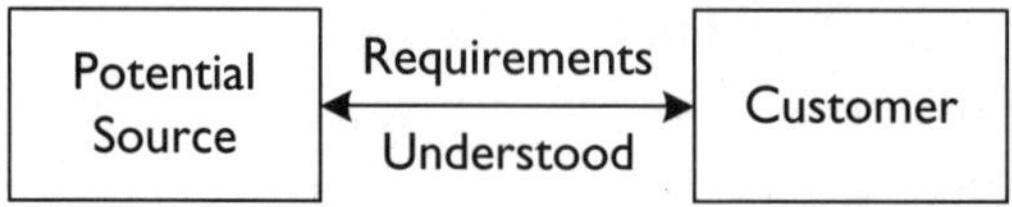

FIGURE 3. Complete Definition of the Potential Source's and Customer's Requirements

sues have been resolved, the potential source will determine how much it will cost them to provide the input to the customer and add to this cost their profit margin, so that a total compensation requirement can be defined. These compensation requirements are then communicated to the customer. Through the negotiation process, a closure of all outstanding issues between the customer and the potential source is reached (see Figure 3). It is important to note that at this point the potential source is not a supplier because the customer often is negotiating with other potential sources to provide the same product or service.

If the potential source represents the best-value option to the customer, the customer agrees to accept the input as long as it is in compliance with the negotiated requirements. The customer also agrees to compensate the potential source for the item or service as negotiated. With an external customer, this act often takes the form of a purchase order. Once the potential source agrees to the provisions defined by the customer, it enters into a contract (formal or informal, verbal or written) to provide the input to the customer that meets the requirements in return for the agreed-to compensation. At this point in the process, the potential source becomes the supplier (see Figure 4). It is important to note that the agreed-to requirements include both the customer requirements and the supplier requirements for compensation.

Now that an agreed-to requirements package has been developed, it is up

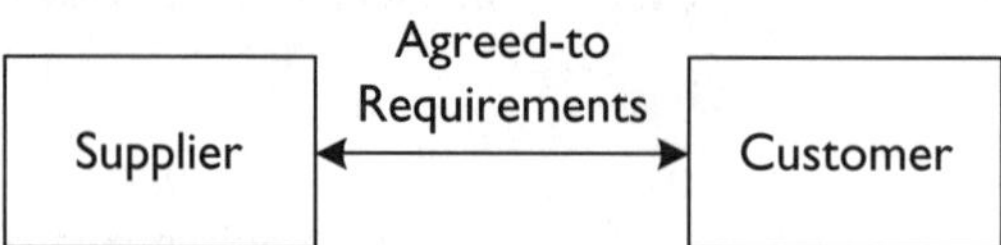

FIGURE 4. Agreed-to Requirements That Both the Supplier and Customer Are Committed to Provide

to both parties to live up to their part of the agreement. The supplier provides the input to the customer, and the customer evaluates the input to determine if it meets the defined requirements. The customer then provides feedback to the supplier related to the performance of the input compared to the agreed-to requirements. This feedback should include both positive and negative data. If the input meets the customer requirements, the customer's feedback that documents positive performance often takes the form of paying the supplier the compensation that was agreed to. We suggest that even if the customer requirements are met, it is a good idea to provide positive feedback to the supplier and suggest ways that the supplier can improve future inputs. All too often, the customer pays the bill but is still not happy with the supplier's output. This represents a major problem with the customer, not the supplier. The suppliers have every right to believe that they are doing a good job if the only feedback they receive from the customer is positive (paying their bills). In the case where the input does not meet the customer requirements, the deviation should be defined so that the supplier can correct the problem. Often, the supplier's compensation is tied into the correction of these problems (see Figure 5).

You will note that in Figure 5 there is a corrective action/improvement feedback flow from the supplier to the customer. This information flow provides the customer with assurance that past problems will be corrected and/or that continuous improvement is scheduled related to the supplier's output.

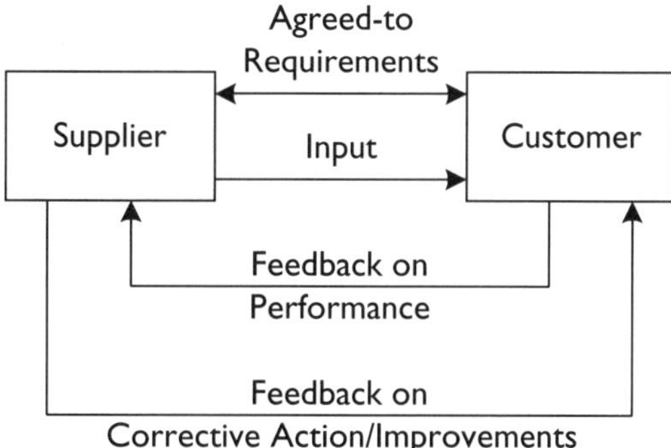

FIGURE 5. The Complete Customer/Supplier Model

What did we learn from this analysis? Two key points:

- A customer/supplier relationship cannot exist unless the requirements of both parties are understood and agreed to. Too often customers expect input from suppliers without understanding their requirements and/or capabilities. On the other hand, too many suppliers provide output without defining their potential customer's requirements and obtaining a common, agreed-to understanding of both parties' requirements.
- Both the customer and the supplier have obligations to provide input to each other. The supplier is obligated to provide the item or service and define future performance improvements. The customer has an obligation to provide compensation to the supplier for its outputs and feedback on how well the outputs perform in the customer's environment.

The customer/supplier process has a domino effect. Usually, when a supplier is defined, that supplier requires input from other sources in order to generate the output for its customer. As a result, it becomes both a customer and a supplier (see Figure 6).

Although the procedures related to internal customer/supplier partnerships are less stringent and have been simplified because the internal customer does not pay for the services that are provided, the concepts are equally valid. Too often we set different standards for internal suppliers than we have for external suppliers. As a result many of the internal suppliers provide outputs that are far less valuable than it costs to produce the outputs.

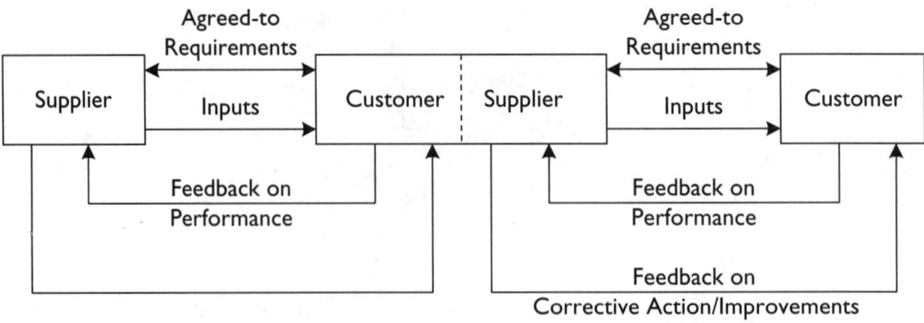

FIGURE 6. The Cascading Customer/Supplier Model

This results in runaway costs and added bureaucracy. With **AAA** you can apply the customer/supplier model to the internal organization and thereby improve quality and reduce cost and cycle time of the services and items delivered both within and outside the organization.

Making the Area Hum

The NWT is the engine that drives the organization. Only by educating, empowering, and continuously communicating with the NWT can any organization perform at an acceptable level. Of course the organization is made up of individuals, each with different personalities and needs that must be managed. But success comes not from each individual doing their own thing but from individuals working together to create outputs that are greater than the sum of the outputs of the single individuals.

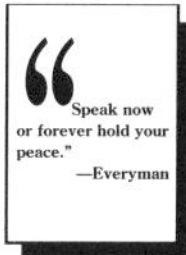

The face-to-face group is as significant a unit of organization as the individual. The two are not antithetical. In a genuinely effective group the individual finds some of his deepest satisfaction.

—DOUGLAS MCGREGOR[5]

Defining customer/supplier relationships is only one part of making an area function effectively. There are many other factors that also must be considered. For example,

- What is the area responsible for?
- How is the area measured?
- What is acceptable performance?
- How does the area fit into the total organization?
- How well do the area's employees understand their roles and the ways they can contribute?
- What are the important activities that the area performs from top management's standpoint?

It is important to note that all of these questions pivot around the activities that the area is involved in. It is for this reason that the **AAA** methodol-

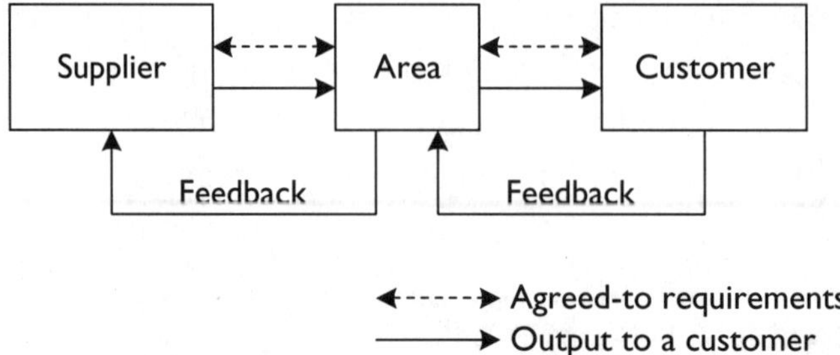

FIGURE 7. **Customer/Supplier Relationships**

ogy broadened its perspective to go beyond the customer/supplier partnership concept to embrace a complete business view of the area. Figure 7 provides a simple view of this enlarged concept.

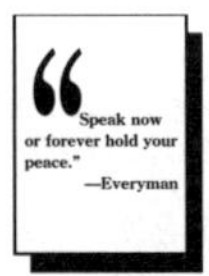

Groups become teams through ***disciplined action.***
—KATZENBACH AND SMITH[6]

The Area Activity Analysis Methodology

The AAA methodology has been divided into seven different phases (see Figure 8 and Table 1) to make it simple for the NWT to implement it. Each of these phases contains a set of steps that progressively leads the NWT through the methodology.

Implementing these seven phases will bring about a major improvement in the organization's measurement systems, increase understanding and cooperation, and lead to reduced cost and improved quality throughout the organization.

Phase I—Preparation for AAA (Chapter 1)

AAA is most effective when it precedes other initiatives such as Continuous Improvement, Team Problem Solving, TQM, Reengineering, or new IT sys-

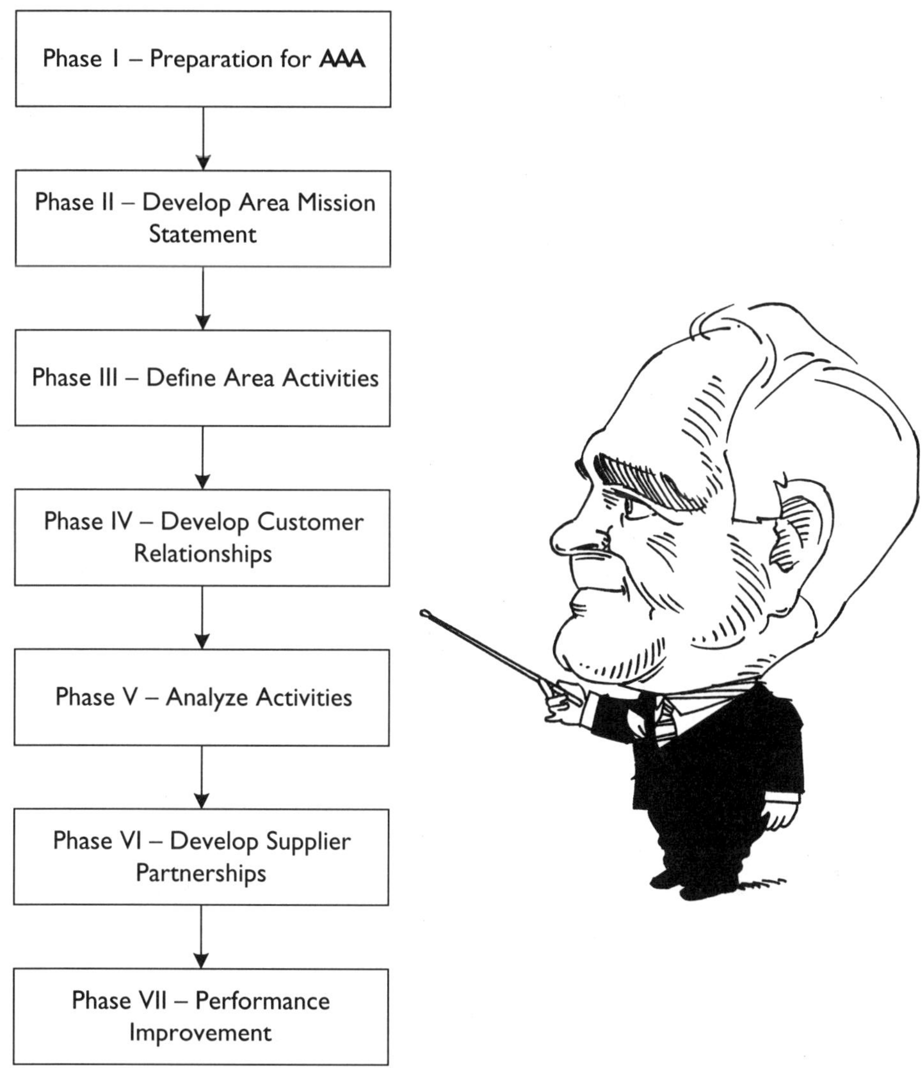

FIGURE 8. The Seven Phases of AAA

tems. It is also best to implement the **AAA** methodology throughout the organization. This does not mean that it will not work if other improvement activities are under way or if it is used only by one area within the total organization. In the preparation phase, the good and bad considerations related to implementing **AAA** within an organization should be evaluated. A decision is

Table 1

Phase	Number of Steps
Phase I—Preparation for AAA	5
Phase II—Develop Area Mission Statement	6
Phase III—Define Area Activities	8
Phase IV—Develop Customer Relationships	7
Phase V—Analyze the Activity's Efficiency	6
Phase VI—Develop Supplier Partnerships	5
Phase VII—Performance Improvement	8
Total	45

made whether to use AAA within the organization. If the decision is made to use AAA, an implementation strategy is developed and approved by management. Phase I is divided into five steps:

STEP 1 Analyze the environment.
STEP 2 Form an AAA project team.
STEP 3 Define the implementation process.
STEP 4 Involve upper management.
STEP 5 Communicate AAA objectives.

Phase II–Develop Area Mission Statement (Chapter 2)

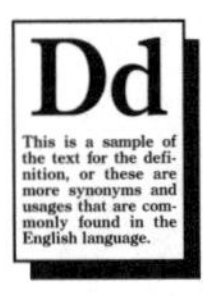

A **mission statement** documents the reasons for the organization's or area's existence. It is usually prepared before the organization or area is formed, and it is usually changed only when the organization or area decides to pursue new or different set of activities. For the AAA methodology, a mission statement is a short paragraph, no more than two or three sentences, that defines the area's role and its relationships with the rest of the organization and/or the external customer.

Every area should have a mission statement that provides the area manager and the area employees with guidance related to the activities on which the area should expend its resources. Standard good business practice calls for the area's mission statement to be prepared before an area is formed. The mission statement should be reviewed each time there is a change to the organization's structure or a change to the area's responsibilities. It should also be reviewed about every four years, even if the organization's structure has remained unchanged, to be sure that the mission statement reflects the current activities that are performed within the area.

Also during phase II, the area's service policy is developed.

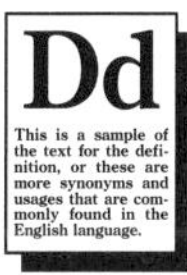

A **service policy** is a short statement that defines how the area will interface with its customers and suppliers.

During Phase II, the **AAA** team will review and update the area's mission statement, or write one if necessary. In all cases, any change to the mission statement must be approved by upper management before it is finalized. Phase II is divided into six steps:

Step 1 Obtain present mission statement.
Step 2 Develop preliminary area mission statement—NWT manager.
Step 3 Develop preliminary area mission statement—each employee.
Step 4 Develop a consensus draft area mission statement.
Step 5 Finalize area mission statement.
Step 6 Develop the area's service policy.

Phase III–Define Area Activities (Chapter 3)

During this phase, the **AAA** team will define the activities that are performed within the area. For each major activity, the **AAA** team will define the activity's output(s) and the customers that receive that output. An activity champion is also assigned to each activity. Phase III is divided into eight steps:

Step 1 Identify major activities—each individual.
Step 2 Combine into broad activity categories.
Step 3 Develop percentage of time expended.

STEP 4 Identify major activities.
STEP 5 Compare list to area mission statement.
STEP 6 Align activities with mission.
STEP 7 Approve of the area's mission statement and major activities.
STEP 8 Assign activity champions.

Phase IV—Develop Customer Relationships (Chapter 4)

During this phase, the **AAA** team will meet with the customers that are receiving the outputs from the major activities conducted by the area to

- Define the customer's requirements.
- Define the supplier's requirements.
- Develop how compliance to the requirements will be measured.
- Define acceptable performance levels (performance standards).
- Define the customer feedback process.

Phase IV is divided into seven steps:

STEP 1 Select critical activity.
STEP 2 Identify customer(s) for each output.
STEP 3 Define customer requirements.
STEP 4 Define measurements.
STEP 5 Review with customer.
STEP 6 Define feedback procedure.
STEP 7 Reconcile customer requirements with mission and activities.

Phase V—Analyze the Activity's Efficiency (Chapter 5)

For each major activity, the **AAA** team will define and understand the tasks that make up the activity by analyzing each major activity for its value-added content. This can be accomplished by flowcharting the activity and collecting efficiency information related to each task and the total activity. Typical information that would be collected is

- Cycle time
- Processing time
- Cost
- Rework rates
- Items processed per time period

Using this information, the **AAA** team will establish efficiency measurements and performance targets for each efficiency measurement. Phase V is divided into six steps:

STEP 1 Define efficiency measurements.
STEP 2 Understand the current activity.
STEP 3 Define data reporting systems.
STEP 4 Define performance requirements.
STEP 5 Approve performance standards.
STEP 6 Establish a performance board.

Phase VI—Develop Supplier Partnerships (Chapter 6)

Using the flowcharts generated in Phase V, the **AAA** team identifies the supplier that provides input into the major activities. This phase uses the same approach discussed in Phase IV but turns the customer/supplier relationship around. In this phase, the area is told to view itself in the role of the customer. The organizations that are providing the inputs to the NWT are called internal or external suppliers. The area then meets with its suppliers to develop agreed-to requirements. As a result of these negotiations, a supplier specification is prepared that includes a measurement system, performance standard, and feedback system for each input.

This completes the customer/supplier chain for the area, as shown in Figure 7 on page 22.

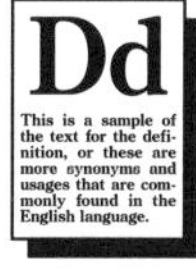

A **supplier** as an organization that provides a product (input) to the customer (source ISO 8402).

Internal suppliers are areas within an organizational structure that provide input into other areas within the same organizational structure.

External suppliers are any suppliers that are not part of the customer's organizational structure.

Phase VI is divided into five steps:

STEP 1 Identify suppliers.
STEP 2 Define requirements.
STEP 3 Define measurements and performance standards.
STEP 4 Define feedback procedure.
STEP 5 Obtain supplier agreement.

Phase VII–Performance Improvement (Chapter 7)

This is the continuous improvement phase that should always come after an activity has been defined and the related measurements are put in place. It may be a full TQM effort or just a reengineering activity. It could be a minimum program of error correction and cost reduction or a full-blown Total Improvement Management project.

During Phase VII, the NWT enters into the problem-solving and error-prevention mode of operation. The measurement system should now be used to set challenge improvement targets, and the NWT should be trained to solve problems and take advantage of improvement opportunities. The individual efficiency and effectiveness measurements are combined into a single performance index for the area. Typically, the area's key measurement graphs are posted and updated regularly.

During Phase VII, management should show its appreciation to the NWTs and individuals who expended exceptional effort during the **AAA** project or who implemented major improvements.

Phase VII is divided into eight steps:

STEP 1 Set up the reporting systems.
STEP 2 Identify the activities to be improved.

STEP 3 Install temporary protection if needed.
STEP 4 Identify measurements or task to be improved.
STEP 5 Find best-value solutions.
STEP 6 Implement solutions.
STEP 7 Remove temporary protection if installed.
STEP 8 Prevent problem from recurring.

Rules That Challenge TQM Principles

We believe that two of the TQM principles need to be challenged, or at least expanded upon, in order to reflect the latest thinking related to organizational alignment. The following rules are used to govern **AAA** activities.

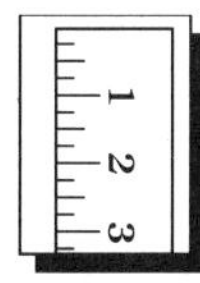

RULE 1. There are three types of customers: primary customers, internal customers, and external customers. Every employee serves at least two of these customers; some employees serve all three (see Figure 9).

The TQM principles recognize internal and external customers but do not address primary customers. The TQM approach focuses on improving the quality of service provided to both the internal and external customers but does not address directly improving the way the individuals service their primary customer. The result is a lot of talk about the importance of the external customer who is paying the bill, but in the real world it is your upper manager who decides which activities you do and whether you are going to continue to do them. From the employees' standpoint, it is always the primary customer's expectations that must be met to be successful, not the external customer's expectations.

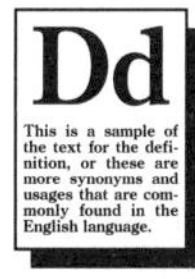

Primary customers are the persons in upper-level management who legalize the activity that an individual or group performs.

Upper management is any level of management that can delegate an activity and its associated responsibility and/or accountability to the spe-

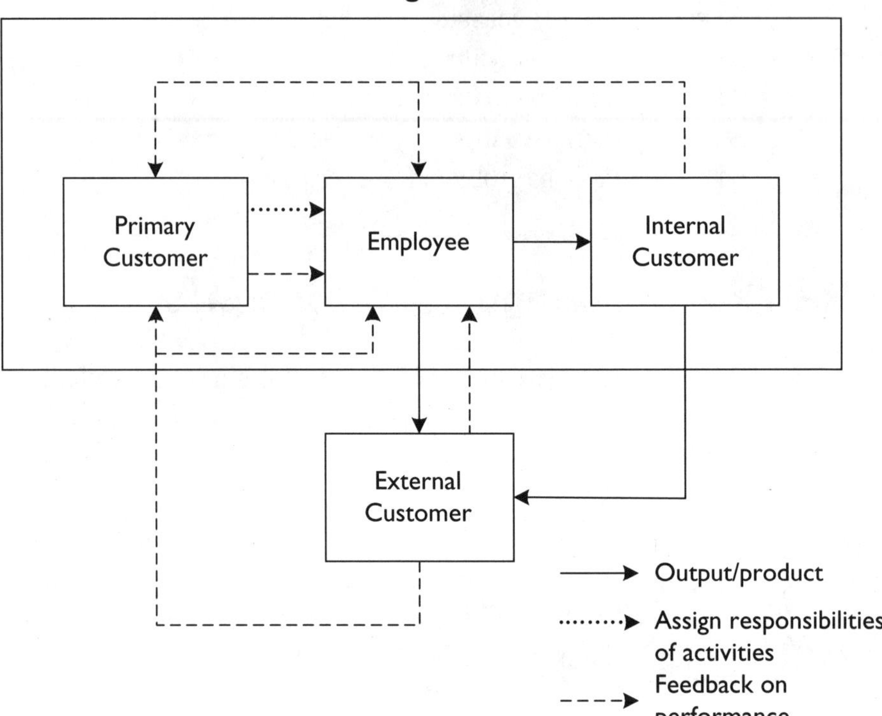

FIGURE 9. View of the Three Types of Customers

cific individual. Upper management to the vice president of R&D would be the president of the organization. Upper management to an accountant would be his or her department manager.

It is absolutely essential that the expectations of all three customers come together if the total organization is going to be successful.

Upper management decides they will assign an activity to an individual or group for the following reasons:

- They are too busy to perform the activity themselves.
- They are not capable of performing the activity due to technical or physical limitations.

- They feel it is more effective and/or efficient to have someone else do the activity.
- They don't want to do the activity themselves.

Upper management is the primary customer that everyone has because they define what activities all individuals need to perform. Everyone at every level of the organization, from the floor sweeper to the president, has primary customers. No matter where you are in the organizational structure, there is an upper manager above you. The upper manager for the floor sweeper is the maintenance supervisor. The upper management for the president of the company is the board of directors. The upper management for the board of directors is the stockholders. If you don't know what your primary customer expects from the activities that he or she has hired you to perform, or if you are not fully fulfilling these requirements, you are not meeting minimum standards. If for some reason you cannot agree to perform the activity as your primary customer requires it to be performed, and you cannot convince this primary customer (upper management) to change the requirements, the only option you have is to find a new assignment. In the movie *On a Clear Day You Can See Forever,* Bob Newhart expresses this view about disagreement with the primary customer when he states, "Academic freedom means if you disagree with the administration, you are free to go to another university."

If conflict arises between your primary customer and either one or both of the other two customers (internal or external customers), the primary customer requirements always prevail. As consultants, we are often asked by external customers to do something or to provide some information that our primary customer does not want us to provide. Your loyalty must always be to your primary customer.

RULE 2. The employee doing the job may know the most about what he or she is doing, but that does not mean that he or she is doing things right or even doing the right things. There is no real value added in doing the wrong thing effectively and efficiently.

The primary customer defines what activities should be done. The employee refines how the activity is conducted to obtain the results that the pri-

mary customer expects. For example, the used car salesperson's primary customer is the car dealership owner. The primary customer needs to make a minimum of 10% profit on each used car sold to cover the cost of overhead and salaries. The external customer wants to buy the car at some amount lower than low blue book (lowest possible price). For the external customer to be extremely satisfied, he or she would buy the car at a price that is less than what the primary customer (the dealer) paid for the car.

- Advertised price for a used car: $9,500
- Used car bought by dealer for: $8,000
- Overhead costs: $800
- Minimum sales price: $8,800
- Low blue book price: $7,900
- Price that the external customer wants to pay: $7,500
- Difference between what the primary customer wants for the car and what the external customer wants to pay: $2,000

There is often a conflict between the requirements of the primary customer and the external customer. The challenge that faces employees is to develop a balance between these two customers that provides a win/win situation for both the primary and external customers.

Chapters 2, 3, and 5 are designed to ensure that the primary customer's requirements are well defined and understood. Chapter 4 is designed to ensure that the natural work team understands the internal and/or external customer's requirements.

Benefits of AAA

The **AAA** methodology provides you with five major benefits:

1. Understanding

The **AAA** methodology is needed because most individuals and groups do not really understand just why they do the things they do. They don't know who their suppliers are, nor who their customers are. Even if they do know, it

is unlikely that they and their customers, suppliers, and management have a common, agreed-to understanding of how their output should be measured and what is acceptable performance related to each of these measures. Improvements cannot be made without understanding these items. **AAA** can provide this understanding because it is a systematic and disciplined method of looking at the inputs from the suppliers, the value-added content of the area, and the outputs the customers receive.

2. Involvement

AAA is a methodology that involves managers and nonmanagers (administrative personnel, accountants, salespeople, operators, technicians, engineers, etc.) in analyzing what goes on within an area and defining what acceptable performance is.

3. Opportunity

AAA's structure makes it an ideal tool for opportunity discovery and problem identification. Defining improvement opportunities is one of the first steps in the improvement journey. Too often, organizations train people to solve problems and then tell them to go out and find a problem to solve. With AAA the employees are provided with information that defines if they have business-related problems, as well as defining the magnitude of the problems. If they do have business-related problems and/or improvement opportunities, the employees are then trained to take advantage of these opportunities. Using this approach, problem solving is truly a value-added business activity.

4. Communication

AAA is designed to capture vital information and keep management and the employees aware of how the area is integrated with the overall goals and strategies of the organization.

5. Measurement

AAA is a methodology that will help an area develop and use meaningful measurements and performance standards. Typically, each area will have three to six effectiveness measurements and three to six efficiency measurements with their associated performance standards. Often, these measurements are combined mathematically to develop a single improvement measurement for the many activities that go on within the area. This measurement system will help to integrate what is done within the area with the overall strategies and goals of the organization.

Advantages

Using AAA has many advantages over some of the other improvement techniques:

- All individuals in the organization can be actively involved in the **AAA** process.
- Those employees that contribute to the success of the organization can be identified and rewarded appropriately.
- The organization's operating skills are improved, especially leadership skills.
- Burning issues and problems are addressed.
- A team environment is established within the area.
- Teamwork between areas is greatly improved.
- The area manager maintains the role of leader of the area.
- Employees become more responsible for their own actions.
- Employee self-esteem improves.
- The system provides realistic and meaningful specifications that have been agreed to by the customers, suppliers, and the employees.
- Critical, meaningful measures of effectiveness and efficiency are identified at the area level for each major activity.
- Employees have a better understanding of how they fit into the area and total organization.
- External customer service is improved.
- An appropriate escalation process is established for those issues that cannot be resolved by the NWT.
- Interpersonal relationships are improved.
- The organization maximizes its knowledge base.
- A firm foundation is developed that leads to major quality improvement and cost reduction.

How to Use This Book

This book is organized to make it easy to read and use. **AAA** is first broken down into a seven-phase process. Each phase has its own chapter. Each phase is then broken down into specific steps that the **AAA** team can follow, which are summarized in each chapter in a block diagram. Each chapter in the book uses the following structure and formats: purpose, key questions, deliverables, phase overview, and steps. This structure provides a step-by-step approach to using **AAA**. Three case studies are followed throughout

Chapters 1 through 6 show how the concepts explained in the chapter can be applied to a production area, a support area, and a service area. This format makes it easy for busy managers to refer to the appropriate section during implementation. The seven chapters are summarized below. We have also included a glossary of terms used in the book in Appendix A.

Chapter 1: Phase I–Preparation for AAA

This chapter examines what should be done to prepare the area to begin implementing **AAA**. It examines the commitment management needs to make to ensure success.

Chapter 2: Phase II–Develop Area Mission Statement

This chapter describes how to prepare a mission statement for the area. It shows you how to assess how well the area's mission statement supports the organization.

Chapter 3: Phase III–Define Area Activities

This chapter defines how to identify the major activities performed within the area. It will also help you determine if they truly support the area's mission.

Chapter 4: Phase IV–Develop Customer Relationships

This chapter introduces the concept of the internal customer and shows how to analyze the area's major activities in terms of what the internal and/or external customers require. This is followed by guidelines on how to define measurements for those requirements and develop appropriate feedback mechanisms.

Chapter 5: Phase V—Analyze the Activity's Efficiency

In Phase V, the activities that are being studied are flowcharted down to the task level. Each task is analyzed to define its value-added content. This assessment is then combined with a "poor-quality cost" analysis. Based on these analyses, efficiency measurements and performance standards are then developed for each activity.

Chapter 6: Phase VI—Develop Supplier Partnerships

This chapter defines how the NWT identifies its key suppliers and works with them to define agreed-to requirements and performance standards for each input. The feedback system to the suppliers will also be defined and agreed to with the suppliers.

Chapter 7: Phase VII—Performance Improvement

At the completion of Phase VI, all of the area's measurement systems and performance standards have been agreed to. This usually results in the NWT identifying many improvement opportunities that it can correct itself. Chapter 7 addresses how the NWT attacks these business-related improvement opportunities to bring about rapid and continuous performance improvement. This is now the time to provide the area's employees with the proper tools to address the specific opportunities that face the area.

Summary

The fast-moving, ever-changing environment has changed the way many organizations look on the organization chart. In the old-style organization chart, top management was at the top of the pyramid, indicating that everyone below them provided services to top management (see Figure 10a). The popular notion is that customer-focused organizations have turned the pyramid upside down, with everyone servicing the employee, who in turn ser-

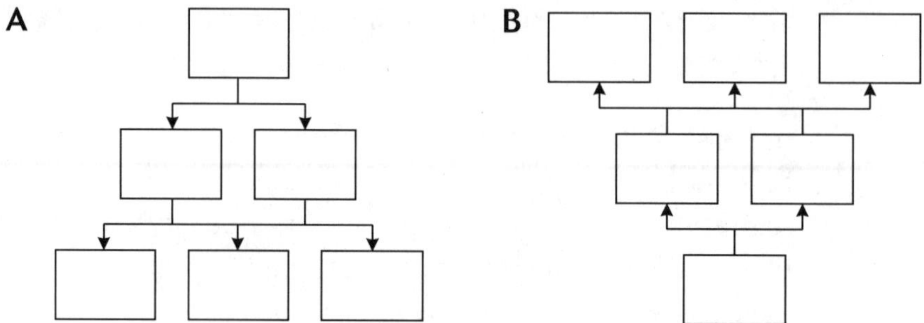

FIGURE 10. (A) Old-Style Organization Chart (pyramid), (B) Customer-Focused Organization Chart (upside-down pyramid)

vices the customer (see Figure 10b). But what could be more unstable than a pyramid resting on its pinnacle? It is obvious that the slightest vibration would cause the upside-down pyramid to topple.

We like to think that the best organization structure looks more like a rectangle (see Figure 11). This way of looking at the organization structure indicates that all activities are important, that five-way communication exists, and that everyone in the organization has an obligation to make the best use

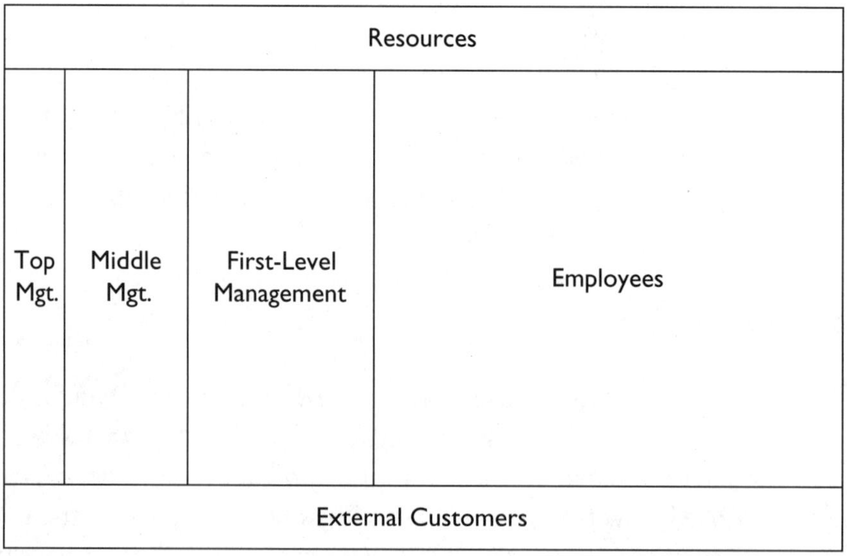

Resources

Top Mgt.

Middle Mgt.

First-Level Management

Employees

External Customers

FIGURE 11. Preferred Organization Structure

of the organization's resources in their efforts to serve their customers. It also lends itself to the concept that organizations use processes that flow across boundaries to conduct the organization's business. It has the advantage of showing that everyone in the organization has an obligation to service the external customers as well as the internal customers. **AAA** provides the understanding and measurement system required to make the rectangular organization operate successfully.

The four major objectives of the **AAA** are as follows:

1. To align the NWT's activities and measurement system with the priorities of the organization and the external customer. Management provides or agrees to what the NWT's mission is and what major activities they are responsible for without telling them how to do the activity.

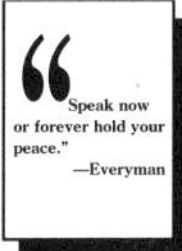

If you tell people where to go, but not how to get there, you'll be amazed at the results.

— General George Patton[7]

2. Develop a spirit of teamwork throughout the organization by defining the internal and external supplier/customer relationship.

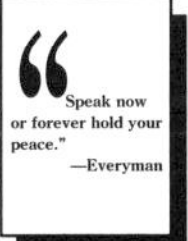

As a spirit of teamwork invades the organization, employees everywhere will begin working together toward quality—no barriers, no factions, 'all one team' moving together in the same direction.

— Peter R. Scholtes[8]

Through teamwork and group activity many of the difficult organizational problems of coordination and control can be solved.

— Douglas McGregor[9]

3. Develop the individual members of the NWT by helping them understand their customers and the activities that go on around them. Only by understanding how the individuals and their activities fit into the organization's vital systems can their energies and talents be best utilized.

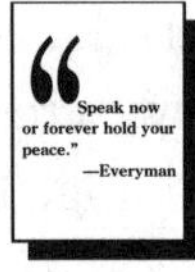

I believe the real differences between success and failure in a corporation can very often be traced to the question of how well the organization brings out the great energies and talents of its people.

— THOMAS WATSON JR., PAST PRESIDENT OF IBM[10]

4. To keep the NWT's improvement activities directed on business issues and not on the process of improvement. All too often, the TQM process becomes the objective rather than performance improvement.

The year that Florida Power and Light won the Deming Award for quality (the first time that a non-Japanese company won the award), they had a net loss of $391 million. This led to the replacement of the company's president. When James Broadhead became CEO of Florida Power and Light, he met with employees and discovered widespread resentment for the quality effort. In the July 1, 1991 issue of *Fortune* Magazine, he was quoted as saying, "I was most troubled by the frequently stated opinion that preoccupation with process had resulted in our losing sight of one of the major tenets of quality improvement, namely respect for the employees."[11] He found "less recognition for making good business decisions than for following the quality improvement process." He also stated that "It (FPL) pushed itself to the brink of nervous collapse in the months before being chosen in 1989."

Many people feel that **AAA** focuses too much on measurements. The truth of the matter is that it is designed to install a complete measurement system that is business focused. Yes, **AAA** does focus on measurements. People around the world want to be measured. They want to know if they are winning or losing. It is only the poor performers that do not want to be measured.

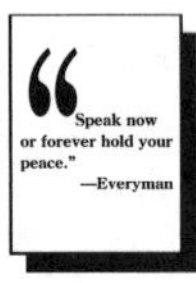

Measurement is the first step that leads to control and eventually to improvement. If you can't measure something, you can't understand it. If you can't understand it, you can't control it. If you can't control it, you can't improve it.

— H. JAMES HARRINGTON[12]

Dave Farrell, senior manager, summed up **AAA** as, "Area activity analysis has, for many clients, proven to be an extraordinarily useful methodology for aligning work groups' improvement activities with the needs and priorities of the organization and its customers."

Comments

Don't think that AAA is only for big organizations. It is for all organizations. We have seen it work in a company of 56 employees and in another company of 320,000 employees. It works for all organizations because it is designed to make better use of and to develop an organization's most valuable asset—its employees.

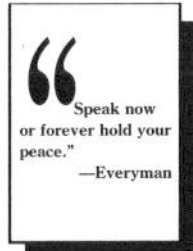

The most important resource in the quest for excellence is people, and in this regard, the smaller companies play to the same set of rules.

—DONALD E. PETERSON, PAST CHAIRMAN OF THE BOARD, FORD MOTOR COMPANY[13]

Take away all my customers and in a month or two I will have a new set. Burn down my office and within a week I will be located in a new building. If my investors pull out their investments I will be fully capitalized again in 60 days. But take away my team (employees) and I am out of business. Truly, the most important thing to me is not my customers, my methodology, my equipment, or my capital. It is the people that work with me to deliver excellent service to our customers.

—H. JAMES HARRINGTON

Notes

1. Dr. H. James Harrington, *The Improvement Process: How America's Leading Companies Improve Quality* (New York: McGraw-Hill, 1987), 86.
2. Dr. H. James Harrington, *Total Improvement Management* (New York: McGraw-Hill, 1996), 13–14.
3. Ibid., 16.
4. Dr. H. James Harrington, *The Quality/Profit Connection* (Milwaukee, WI: American Society for Quality Control (ASQC)-Quality Press, 1989).
5. Douglas McGregor, *The Human Side of Enterprise* (New York: McGraw-Hill, 1985).

6. John R. Katzenbach and Douglas K. Smith, *The Wisdom of Teams: Creating the High-Performance Organization* (New York: Harper Business, 1994).
7. Helio Gomez, *Quality Quotes* (Milwaukee, WI: American Society for Quality Control (ASQC)-Quality Press, 1996, 57).
8. Peter R. Scholtes, *The Team Handbook* (Madison, WI: Joiner Associates, Inc., 1988).
9. Douglas McGregor, *The Human Side of Enterprise* (New York: McGraw-Hill, 1985).
10. Dr. H. James Harrington, *Excellence—The IBM Way* (Milwaukee, WI: American Society for Quality Control (ASQC)-Quality Press, 1988).
11. James Broadhead, *Fortune* Magazine (July 1991).
12. Dr. H. James Harrington, *The Improvement Process: How America's Leading Companies Improve Quality* (New York: McGraw-Hill, 1987).
13. Dr. H. James Harrington, *Total Improvement Management* (New York: McGraw-Hill, 1996).

Putting the Puzzle of AAA Together

In this Introduction, we have defined area, activity, and analysis. In addition, we have described the seven-phase approach used by the **AAA** methodology. Our puzzle is beginning to take shape.

CHAPTER 1

Phase I—Preparation for AAA

To Succeed Remember The Five Ps: Proper Planning Prevents Poor Performance

Chapter Purpose

This chapter provides insight on how to prepare your organization to use effectively Area Activity Analysis (**AAA**). During this phase, we discuss the five steps required to prepare the organization to start an **AAA** project. To start, let's define preparation.

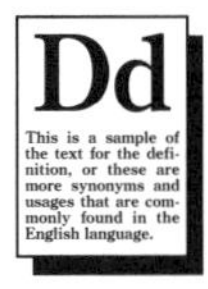

Preparation is the activities that are performed to ensure that a project will succeed in the organization.

AAA is used to help people understand their jobs better and to establish the area's performance measurement system. In most cases an **AAA** initiative is undertaken because management wants to establish an internal customer/supplier relationship within the organization or because management wants the *natural work teams* (NWTs) to take on more responsibility related to solving their own problems and improving their performance. **AAA** can also be used by individuals in their daily work activities. **AAA** leads to developing a better understanding of how the individual and/or area fits into the total organization and defines how they should operate. (Note: Throughout the remainder of this book, whenever the term "the customer" is used, it will refer to both the internal and external customer unless otherwise specified.)

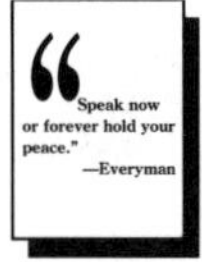

Organizations—which, after all, are merely collections of people—exist for only one purpose: to help people reach ends together that they could not achieve individually.

—ROBERT H. WATERMAN JR.[1]

Very often it is difficult for the members of the NWT to understand how organizations function in today's complex environment, let alone understand how they support the organization's objectives. Figure 1-1 was an organiza-

DATA FLOW

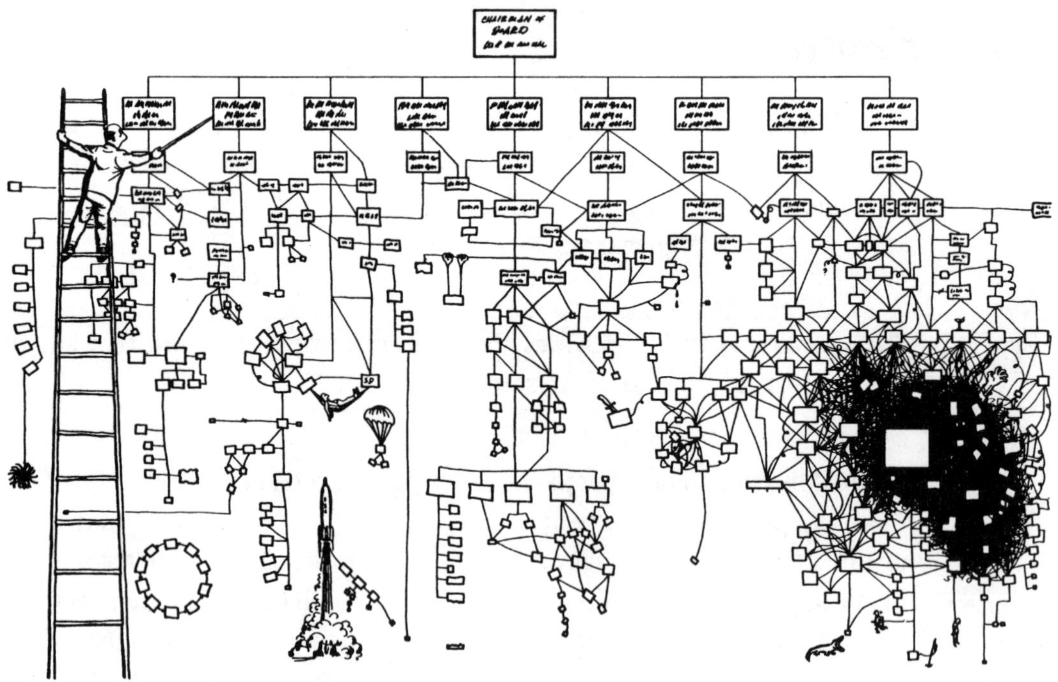

FIGURE 1-1.

tional chart that was unofficially circulated through IBM after one of their reorganizations. It provides an excellent picture of how many members of a NWT view the organizational structure.

How Can an AAA Project Be Implemented within an Organization?

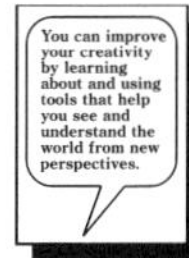

We have seen the **AAA** methodology implemented in many different ways in different organizations. The following are a few popular approaches.

1. The chief operating officer (COO) included **AAA** as part of the strategic operating plan. The COO instructed each location to budget for support of the project and plan to have it completely in place before the end of the budgeted period (top down).
2. Top management set aside training resources for the **AAA** methodology and required each area to absorb the cost of preparing the area's **AAA** (top management direction).
3. Top management supported **AAA** by providing required resources throughout the total location (top management leadership).
4. A vice president set aside resources to do **AAA** in every area that he or she was responsible for (upper management support).
5. Upper management set aside resources to help any area that wanted to use **AAA**, but it was not a requirement (upper management support).
6. A middle manager budgeted for a project to install **AAA** throughout all of the departments that reported to him or her and required each department to complete the process in the next six months (middle management leadership).
7. The Human Resource Department budgeted to support the **AAA** methodology by providing training to all managers and then required that the **AAA** approach be used as part of the individual's performance planning and evaluation cycle (HR direction).
8. A first-line manager used **AAA** to improve morale and productivity within his or her department without asking for a budget increase (manager leadership).

9. Individual employees used **AAA** to better understand their assignments and to improve their performance, thereby helping them to advance faster within the organization (self-imposed).

Each of these nine approaches to implementing **AAA** was successful, although they were not equally effective. In order to help define your improvement strategy, we put the nine different approaches in order—number one being the most effective approach, and number nine, the least effective. We feel that the first six approaches are all reasonable ways to go about implementing **AAA** within an organization. Therefore, we proceed by assuming that the organization will use one of the first six approaches. If this is not the case in your organization, the concept presented throughout the remainder of the book can easily be modified to your implementation strategy.

The following are some definitions that we will be using throughout this book.

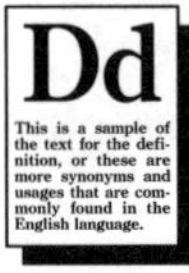

AAA Methodology—a proven approach used by each natural work team (area) to establish efficiency and effectiveness measurement systems, performance standards, improvement goals, and feedback systems that are aligned with the organization's objectives and understood by the employees involved.

AAA Process—the activities required to implement the **AAA** methodology within an organization.

Project—a temporary endeavor undertaken to create a unique product or service.*

AAA Project—the combination of resources, planning, and commitment required to implement the **AAA** methodology within a specific organization. It usually will include a project plan and the follow-up activities to execute the project plan.

Project Plan—a formal, approved document used to guide project execution and project control. The primary uses of the project plan are to

---

*Source: Project Management Body of Knowledge—PMBOK.

document planning assumptions and decisions, to facilitate communication among stakeholders, and to document approved scope, cost, and schedule baselines. A project plan may be summarized or detailed.*

AAA **Project Team**—the group of individuals assigned to develop the AAA project plan and coordinate its implementation throughout the organization.

AAA **Project Team Leader**—the individual who will act as the AAA champion throughout the organization.

Organization—a company, corporation, firm, enterprise, or association or any part thereof, whether incorporated or not, public or private, that has its own functions and administration.†

Key Questions

Reaching a consensus on the following key questions before the AAA project team starts planning for AAA will help it select the best alternatives.

- Who should use AAA?
- Have the desired outcomes been stated?
- Are there adequate resources available to do AAA in the area?
- What else needs to be done to make an AAA project successful?
- Who will champion the AAA project?
- How will the organization measure the success of AAA?

Deliverables

At the end of the preparation phase, the organization will be ready to begin an AAA project. An AAA project team has been assigned, and they have completed a project plan. A cost/benefits analysis has been completed, and a budget to support the AAA project has been approved.

*Source: Project Management Body of Knowledge—PMBOK.
†Source: ISO 8402: 1994.

Process Overview

AAA can be used by managers at any level of the organization to improve the effectiveness of their operations. It can be used by an individual area or as part of a coordinated, organization-wide effort. Unlike so many other approaches, it does not require organizing a cross-functional team. This means that an individual manager can implement **AAA** without it being implemented in other areas.

The ideal way to implement **AAA** is throughout the total organization. With this approach every manager will serve as a member of the **AAA** team, led by his or her manager, and will lead an **AAA** for the NWT made up of the employees that report to him or her. Figure 1-2 shows how this would work in a five-level organization.

Since **AAA** is completely within the authority of the individual manager to implement, it simply requires making the decision to begin and the com-

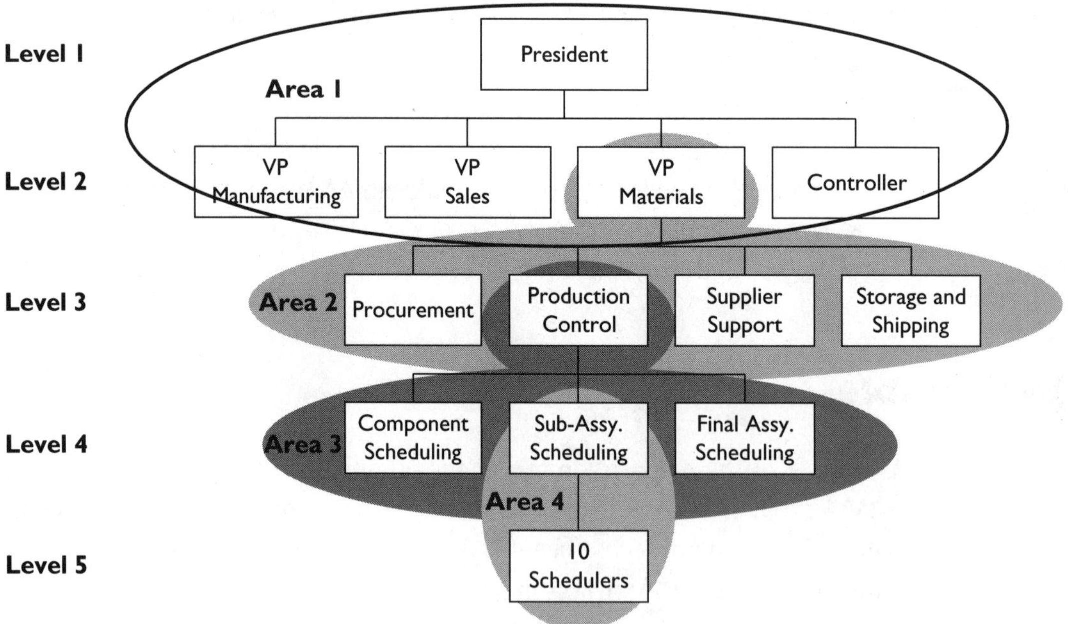

FIGURE 1-2. How AAA Works in a Five-Level Organization

mitment to follow through once the process has begun. There is no special team that has to be organized, just the natural work group that reports to the manager. There is no large expenditure of capital since it requires no special equipment. The only major expense is the employee's time and some training support.

Process Redesign versus AAA

There are thousands of processes that make up most organizations. These processes are divided into tens of thousands of activities, which can be further broken down into hundreds of thousands of tasks. Process redesign and process reengineering usually look at between 10 to 35 of the major processes, and then only for a short period of time. **AAA** sets up a total measurement system that will be used for years.

Although process redesign and reengineering activities produce exceptional results, these gains decay with time if left to the normal routine. Because reengineering can only be applied effectively to a very small percentage of the processes, its impact is difficult to detect at the bottom line. As a result, for an organization to sustain ongoing significant improvement in performance, it needs to focus its improvement effort on the tens of thousands of activities that go on in the organization each day. **AAA** sets the stage for this improvement effort.

Involving Everyone

One of the major problems that faces the team process when you try to get everyone involved is that there are individuals who just don't want to participate in team problem-solving projects. Although these loners do a good job, they are only interested in their individual assignments. They feel that taking part in team activities detracts from rather than complements their work performance. You'll hear statements like "I'm busy already. If I take an hour to attend a team problem-solving session, I'll just have to stay another hour later to do the work that didn't get done," or "If I go to this meeting, what do you want me to omit from my present work load?" You have to admit that these are legitimate concerns from the employee's standpoint.

AAA, on the other hand, is a project that lasts for a set period of time. Its goal is to understand how the area fits into the organization and to establish performance measurements for the area. It is reasonable for management to require every employee in the area to understand both how the area functions and the area's required performance level. Our experience indicates that once employees gain this basic understanding of what is expected from the area and discover that there are performance issues that the area needs to improve, most employees are anxious to correct these defined performance problems. The employees now look forward to problem-solving training that is quickly put to use solving real business problems.

The area manager should focus on the fact that **AAA** is not something separate from everyone's daily jobs. **AAA** is a basic job responsibility for everyone in the area to individually and collectively understand what to do and how to do it.

One of the most important benefits that the organization receives from implementation of **AAA** is that it builds a strong feeling of loyalty to the group or NWT that they work with. Rensis Likert stated,

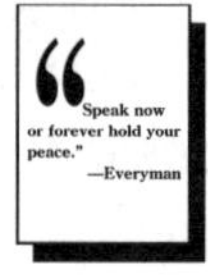

The greater the loyalty of the members of a group toward the group, the greater is the motivation among the members to achieve the goals of the group, and the greater the probability that the group will achieve its goals.

—Rensis Likert[2]

Phase I Breakdown

The block diagram in Figure 1-3 shows the five steps that make up Phase I—Preparation for **AAA**. Each of the steps is explained in detail.

Step 1–Analyze the Environment

For the **AAA** methodology to work effectively, it should be applied in the correct type of organization. The organizations that are most effective at using **AAA** are ones that have a sincere concern for their customers and their em-

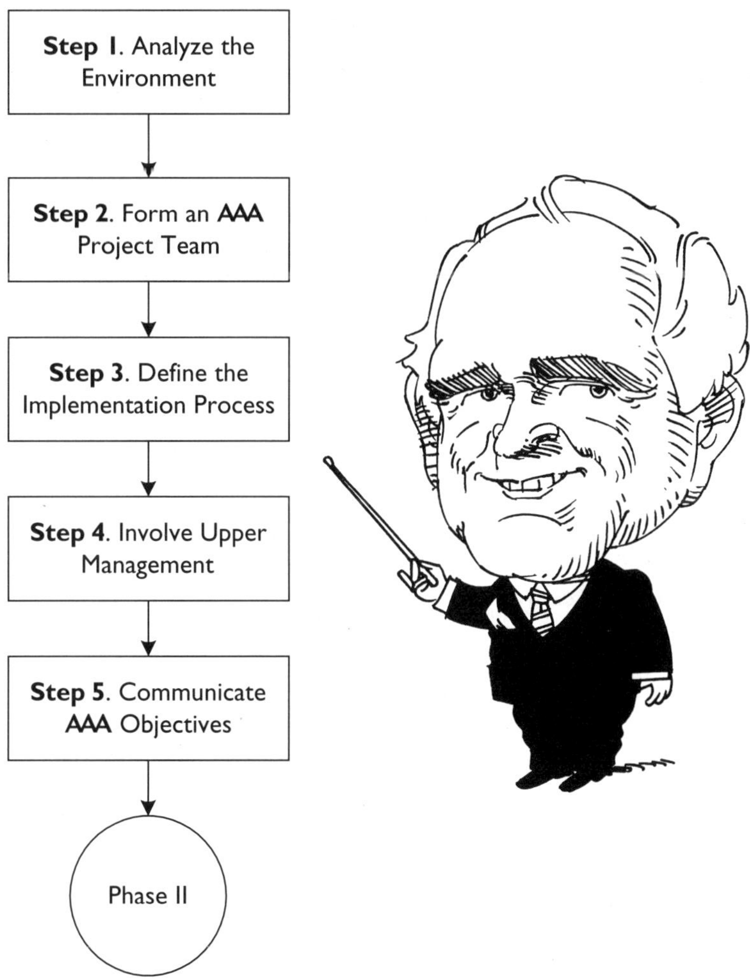

FIGURE 1-3. **The Five Steps That Make Up Phase I**

ployees. These organizations have developed, are in the process of developing, or want to develop an environment that embraces the following characteristics:

- External customer focus.
- Employees take pride in their output.
- Employees understand and relate to the organization's objectives.

- Employees are involved.
- Employees are considered an investment.
- Performance is continuously improving.
- Change is regarded as an opportunity, not a problem.
- Preventive rather than reactive orientation.
- Commitment to providing a fair return on the stockholders' investment.
- Open communication with all stakeholders.
- Excellent systems for measuring short- and long-term progress.

Organizations that have the correct environment are ones that realize that there is a need to continuously improve. These organizations want all of their employees to solve the problems that they face, to overcome the roadblocks that prevent improvement, and to be quick to recognize opportunities for improvement. These organizations develop a management system that encourages teamwork throughout the organization. Through the use of **AAA**, an organization can go a long way toward making the described environment a reality.

If your organization has developed or wants to develop an environment similar to the one that we have just described, you are ready to move to Step 2.

Step 2–Form an AAA Project Team

The **AAA** process is usually started by someone within the organization who has come in contact with the **AAA** methodology and believes that it can help improve the organization's total performance. This individual or group of individuals takes it upon themselves to sponsor the implementation of the methodology throughout the organization. This sponsor will then set about convincing the appropriate management to set up an **AAA** project team to develop a cost/benefits analysis related to implementing the **AAA** methodology within the organization. The chairperson of the **AAA** project team is often referred to as the **AAA** champion.

Management should hold the **AAA** project team accountable for

- Understanding **AAA**
- Defining how the methodology will be implemented

- Developing a project plan
- Doing a cost/benefits analysis

Organized Labor Involvement on the AAA Project Team

Although the improvement process starts by getting management involved first, eventually all employees need to become active participants in the process. It is a fatal error to ignore the unions during the planning and execution phases of the process. Appropriate union representation should be considered for membership on the EIT, the Improvement Steering Council, and even on the board of directors. Even if involving organized labor in the early parts of the improvement process slows down the process, the time and effort expended will more than pay for itself during the implementation phase.

The labor movement is undergoing a revolutionary transformation. You can see it among the communication, rubber, and textile workers. Organized labor is working with companies like AT&T, Ford, Goodyear, and Xerox to help save jobs by making the organizations more competitive. GM's Saturn plant's interface with the United Auto Workers is a good example of flexible collaboration. Kenneth Coss, leader of the United Rubber Workers, stated, "Our goal, really, is to preserve the industrial base. We told the companies that this industry is self-destructing. We'd better work jointly using all our intelligence, our initiative, to make world-class facilities."[3] Lynn Williams, leader of the steelworkers, stated, "When it comes to dividing up the pie, we'll be adversaries. But now we have to grow the pie, and that means working together."[4]

Xerox's relationship with the Amalgamated Clothing and Textile Workers Union (ACTWU) is an outstanding example of how unions and management can work together in implementing employee involvement. As early as 1980, contracts between Xerox and ACTWU included clauses supporting joint improvement efforts.

Working together, the clothing workers' union and Xerox have changed their interface.*

---

*Source of data: *Fortune* Magazine, February 8, 1993.

- Xerox can use temporary workers because they granted union members job security for the duration of their contract.
- No-fault termination dropped absenteeism from 8.5 to 2.5%.
- Cooperation teams—one team working on improving the wire harness process saved $3.5 million. This allowed the process to stay in the United States, saving 240 jobs.

Buddy Davis, St. Louis district director for USW, said, "Now 100 percent of our members are on a committee, and because these committees work out day to day a lot of smaller problems that used to be saved up for the bargaining table, the bargaining goes fast and smooth."[5]

It isn't all peaches and cream. Many hard-core, rank-and-file people still reject the whole team concept, but things are changing. If you want organized labor helping your organization improve, involve them early in the planning process and keep them informed. If you want them to agree to new work rules, then the organization needs to open up the books to them, providing cost and profit data. We need to convert what in many cases is an adversarial relationship into a partnership.

Understanding the AAA Methodology

The **AAA** methodology is not difficult to understand. It is a relatively straightforward concept. The proper level of understanding for the **AAA** project team can be obtained by each member reading this book and then discussing how the concepts presented can be applied to the organization with the entire **AAA** project team. We suggest that these discussions take place after each chapter is read.

Another approach is to have a consultant who has experience in the use of the **AAA** methodology conduct a two-day class. The advantage of this approach is that the consultant can apply his or her experience to your organization, thereby helping you avoid some of the pitfalls that other organizations have overcome.

Defining How the Methodology Should Be Implemented

Even though the **AAA** methodology is very straightforward, we find that many organizations underestimate the work that is required to implement the methodology and the benefits that are derived from its implementation. Some organizations have major problems in establishing an environment that accepts a systematic measurement process that defines the expectations for all of the organization's major activities. Other organizations resist change because they are already undergoing more change than the employees can handle or because past improvement efforts have not been as successful as projected. To overcome some of this resistance to change, **AAA** project teams often utilize Organizational Change Management concepts in support of the project. There is a book in this series related to Organizational Change Management that should be read by the project team if your organization does not readily embrace change.*

Step 3—Define the Implementation Process

Implementation is the real key to the success of most improvement processes. Usually, organizations fail to improve their performance because the methodology was poorly implemented. The Ernst & Young book *Total Quality: An Executive's Guide for the 1990s* (Business One Irwin, 1990) provides a good implementation rule: "A useful motto during the start-up phase is, 'Think big—start small.' "[6]

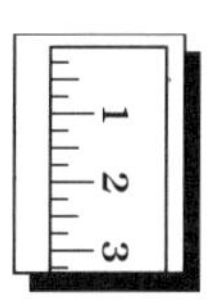

One of the first questions that the **AAA** project team needs to answer is, What areas should use the **AAA** methodology? The next question is, In which areas should **AAA** be applied first? The third question that the **AAA** project team needs to answer is, What support does the area need to implement the methodology? Then the project team should ask, How will the **AAA** methodology benefit the organization, and how can it be measured?

AAA can be implemented in a small portion of an organization, in the total organization, or in specific functions within the organization. We recommend that it be implemented by every natural work team throughout the organization. If the total organization is going to use **AAA**, there are two general approaches that can be used in rolling out its implementation: the organizational structure approach and the supply chain approach.

---

*Other books that relate to this subject are *Managing at the Speed of Change,* by Daryl R. Conner (Villard Books, a division of Random House Inc., New York, 1993), and *Total Improvement Management,* by H. James Harrington (McGraw-Hill, New York, 1995)

Many organizations roll out the **AAA** methodology following their organizational structure. There are major advantages in starting at the top and coming down through the organization because the mission statement and major activities for each lower-level area should support the higher-level area's mission statement and activities.

In other organizations, the supply chain approach is used starting with the external customer. Organizations use this approach because they want to ensure that the needs of the external customer are reflected back through the rest of the organization. To ensure that the supply chain approach works well, it is best to start the **AAA** implementation activities with the areas that are the closest to the customer (marketing and sales) and work back through the supply chain. With the supply chain approach, the support groups complete their **AAA** activities near the end of the **AAA** project.

If your organization is not ready to make this degree of commitment to the **AAA** process, it will be necessary for the **AAA** project team to trim back on the project and select specific areas to implement **AAA**. Again, there are two generally accepted ways of cutting back: the engineered approach and the volunteer approach.

Engineered Approach

The engineered approach analyzes the organization to define which areas will benefit most from the methodology and develops a project plan around implementing the methodology in these areas only. Although the production areas receive a great deal of benefit from gaining a better understanding of their customer needs and how their areas perform, we find that the production areas already have a fairly good set of efficiency and effectiveness measurements. In addition, we have found that the production areas are not the areas that are the biggest source of most organizations' problems. As a result, we recommend that, if there is a need to cut back **AAA** activities, you start with eliminating the **AAA** project from the production areas.

The following functions are listed in priority order based on the benefits that most organizations will derive from their implementation of the **AAA** methodology. If you need to cut back, we suggest that you start with the functions at the bottom of the list and work your way up until you reach an acceptable commitment level.

- Product engineering
- Sales and marketing
- After-sales service
- Production control
- Finance
- Purchasing
- Manufacturing engineering
- Maintenance
- Human resources
- Quality assurance
- Manufacturing

This approach to cutting back the **AAA** program keeps each of the selected functions in line with the total organization's mission, visions, and goals.

Volunteer Approach

The volunteer approach relies on individual managers evaluating the **AAA** methodology and realizing that it would be beneficial to apply the methodology to their area. There are a number of advantages and disadvantages to this approach. Here are some of the disadvantages:

- It is harder to provide the required linkages to higher-level mission statements, activities, and goals.
- It requires that a very good communication system be established and used by all the managers to ensure they understand what **AAA** is before they commit to using it.
- There is a lower level of commitment between suppliers and customers that are not using **AAA**.
- There is more work involved in gaining supplier agreement to the customer specifications.

Some of the advantages of the volunteer approach are these:

- The managers that volunteer want to use the process.
- The areas that volunteer usually have a current need to develop better understanding of their processes and to establish an effective measurement system.

- Usually, there is a better short-term return on investment in the volunteer areas.

There is no right or wrong way to implement **AAA**. Any one of the previously mentioned approaches works and provides good results. Most organizations that start the **AAA** program on a limited basis soon see its benefits, and the **AAA** program expands to the other areas within the organization. Now the **AAA** project team will need to define what type of support the individual areas will require when implementing the **AAA** process.

We also find that the individual area completes the assignment more efficiently and effectively if a trained **AAA** facilitator is available during the initial meetings. The facilitator will also serve as a resource to answer questions during the **AAA** process and to provide the required training. The **AAA** project team should identify what facilitative resources are required to support the project and ensure that the facilitators have the required training. The selected facilitators need to be trained in basic facilitating skills and the **AAA** methodology.

Because of the short length of a typical **AAA** project, organizations frequently use consultants to serve as **AAA** facilitators, which has a distinct advantage because of the vast number of different measurement systems the consultant has come in contact with. The facilitator must have the following skills:

- Complete understanding of **AAA** methodology
- Activity-based costing
- Poor-quality cost
- Team dynamics
- Flowcharting
- Graphics presentation
- Conflict resolution
- Activity value analysis

The **AAA** project team will also be responsible for defining what problem-solving tools will be used to support the areas during Phase VII (Continuous Improvement) and for scheduling the required training.

Typical tools and techniques that are used during the continuous improvement phase include the following:

- Brainstorming
- Check sheets
- Graphs
- Nominal group technique
- Force-field analysis
- Cause-and-effect diagrams
- Flowcharting
- Affinity diagrams
- Interrelationship diagrams
- Statistical process control
- Tree diagrams
- Matrix diagrams
- Prioritization matrix
- Process decision program charts
- Arrow diagrams*

AAA Project Plan

The AAA project team should also develop a project plan that will be used to direct the implementation of the AAA project. The project plan should include subjects such as these:

- Scope of the project
- Implementation plan
- Implementation schedule
- Training plan
- Resource plan
- Project budget
- Support resources plan
- Project objectives and goals
- Measurement plan
- Communication plan

---

*These tools and techniques are discussed in the team book in this series. They are also discussed by H. James Harrington in his book *Total Improvement Management* (McGraw-Hill, 1995).

- Project risk management plan
- Organizational change management plan

The AAA project team will also develop a communication plan to explain to the entire organization why an AAA project is being undertaken, what results the organization expects to achieve, what the AAA methodology is, and the role that each employee will play in the project. The communication plan should also include a regular status report that is distributed to the total organization.

The AAA project team should prepare a budget to support the AAA project so that management will have a good understanding of the total investment. Having an approved budget helps the individual managers understand that upper management supports the AAA project because it has funded it. There is no better way for upper management to telegraph the unimportance of a project than to take the position that the project's resources should be absorbed in the area's current budget.

Typically, this AAA project team prepares the project plan and a supporting budget and submits it to upper management for its approval. Once the project plan and budget are approved, the AAA project is ready to be activated.

A typical AAA project is completed in 60 to 90 days for a medium-size location (2,000 employees). As a result, this project team is usually left intact throughout the project to handle any unforeseen problems and to keep upper management informed about the project's progress. By no means is the project a full-time job for any member of the team unless that member is serving as an AAA facilitator.

Return on Investment

The AAA project team needs to evaluate what impact AAA will have on the organization. It is very easy to discuss the soft impact AAA has on the organization, for example

- Improved morale
- Improved customer satisfaction
- Increased employee involvement

- Aligned employee and organization goals
- Improved measurement systems

It is much more difficult to convert these soft impacts into financial returns that can be measured and compared to implementation cost. One of the biggest advantages of **AAA** is that it establishes efficiency measurements for all areas. Improvement in the efficiency measurements has a positive impact on the bottom line. Typically, by applying the continuous improvement approach, an area will improve its efficiency between 10 to 15% a year. It takes less than 0.5% of the area's yearly resources to complete Phases II through VI of the **AAA** process and about 1 to 2% of the area's resources during the continuous improvement phase of **AAA**. Based on these assumptions, the return on investment (ROI) will run between 8:1 and 15:1.

The project team can prepare its estimates of the ROI for **AAA** by contacting a sample of the management team and having them estimate how much their area's efficiency would improve if the area had good efficiency and effectiveness measurements and had the training required to improve their performance. Usually, these estimates are more conservative than the real measured results.

Effectiveness measurements are directed at improving external customer satisfaction, either directly or indirectly. (Improving internal customer satisfaction should result in improved external customer satisfaction.) It is fairly easy to measure the level of external customer satisfaction through customer surveys. The reason that an organization wants to increase external customer satisfaction is because it should result in increased market share. As a result, the only true measure of effectiveness is increased market share. This makes it very difficult to measure the ROI from effectiveness improvements at the individual area level. However, the savings from using **AAA** can be measured for the total project by evaluating the increased profit that results from increasing the organization's market share. Usually, the marketing department can provide an estimate for increased market share that results from a percentage point improvement in the external customer satisfaction index. Typically, **AAA** will lead to a 5% per year improvement in the customer satisfaction index. The **AAA** project team should estimate what impact **AAA** will have on the external customer satisfaction index, then use these data to define increased ROI.

As the **AAA** process is implemented, each area establishes systems for measuring and reporting its efficiency and effectiveness improvements. These real data can be used to measure actual ROI.

Step 4–Involve Upper Management

When the project plan is completed, it should be submitted to top management along with the **AAA** project team's recommendations. If the project is approved, a budget to support the project should be established, and then the project is ready to move on to Step 4.

The **AAA** project requires more than resources to make it part of the way the organization manages the business. The employees will soon begin to believe that management is taking advantage of them if measurement systems are only established for the activities that the employees are involved in. After all, no one is perfect, and the errors that are made by upper management are far more costly than the ones made by the employees.

If upper management is in full support of the **AAA** project, the executive team (president and the people who report to the president) will be the first area to undertake the **AAA** process cycle. This is the logical starting point because the mission statement of the lower-level areas should support the executive mission statement. Grandmother Harrington gave some good advice that applies here: "If you're going to sweep the stairs, always start at the top."[7]

Starting at the executive team level transforms the executive's words into action, making believers out of the total organization. The real problem is that the top management team in many organizations is less of a team and more of a group of people working in an organization that are competing with each other for power. Outwardly, they talk about teamwork, but their actions tell another story. Top management should be managers, not engineers, accountants, salespersons, or lawyers. Any top manager should be able to manage any function. We would like to see top management rotated every three to four years and never back to the same function until they have managed all of the other functions.

Making an accountant the chief financial officer only serves to build the financial smokestack functions. Starting the **AAA** with the top management NWT helps bring the organization together.

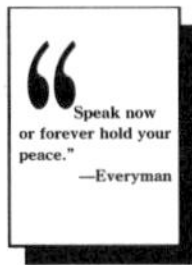

Most so-called managerial teams are not teams at all, but collections of individual relationships with the boss in which each individual is vying with every other for power, prestige, recognition, and personal autonomy.

—DOUGLAS MCGREGOR[8]

We are always surprised at the transformation in behavioral patterns that takes place when the executive team defines who its customers are and finds out how poorly it is fulfilling its internal customer requirements.

It is not enough for top management to set up their own measurement system and report progress related to the measurements to the total organization. They should show their interest by taking an active role in the **AAA** communication process. They should also reinforce desired behaviors by rewarding them when they occur. This is often accomplished by assigning each top manager a number of areas to work with to encourage and help them as they go through the **AAA** process. We suggest that each executive is assigned three to five natural work teams to sponsor. As their sponsor, the executive will help them overcome any bottlenecks they encounter and review their progress on a regularly scheduled basis.

Step 5—Communicate AAA Objectives

It is important to be sure that the total organization understands that the **AAA** methodology is being implemented, what the **AAA** process is, how it will affect the way the organization is managed, and which areas are going to apply the methodology. There are a number of ways that this can be accomplished. Some of the more common areas are as follows:

- An article is printed in the organization's newsletter authored by the president of the organization.
- A notice is posted on the bulletin boards throughout the organization.
- Brochures are prepared and distributed to each employee.
- The president announces it over the organization's broadcast system.
- Individual department meetings are held and an audio/videotape of the president is played where he or she explains the **AAA** methodology and how it will be applied to the organization. This is followed by the manager of the area explaining how **AAA** will affect the area.

- For small organizations, it may be effective to have a meeting of the entire organization and have the president explain how the **AAA** methodology will be applied within the organization.

Preparing for the First Meeting

Typically, a brochure is prepared to provide detailed information about the **AAA** process for the employees who will be involved in the project. This brochure is normally distributed about two weeks before the first area meeting. Advise members that they should be thinking about what they do and who they do it for. Their manager should inform them that a formal meeting will be held in about two weeks. The manager should clearly state the desired outcome of **AAA**.

It is very important that the people know what is expected of them by giving them an overview of the entire **AAA** process and why it is being used. The manager should describe to people why he or she thinks that the **AAA** process will be so important to the organization as a whole and to the individual employees. The manager should point out that an organization is like any other living organism—each part has a vital function to play in concert with every other part if the organization is to be healthy and survive—and **AAA** will help these parts work together better. The manager should also explain that **AAA** provides a checkup to keep everyone on track and make sure they are fulfilling the roles that the organization expects them to perform. **AAA** helps the area to focus more effectively and to avoid the frustrations of being pulled in several directions at once.

Things That Can Help

Some things that are not required but that facilitate the implementation of **AAA** are

- The organization has a long-term business plan, and this plan is well communicated to the total organization.
- The **AAA** project is part of the strategic plan.

- The role of each area is defined in relation to the grand scheme of things for the organization.
- Individuals have an understanding of the goals of the organization.
- Individuals have an understanding of the improvement process the organization is using.
- The top management team uses **AAA** to define its measurement systems and improvement needs.
- The **AAA** measurements are connected to the individual's performance measurement process and reward system.
- Individuals have an understanding of data collection methods.
- Individuals have an understanding of problem identification tools and methodologies.

Having an awareness of organization policies and open communication will put **AAA** in the proper perspective and prevent it from being seen as a stand-alone program.

Examples

Throughout the rest of this book, we will provide you with examples from specific industries. The three companies that will be used are

- Insurance—Insurance Policy Processing Dept., No. BIC 421
- Product manufacturing—BAK Final Assembly Area, No. 301
- Computer manufacturing and service—Customer Service Support Dept., No. 107

Insurance Company Example. In the case of the insurance company, the **AAA** project team decided to start the **AAA** process by implementing it in its financial and policy preparation functions only. The project plan called for the first project to be implemented by the functional managers and all of the managers reporting to them. The managers were then scheduled to use the **AAA** methodology in their own departments. After the project plan was approved by the executive committee and the budgets were approved, the project team was disbanded.

Ben Novell, manager of Customer Service Assurance, was put in charge of the **AAA** project. Ben already had trained facilitators reporting to him who had helped implement the problem-solution teams two years earlier. This allowed him to upgrade his experienced facilitators quickly to the point that they were able to support the area managers during their **AAA** meetings. To speed up the process, Ben hired a consultant to develop a training package and to train his facilitators how to use it. During the remainder of this book, we will use Bob Wilson's department number 351 as our insurance company example. This department, the Insurance Policy Processing Department, is located in the headquarters office in Hartford, Massachusetts.

Manufacturing Company Example. In the case of the manufacturing company, the **AAA** project team decided to use the **AAA** methodology throughout the organization. The first group that was scheduled to use the **AAA** methodology was the president and all of the staff and vice presidents that reported directly to him. It would then be rolled down through the organization, involving middle managers, then first-line managers. The project team made a rule that no manager could start an **AAA** project unless his or her manager had already started an **AAA** project. To get the project started, the team hired a consultant to train the organization's facilitators and to work with the executive and middle managers in conducting their meetings. The organization kept the **AAA** project team intact while the **AAA** methodology was being implemented. The consultant reported to the chair of the **AAA** project team, Betty Maas. The project team met for one hour each week for three months. Once a month, the project team reported the status of the **AAA** project to the executive committee. During the remainder of this book, we will use Sheila Lomax's department number 301, BAK Final Assembly Area Department, as the product manufacturing company example.

Computer Manufacturing and Service Company Example. In the computer manufacturing and service company, the **AAA** project team found that upper management supported **AAA**'s concepts but felt that they did not have the time to go through the **AAA** process themselves. The **AAA** project team did find that there was a need and a desire to use the methodology in some areas throughout the business. As a result, the team decided to make the **AAA** methodology an option that could be used by any area. It was decided by management that the HR department would be put in charge of the **AAA** project and be held responsible for developing the training materials and implementing the communication system. The HR department was also given the responsibility for providing facilitators to help the areas run the **AAA** meetings.

Bill Warren's department number 107, the Customer Service Support Department, was one of the first departments to volunteer to implement the **AAA** methodology. As a result, throughout this book, we will use the Customer Service Support Department as the example related to the computer manufacturing and service company.

Summary

During Phase I, the following should be accomplished.

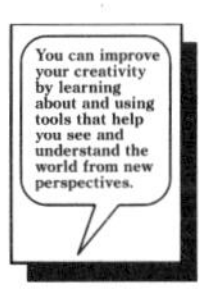

- A champion for the **AAA** methodology should emerge from within the organization.
- An **AAA** project team should be assigned.
- An **AAA** project plan should be developed and approved by the executive team.
- If needed, an **AAA** consultant should be selected.
- **AAA** facilitators should be assigned and trained.
- A decision should be made whether a special organizational change management effort should be implemented in support of the **AAA** project.
- The project and its supporting budget should be approved by upper management.
- A communication plan should be prepared and the initial communication activities should be completed.
- Management that will be using **AAA** should be trained related to the concept.

Preparing each area before **AAA** starts allows for smoother implementation. It is very important that those who will be using the **AAA** process understand it before they find themselves in the middle of implementing it. The importance of a good communication plan cannot be overestimated.

The rest of the **AAA** process is broken down into easily understood phases and implementation steps. Remember the rule: Plan for success, rush into failure. The choice is yours.

Notes

1. Robert H. Waterman Jr., *The Renewal Factor: How the Best Get and Keep the Competitive Edge* (New York: Bantam Books, 1988).
2. Rensis Likert, *The Human Organization: Its Management and Value* (New York: McGraw-Hill, 1967).
3. Dr. H. James Harrington, *Total Improvement Management* (New York: McGraw-Hill, 1996).
4. Ibid.
5. Ibid.
6. The Ernst & Young Quality Improvement Consulting Group, *Total Quality: An Executive's Guide for the 1990's* (Homewood, IL: Business One Irwin, 1990).
7. Dr. H. James Harrington, *Total Improvement Management* (New York: McGraw-Hill, 1996), 59.
8. Douglas McGregor, *The Human Side of Enterprise* (New York: McGraw-Hill, 1985).

Putting the Puzzle of AAA Together

In this chapter we found where "preparation" fits into the **AAA** puzzle.

CHAPTER 2

Phase II—Develop Area Mission Statement

An Area without a Written Mission Statement Is like a Boat without a Rudder

Chapter Purpose

W. G. Scott stated: "A formal organization is a system of coordinated activities of a group of people working cooperatively toward a common goal under authority and leadership."[1] The objective of Phase II is to define or redefine the mission or purpose of the area. This needs to be done whether the area is new or has existed for a long time. All well-managed organizations should always prepare a mission statement for a new area before it is formed so that it will execute the activities that it was created to perform. The mission statement is also used to get everyone in the area pointed in the right direction and off to a good start.

The remainder of this book is directed at how an individual area implements an **AAA** project. The natural work teams (NWTs) are responsible for preparing and implementing an **AAA** project in their area. In most cases, the manager or superintendent who leads the NWT serves as the project team leader. However, in some areas that are already using structured team concepts, one of the team members assumes this role.

Most of the areas that undertake an **AAA** project will have been in operation for some time. Some may already have had their mission defined by their management. Over time, however, most areas take on more and more responsibilities. New people are hired into the area and new activities are assigned without updating the mission statement. As a result, the clarity of the original mission begins to fade. Thus, it is good business practice to review and update if necessary each area's mission statement every two or three years.

Let's be perfectly clear—upper management has the responsibility for defining all areas' missions. They are the only ones who can delegate responsibility. In most organizations, management has done a poor job of fulfilling this role. As a result, the employees who work in the areas throughout the organization and are the closest to the activities are in an excellent position to take a first cut at a mission statement if one does not exist. They are also in the best position to review the present mission statement to ensure that it is in harmony with the work that is going on within the area. In all cases, new or revised mission statements must be signed off by upper management to legitimize them. Our experience indicates that, in most cases, upper management sign-off is only a rubber stamp. However, we have seen a number of mission statements where this was not the case, and the proposed statement was modified significantly. This usually occurs when

- Upper management is unaware of what the area has been doing.
- The employees are defining what they would like to be doing, not what needs to be done.
- The employees are empire building.
- There is more than one area doing the same activity.

In any case, the mission statement should reflect what is going on in the area at the present time. It should not include additional activities that are not part of the area's present assignment. If it makes good business sense to expand the area's responsibilities, these suggestions should be noted separately and submitted to upper management. If approved, the mission statement should then be adjusted to reflect the increased responsibilities, and a new budget should be approved to cover the additional activities.

Either way it is important that there is common understanding, agreement, and support of the area's mission between management and the employees. Be sure that the NWT manager, the employees that make up the NWT, and upper management agree with the mission. Most areas exist to provide a service or a product. Studies have shown that more than two-thirds of the areas in an organization provide a service. Writing a mission statement and getting it approved may seem to be a bit formal. Put in perspective, it sets the boundaries for which the area is responsible and accountable. We will give you a six-step method to develop a mission for the NWT and a service policy statement.

Key Questions

Before writing the area's mission statement, the NWT should answer the following questions, which will help establish needed area direction, alignment with organizational goals, and a strong sense of common purpose:

- Does the area have an approved mission?
- Would it be helpful to have an approved mission statement?
- What is the mission of the area?
- What unique value does the NWT add to the organization?
- Do other areas expect the NWT to do things that are not in its mission?
- How well does this mission align with the next-level management's expectations for the area?
- How does this mission support the objectives of the organization?
- Does the NWT do things that are not in line with its mission?

Deliverables

At the end of Phase II, the area will have a clear, approved definition of what types of activities should occur within the area and the boundaries within which they should function. This determines which activities should be reassigned or if new activities should be added. The area's employees will also understand how the area's mission aligns with their management's expectations and overall organizational goals. In addition, the NWT's service policy statement was developed and agreed to.

Process Overview

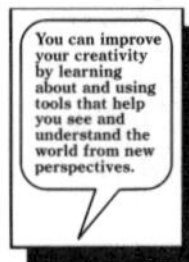

Writing a formal mission statement should not take a significant amount of time and energy. The small amount of resources invested to prepare an area's mission statement is definitely worth it. It is best to begin the process with the official written mission statement if one is available. It is good business practice for management to prepare a mission statement before the department is formed; however, it is not uncommon for an area to spring into existence with little conscious thought or effort and operate for years without a formal mission statement.

If there is not a formal roll-out plan, the NWT manager should inform (or ask permission of) his or her manager to begin the **AAA** process. When the NWT manager has upper management's permission, it is time to review and/or develop the area's mission statement.

In this chapter, we begin to develop a model of how the **AAA** process is implemented within an area, beginning with the NWT manager and the area's mission statement shown in Figure 2-1.

It is often amazing how different the NWT's view of its mission is than its true mission statement. The members of the NWT often lose sight of the true purpose of why they were pulled together because they try so hard to do their job better without considering what management and/or their customers require from the organization.

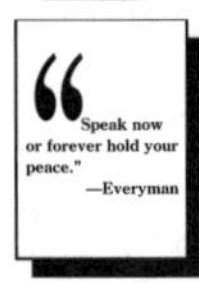

Sometimes the accounting people act as if they think the organization exists so they can keep books on it.

—Karl Albrecht and Ron Zemke[2]

We have found it to be most effective for the manager of the area that is using the **AAA** process to develop a draft mission statement of what he or she

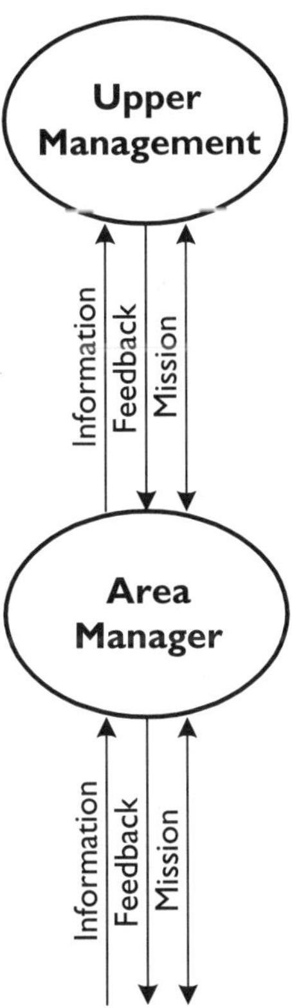

FIGURE 2-1. NWT Manager

believes is the area's mission. At the same time, the NWT manager should ask each member of the area to develop what she or he believes is the area's mission. A mission statement should be a short, concise statement of what the area is assigned to do. A good mission statement is normally three sentences or less and does not contain measurements or targets. It should always reflect what the area is budgeted to do, not what people who work in the area would like to be doing.

At a meeting of all members of the NWT, a consensus is reached on the area's mission statement. They will then compare the mission statement that has just been developed with the existing statement. Any differences will need to be resolved with upper management.

Phase II Breakdown

The block diagram in Figure 2-2 shows the six steps that make up Phase II.

Step 1–Obtain Present Mission Statement

The NWT manager should get the current mission statement from upper management if it exists. The current official mission statement provides a reference point to ensure that the area is still performing its assigned mission.

The NWT manager should also request a copy of the mission statement from his or her manager's area. This higher-level mission statement is important because the higher-level managers can only delegate responsibilities for activities that are under their span of control. It is absolutely essential that these two mission statements are in close harmony. This is a good time to review the area's current mission statement with the next-level manager and get his or her opinion if it needs to be updated. If it does, the NWT manager should find out what changes the next-level manager would like to include.

Also in this step, the NWT manager should notify (get permission from) upper management that the area will be implementing an **AAA** project and provide the next level manager with a preliminary time schedule. Depending on the organization and/or the **AAA** project plan, getting upper management's permission may not be required since the **AAA** project will already be included in the organization's business plan. In other organizations it may be easier to ask forgiveness than permission.

Step 2–Develop Preliminary Area Mission Statement–NWT Manager

The NWT manager should develop a preliminary version of the area's mission statement, based on the input from upper management and the NWT manager's knowledge of what the area is doing. This mission statement will

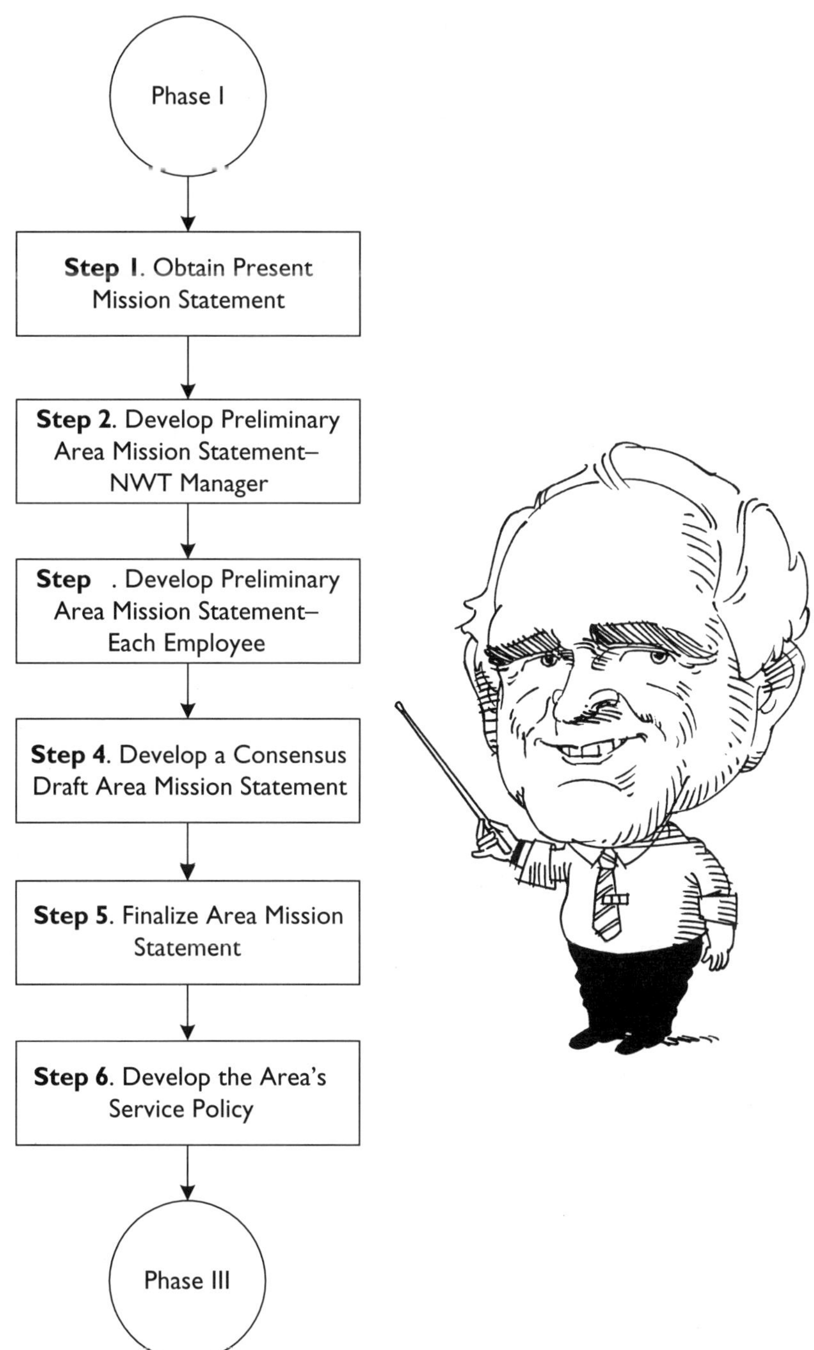

FIGURE 2-2. **The Six Steps That Make up Phase II**

help the NWT manager clarify his or her understanding of the responsibilities assigned to the NWT. It should not be shared with upper management or the individuals that work in the area at this time.

The NWT manager should schedule a meeting of everyone in the area to refine the preliminary mission statement for the area. If the organization is using facilitators, the NWT manager should identify the facilitator assigned to the area. The NWT's manager should then meet with the facilitator to plan for the first meeting and outline the meeting agenda.

Step 3–Develop Preliminary Area Mission Statement–Each Employee

The NWT manager should ask each individual to write a mission statement, which can be done in a regular group meeting, by memo, or in individual sessions. The manager should explain what a mission statement is and what it does and does not contain.

It is important that the manager acknowledges that it may be difficult for some individuals in the area to prepare a mission statement for the total area because they may not have a good understanding of all the activities that go on within the area. Even if the mission statements prepared by the individuals cover only the parts of the area that they understand, they will still provide key inputs into the combined mission statement.

We have found that if each individual documents on flip chart paper the mission statement that he or she developed, it makes the next step easier.

Step 4–Develop a Consensus Draft Area Mission Statement

We recommend that the meetings used to implement the **AAA** methodology within an area are held in a quiet, comfortable conference room if possible. The conference room should be well equipped with two or three flip charts and room to post used flip chart pages for future reference. The first meeting should be scheduled for three hours, because the agenda will include training on **AAA**, developing a meeting code of conduct, and developing the area's preliminary mission statement. All meetings should have an agenda prepared and distributed well in advance of the meeting.

The first meeting should start with a detailed review of the **AAA** process, followed by a discussion about how the area and the individuals within the area will benefit from implementing the **AAA** process. It is often beneficial to do a force-field analysis based on this question: "How well do we understand the area's customer's and management's expectations of the area?"

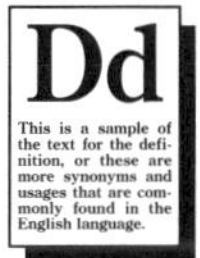

Force-field analysis is a tool that looks at the positive and negative forces that cause a situation to exist.

These two forces are called "driving or facilitating forces" and "restricting or inhibiting forces." The two force fields push in opposite directions. While the stronger of the two will tend to characterize the situation, a point of balance is usually achieved that gives the appearance of a steady-state condition. The force-field approach allows the individuals to analyze the negative and positive forces that cause the situation to exist. This allows them to establish action plans that reinforce the positive forces and minimize the negative forces, thereby bringing about improvements in the situation.

The next point of business at this meeting is establishing a code of conduct that will be used at all **AAA** meetings. If the area already has a code of conduct for its other meetings, it should also be used for the **AAA** meetings. If a code of conduct does not exist, the NWT should prepare one.

A meeting code of conduct defines the acceptable behavioral patterns related to participating in a meeting. These behavioral patterns are not based on preset rules developed by other sources but are the rules that the NWT places on itself while relating to each other during meetings. The following are typical items that might be included in a meeting code of conduct.

- It is unacceptable to be more than five minutes late to a meeting.
- All meetings will begin within five minutes of the scheduled start time.
- All meetings will end on or before schedule.
- Agendas will be sent out at least three days in advance of the meeting.
- Decisions will be based on a consensus of the group, not by vote.

- All reports to be presented at the meeting will be distributed in written summary form 24 hours before the meeting.
- No one will talk unless recognized by the chairperson.
- No item that is not on the agenda will be discussed during the meeting unless the agenda is modified by a three-quarters majority vote.
- Each presentation will be scheduled for a specific time period, and the chairperson will stop the presenter when that time allotment expires.
- The chairperson is accountable for ensuring that the meeting progresses on schedule.
- All people who attend the meeting should express their ideas.
- Minutes of the meeting will be distributed within 24 hours of the meeting by the meeting chairperson.

Once a code of conduct is agreed to by the NWT, the NWT should channel its efforts to developing a preliminary mission statement. A very effective way to get this process started is to have each NWT member post his or her draft version of the area's mission statement and explain why selected phrases used to describe the area's mission were chosen.

The objective of this step is to elicit ideas from everyone about the mission of the area. Some people will be skeptical about the process; others will be reluctant to share their opinions. It is critical to set up an environment that is safe for people to express themselves. Each person should present his or her area's mission statement, explaining why key words were selected, and relating the mission statement to the work that goes on in the area.

The NWT members should then read through all the ideas posted on flip chart paper and look for overlaps, similarities, and themes. Several ideas can usually be combined at this point to reduce them to a more manageable number. Make a list of phrases that the employees think are particularly descriptive.

If the remaining ideas are complementary, then move on to the next step. If there are significant differences, then stop to allow further discussion. Ask if the differences are related to ends or means. Often people can agree at a strategic level and disagree on tactics. Refocus the discussion back on the mission statement of the area, and defer discussion on tactical issues to the next meeting where major activities will be defined.

To make this transition effectively, it is good practice to record key tactical points that are being discussed on the "parking board" so you can readily refer back to them during Phases III and V.

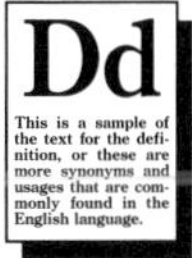

Parking board is a list of subjects or ideas that will be addressed later. Usually these subjects or ideas are not relevant to the meeting's agenda but warrant discussion at a later time.

The NWT should now direct its efforts to drafting a mission statement from the diverse input that everyone feels comfortable with. This is the critical time when people's thinking begins to converge and consensus is achieved. By listening closely to people when they present their ideas and asking questions of one another, it is possible to identify those common threads that can now be woven into the fabric of common purpose.

A mistake that is often made at this step is that the NWT prepares a mission statement that reflects every job that takes place within the area because each individual wants to see his or her job reflected in the mission statement. Take the case of the area that enters orders into the scheduling system and has a secretary who handles clerical activities related to the area's operation (not the order-processing activities). In addition, the area has a programmer who writes specific programs to allow different customer orders to be processed. In this case, there would be no need to reflect directly the secretary's activities and little need to reflect the programmer's activities in the mission statement, because their jobs are indirectly reflected in the area's general mission. Their assignments would be considered at the activity level.

Another mistake frequently made at this point is that the mission statement is prepared defining what the area would like to do, not what it is doing. There is nothing wrong with identifying expanded responsibilities that the NWT feels would be value added to the total organization. However, they should not be included in the mission statement. When these types of ideas arise, the NWT manager should record them on a parking board to be investigated outside of the **AAA** process activities. A typical mission expansion idea would be: We should buy our own stationery supplies instead of going through purchasing. If the list of expanded responsibilities becomes too long or there is a single idea that the NWT feels is very important to the area's mission, the NWT manager will need to get the item resolved by upper management before the mission statement is completed.

A third mistake that is often made is that the mission statement is written so specifically that it is soon out of date. Example: Department 324 develops and releases analog circuitry for the 7501 disk drive. In this case, the mission statement will be out of date when the next development cycle starts for the 8501 disk drive. A better, more long-lasting mission statement would be: Department 324 develops and releases analog circuitry for disk drives. This would be a good mission statement unless another department already has the responsibilities for developing and releasing analog circuitry of other disk drives within the organization.

We recommend that the NWT generate a first-draft statement at this meeting and that the employees take it back to their work area to consider it for about a week. During this gestation period, the NWT manager should share the draft mission statement with his or her manager to obtain his or her comments. This can go a long way toward preventing the next draft mission statement from being rejected when it is formally submitted to the next-level manager for approval. Although it is up to management to determine the organization's mission, and management must ultimately prevail, it is critical to get as much buy-in from NWT members as possible because they will be held accountable for implementing the assigned activities.

Approximately one week later, the NWT manager should schedule a second meeting during which the area's draft mission statement will be revised if necessary. At this meeting, a second discussion about the draft mission statement should be undertaken. This allows the members of the NWT to express any second thoughts or new ideas that they may have had related to the area's mission statement.

The NWT should then review the higher-level mission statement to be sure that the area's mission statement supports it. If it does not support the higher-level mission statement, one or both of the mission statements need to be changed. Remember that the area's preliminary mission statement is not a working document at this point since it still needs to be signed by upper management before it becomes official. One of management's primary jobs is to delegate responsibilities. The mission statement is one way to delegate specific assignments. As such, management is responsible for mission statements. Employees and lower-level managers take the responsibilities that have been assigned and design processes to accomplish the assignments.

The NWT should then compare the mission statement it generated to the official mission statement that presently identifies the area's responsibilities. Take time to discuss all differences because often an area takes on responsibilities that upper management neither knows about nor wants the area to perform.

Elicit people's ideas and feel free to volunteer your own at this point. Look for themes or threads of continuity that could serve as the basis for a single mission statement. Look for portions of the statement or key words that people agree on, and then try to tie up the loose ends. This discussion usually results in the mission statement being refined.

If possible, do the final "wordsmithing" in this meeting, then push for closure. If you have a general statement but run out of time working out the details, ask someone in the group with good writing skills to be responsible for finalizing and distributing the statement prior to the next meeting.

Step 5—Finalize Area Mission Statement

If there are no differences between the original written mission statement and the one prepared by the NWT, the manager should get agreement from everyone in the NWT that the original mission statement is still valid.

If the mission statement already approved by upper management is rewritten, the NWT should schedule a meeting with upper management to resolve any differences. If the proposed mission statement is not accepted by upper management, the NWT should revise it and have it reviewed by upper management until it is acceptable. When an agreed-to mission statement has been prepared, it should be signed off by all concerned. This includes the NWT, the NWT manager, and upper management. Figure 2-3 is a typical form that could be used.

We suggest that all NWT members sign off on the mission statement. This approach builds commitment and demonstrates understanding on the part of the employees.

Area Name: ______________________________

Area No.: ______________ Revision Date: ______________

Area Mission Statement: ______________________________

____

____

____

____

____

____

____

____

____

Prepared by:

______________	______________	______________
______________	______________	______________
______________	______________	______________
______________	______________	______________
______________	______________	______________
______________	______________	______________

Date Prepared: ______________

Approved By: ______________________

NWT Manager: ______________________ Date: ______________

Next-Level Manager: ______________________ Date: ______________

FIGURE 2-3. A Typical Mission Statement Form

Step 6—Develop the Area's Service Policy

All areas provide some type of services to internal or external suppliers and customers. In this step, the NWT will develop a policy statement that defines how the NWT will interface with its suppliers and customers.

It is easy to understand and define how the NWT should serve its customers. Typically, this is expressed in meeting their requirements, on time, at a reasonable price, and at a high quality level. It is much more difficult to understand how the NWT should serve its suppliers. The truth of the matter is that we all have an obligation to service our suppliers also. The NWT services its suppliers by providing them with a well-defined set of requirements, allowing adequate time for their suppliers to deliver their inputs, and providing feedback on how well the suppliers are performing. A typical NWT's service policy for a department initiated "order entry" would be the order entry service policy:

> We provide our internal and external customers with service that meets or exceeds their requirements on or before the scheduled date. We continuously improve our output demonstrating measurable improvement to our customers and management. We build supplier partnership by providing them with measureable requirements and adequate time for them to schedule our work in with their other activities, and we report their performance back to our suppliers on a continuing basis.

Things That Can Help

Some of the things that are not required but that facilitate the development of an area's mission statement are

- Give people an idea of what a mission statement is by showing them examples.
- Ask everyone to write down their individual ideas about what they think the mission of the area is prior to the meeting.
- Set a date for the meeting with enough lead time to allow people to think about the mission and document their ideas.
- If a mission statement has already been prepared for the next higher level in the organization, hand it out to the NWT members and ask them to think about the area's mission in that context. The mission statement from each organizational level should be consistent with and complement the higher-level mission statement.

- Reinforce the idea that you expect everyone to come to the meeting prepared and ready to participate. Let them know that your door is open to discuss any questions or concerns they may have.
- The first meeting should be scheduled for two to three hours, depending on the complexity of the organization.
- The NWT manager should talk with several people informally prior to the meeting to see who is well prepared and willing to share their ideas, then ask the NWT members who are best prepared to present their ideas first in order to get the meeting moving.
- If participation at the meeting is good, then let people volunteer at random. If not, it may be necessary to go around the table to encourage each person to express his or her ideas.
- Open the meeting by reviewing the **AAA** process and objectives. Ask if anyone has any questions or concerns they would like to bring up.
- Review the rules of brainstorming: The objective is to get as many ideas as possible in a short time period, all ideas are welcomed without judgment, work quickly, everyone must contribute, and ideas will be evaluated and prioritized later.
- Reinforce the rules of brainstorming by discouraging criticism of people's ideas during this stage and keeping the pace of the meeting fast. When most, if not all, people have contributed and the energy in the group begins to wane, go ahead and contribute your idea for a mission statement. The NWT manager should wait to share his or her thoughts so that those thoughts do not overly bias others in the meeting. Then, ask if there are any more last-minute ideas and bring the brainstorming phase of the meeting to a close.
- Don't try to be an empire builder. Do what has been assigned.
- Don't add new duties without upper management's approval.
- Don't write a mission statement that is a vision statement. A mission statement defines what you are doing, whereas a vision statement defines how you would like to be in the future. Remember, if the NWT is not doing everything required to support its mission, the area is failing to perform satisfactorily.

- A mission statement should be in the present tense and no more than three sentences.

Examples

Throughout the rest of this book, we will provide you with examples of the major output from each phase for three typical areas. These three areas will be used as examples at the conclusion of Chapters 2 through 6, providing the reader with three complete case studies on how to use the **AAA** methodology. These areas are

1. An area (department) in an auto insurance company that is responsible for issuing the actual policy to the agent for delivery to the insured. The department name is Insurance Policy Processing, and its department number is 351. Its manager is Bob Wilson.
2. An area of a manufacturing line that is responsible for making subassemblies that are shipped to a major car maker. The area's name is BAK Final Assembly, and its department number is 301. The area's manager is Sheila Lomax.
3. An area of a major computer company that provides support to its customer service representatives for hardware and software problems. The area's name is Customer Service Support Department, and its department number is 107.

The mission statements for each area are

Insurance Policy Processing Department. Our mission is to process efficiently and effectively insurance policies that conform to the individual requirements defined by our agents.

BAK Final Assembly Area. Our mission is to assemble efficiently and effectively the component parts we receive into assemblies that are delivered on schedule to our customers so that their product lines are never interrupted.

Customer Service Support Department. Our mission is to provide timely, effective solutions to our field service engineers for hardware

> and software problems that they cannot handle by themselves. We are responsible for interfacing with all appropriate departments and vendors to resolve software and hardware issues in a minimum amount of time.

Developing a meaningful mission statement will provide a focus for everyone who works in the area. In addition, each area's mission statement provides the basis for aligning the work that is done in the area with the organization's direction and goals.

Summary

During Phase II, the NWT should accomplish the following:

- Train to understand the AAA methodology.
- Develop an understanding of the next-level manager's mission statement.
- Gain an understanding of the area's present mission statement.
- Prepare a preliminary new mission statement.
- Gain upper management approval of the new mission statement.
- Prepare the NWT service policy.

The NWT is now in a position to define what activities go on within its area to support its approved mission statement.

Stop to Think

Peter Drucker tells a story about three stonecutters who were asked what they were doing. "The first replied, 'I am making a living.' The second kept on hammering while he said, 'I am doing the best job of stonecutting in the entire country.' The third one looked up with a visionary gleam in his eyes and said, 'I am building a cathedral.' "[3]

Notes

1. Helio Gomez, *Quality Quotes* (Milwaukee, WI: American Society for Quality Control (ASQC)-Quality Press, 1996), 12.
2. Karl Albrecht and Ron Zemke, *Service America!: Doing Business in the New Economy* (New York: Warner Books, 1990).
3. Helio Gomez, *Quality Quotes* (Milwaukee, WI: American Society for Quality Control (ASQC)-Quality Press, 1996), 58.

Putting the Puzzle of AAA Together

In this chapter we have found where the area's mission statement fits into the **AAA** puzzle.

CHAPTER **3**

Phase III—Define Area Activities

To Succeed, Be Sure You Understand What You Should Be Doing. . . . Then Do It in a Superior Manner

Chapter Purpose

The objective of Phase III is to identify all major activities that people in the area are engaged in and make sure that these activities are directed to support the area's mission statement. Although it would be nice to be all things for all people in the organization, we know this is an impossibility. In a world where resources are always constrained, people must focus on those activities that are directly tied to accomplishing the mission of the area in which they are assigned to work.

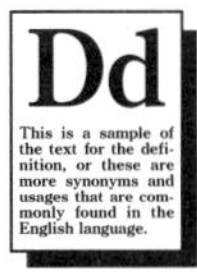

Activities are the actions that are taken by the NWT members to produce the area's outputs.

Typically, there are between three and six major activities going on in an area. Usually, there will be a few of the area's people doing the same thing, a few more doing something different, a few more doing something else, and so on. In most organizations, there will be people working on a number of activities at different times throughout the month. There are some situations where everyone is doing the same things and there are situations where everyone is doing something different. Each activity in the area can be shown in an activity (process) model.

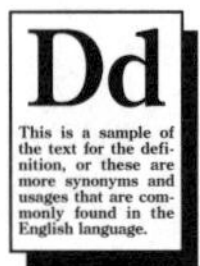

An **activity model** is a flowchart that pictorially presents the relationships of the tasks that are included in the activity.

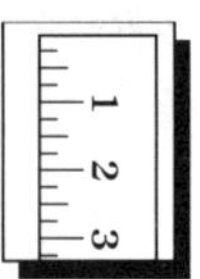

The number of activities in an area can vary widely, anywhere from 1 to more than 20. For the purpose of **AAA**, the area should analyze activities that account for a minimum of 10% of the area's total workload. Using this as a guideline, it is easy to see that a maximum of 10 activities will be classified as major activities. If the area has a long list of activities, the **AAA** team should look for supporting or common activities that can be combined. Remember that for each activity analyzed, there will be a minimum of one efficiency and effectiveness measurement that will be developed and maintained. If the area has 10 major activities, it means that it will have someplace between 25 and 35 measurement data systems to maintain and report on. Very few areas have more than 6 major activities and most have 4 or less.

Key Questions

The NWT should ask itself the following key questions. Reaching a consensus about the answers will help the NWT understand what activities are currently occurring in its area. It will also help the NWT understand what activities are being done that upper management is unaware of and that the area may not need to perform.

- What are the major activities that take 10% or more of the area's time?
- What activities are the NWT doing that account for less than 10% of its time?
- What percentage of the total area's time is spent on each activity?
- What is the NWT doing that is outside of its mission and should be performed by another area?

- Is the NWT doing things that are aligned with what upper management expects from it?
- Why is the NWT doing the identified activities?

Deliverables

At the end of Phase III, the NWT will have a clear picture of what is going on in the area. The NWT will have identified the activities that are conducted within the area and which of them account for more than 10% of the area's resources (major activities). Each major activity will have an activity champion assigned to it.

Process Overview

During this phase, the NWT will develop a list of short, descriptive phrases (two to five words) that describe the major activities that are conducted within the area. These phrases should be worded in such a way that another reader can easily understand that activity.

Defining the area's activities is not difficult, but it does take some time and effort to complete. Understanding what the area is doing enables the NWT to effectively align its activities with upper management's expectations. It also allows the NWT to focus on its customers and suppliers later in the AAA process. It is also important to realize that management must delegate the responsibilities for the activities to the NWT. This is why the activities that the NWT performs must directly relate to the area's mission statement. The area's customers should not tell the area what it is responsible for. If the customers' needs are not aligned with the area's responsibilities, the area should bring these new requirements to management's attention so they can be assigned to the area that is best qualified to fulfill these needs.

After the mission of the area is defined, the NWT manager should ask everyone to keep track of the way they spend the major part of their efforts. Usually, this data-collection period takes about two weeks. Less than a two-week period causes activities to be missed or to be misclassified. You may want to increase the time to four or five weeks if the NWT performs different activities at different times in the month and these activities represent a significant workload.

The NWT manager should then call a meeting to define the major activities that the area is involved in. At this meeting, each individual should provide a list of the major activities he or she performs. The team will then combine all the individual activities to make a list of the area's total activities, which will then be compared to the NWT's mission statement to determine if they support that statement. As a result of this comparison, each activity will be put into one of the following four categories.

- Directly supports the mission statement
- Indirectly supports the mission statement
- Needed to run the area, but does not support the mission statement
- Does not support the mission statement

The model of how **AAA** works has been expanded. We have added activities to the model shown in Figure 3-1. For clarity's sake we have eliminated the upper management link. It is still there; it has just been removed from the drawing.

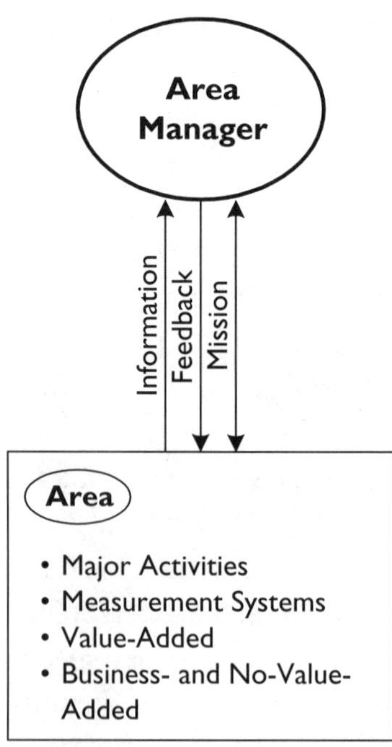

FIGURE 3-1. Area Activities

Phase III Breakdown

The block diagram in Figure 3-2 shows the seven steps that make up Phase III. Each step is explained in detail in the text.

Step 1—Identify Major Activities—Each Individual

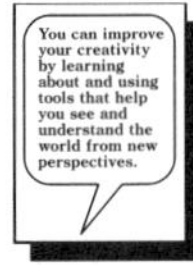

Each employee in the area should now keep track of the way they spend their time for at least two weeks. They should at least identify those activities that occupy 10% or more of their time. In most organizations, employees spend more than 10% of their workday doing personal things (taking breaks, getting coffee, etc.). It is not unusual to have one item on the data log labeled "personal time." Figure 3-3 is one form that can be used to collect the data. You will note that there is room on the form for only nine activities plus one column for miscellaneous. The nine activity columns are more than any individual should need.

There are a number of ways that the data can be collected. Some areas do it by hour, listing what goes on during each hour of the day. Example: 8:05–8:20, telephone call to client; 8:20–8:45, reading general mail; 8:45–9:05, unscheduled meeting with Cathy on budgets, etc. Although this approach is the most accurate, this degree of accuracy is usually not required at this point in the **AAA** process. It is usually sufficient for each individual to mentally review at the end of the day what activities they performed and approximately how much time they spent on each activity.

It is very important that the data collected relate to activities, not tasks. Most people think about what they do from a task standpoint. Typical tasks are using the phone, answering mail, attending meetings, and preparing reports. Typical activities would be conducting performance reviews, building prototype models, certifying suppliers, and planning monthly product schedules. You can see how tasks like going to meetings, making phone calls, and preparing reports are part of each of these four typical activities. Be sure the stage is set for Phase III by having the NWT discuss what the differences are between activities and tasks during Phase II after it has prepared the area's mission statement.

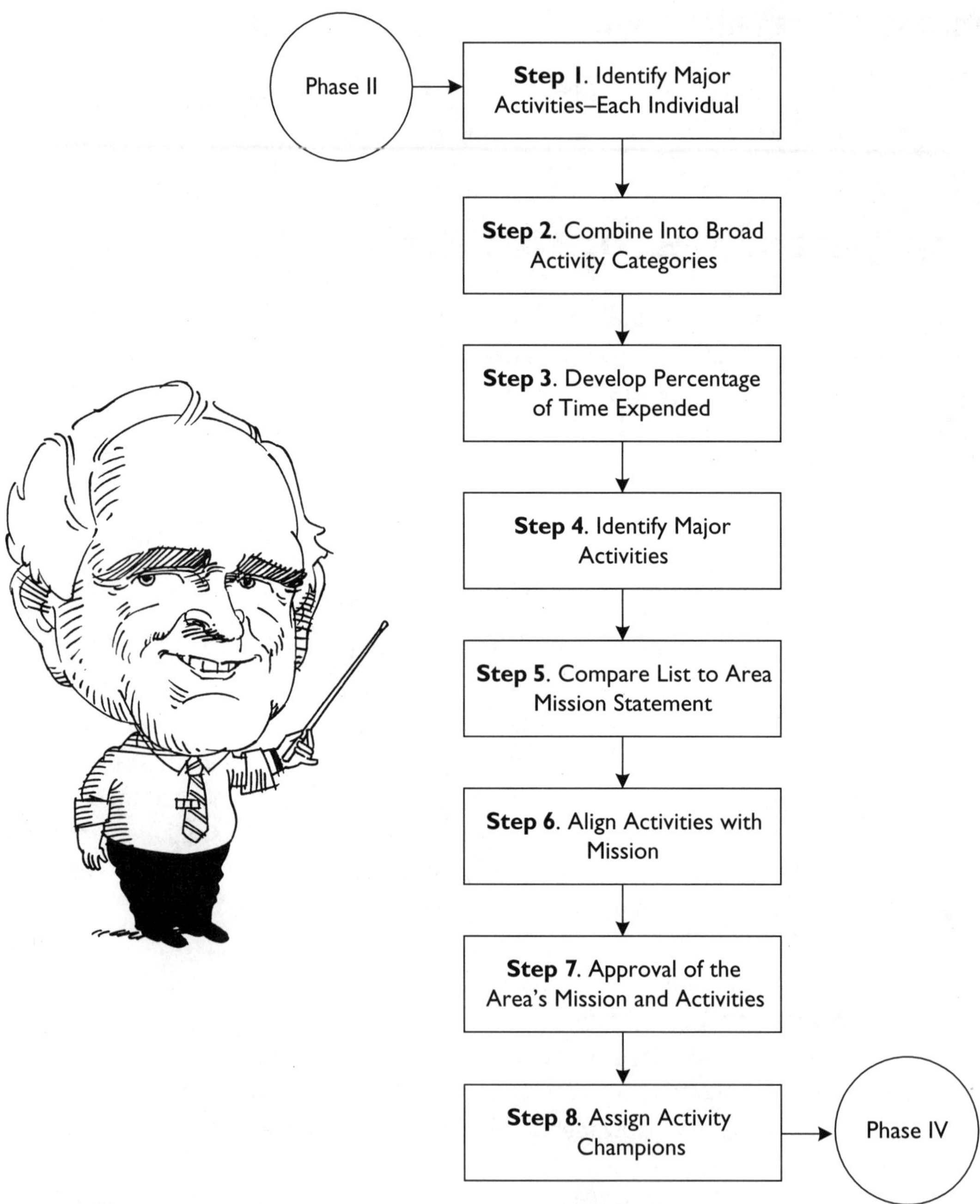

FIGURE 3-2. The Eight Steps That Make Up Phase III

ACTIVITY	HOURS PER DAY						
	Mon.	Tues.	Wed.	Thurs.	Fri.	Sat.	Total
1. 2.							
3.							
4.							
5.							
6.							
7.							
8.							
9.							
10. Misc.							
Total							

FIGURE 3-3. Data Collection Form

Encourage people with similar job functions to work together on developing their lists of activities. Often the NWT manager will prepare a list of activities that are going on in the area, which is then used to collect the data.

Step 2—Combine into Broad Activity Categories

The objective of this step is to elicit input from the NWT about their major activities and consolidate the input into a list of the major activities performed by the NWT. This should be done at an NWT meeting. The simplest way to get the meeting going is to go around the room and ask people to read their top three major activities that take the largest percentage of their time. Have them record each activity on a 3 × 5 card along with the average number of hours per week spent on the activity. Collect the cards after they are read.

Rotate around the table again and get people to share their next three

ACTIVITY	PERSON HOURS/WEEK								
	Mary	Ruth	Bill	Fred	Renee	Jim	Total	Major Activity	Classification
Process expense accounts				30		20	50	yes	1
Arrange for trips		30				4	34	yes	1
Schedule meetings					8		8	no	3
Process petty cash	8				10	10	28	yes	1
Process check requests					12		12	no	1
Publish monthly travel report	8						8	no	3
Negotiate travel contracts		5					5	no	1
Deliver tickets	18						18	no	4
Arrange for outside conferences			32				32	yes	1
Attend department meetings	5	3	3	3	3	3	20	no	1
Misc.	1	2	5	10	7	3	28	no	2

FIGURE 3-4. **Typical List for a Travel Department**

highest-percentage activities and continue until all activities that take more than 10% of the employees' time have been identified. Post the cards where everyone can see them, grouping the same activities together.

Ask people to combine activities where overlaps and redundancies seem clear, while avoiding creating such broad categories of activities that they lose the true meaning of the individual activities themselves. Figure 3-4 is a typical list filled out for a travel department.

Step 3—Develop Percentage of Time Expended

After recording and combining people's individual activities, they must be reevaluated in terms of the estimated percentage of time such activities take for the area as a whole.

Define those activities that account for a minimum of 10% of the NWT's time. (Example: six people on the team × 40 hours per week × 10% = 24 hours.) The team may want to combine some of the miscellaneous activities under a new title that will add up to 10% of the team's efforts. Note that there can be no more than 10 activities on the final list. Normally there are between 3 and 6 major activities on the final list. In the example shown in Figure 3-4, there are 4 major activities (including miscellaneous) based on using the 10% rule only. (Six employees × 40 hours per week × 10% = 24 hours minimum.)

Step 4—Identify Major Activities

This is usually the easiest step, since the objective is simply to reduce the number of major activities down to a more manageable number based on their percentages and their impact on the organization.

Rank the activities from largest percentage of staff time to the smallest. Draw a line separating those that do not occupy 10% or more. The activities with values of 10% or greater will normally be considered the area's major activities.

Examine this reduced list as a group and ask if there is some critical activity that has been overlooked or eliminated because it did not meet the 10% rule. If someone feels strongly that another major activity needs to be added to the list, feel free to do so. Ten percent is an arbitrary cutoff point, and it is more important to have everyone feel the list is accurate and complete. Sometimes there are critical activities that are major but do not take a large percentage of time, such as closing the books at the end of the month or year. These should not be overlooked.

Additional activities might be selected if 1 or 2 activities account for more than 90% of the area's total resources or when a specific activity is very important to the area's function but does not require a great deal of time to perform. (Example: In the quality assurance area, probably less than 10% of the area's resources are dedicated to following up on external customer complaints, but the activity is very important to the organization's reputation.) Remember, the 10% rule is a guideline. The important thing is that the end list should have a maximum of 10 very important activities on it that directly support the NWT's mission statement.

Step 5—Compare List to Area Mission Statement

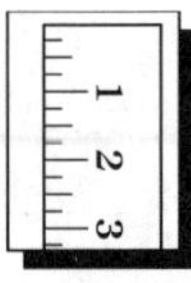

Comparing the major activities to the area mission statement of the area to identify areas of alignment and misalignment is a very important task. One of the ways to get more time to do the important things that need to be done is to not do other things that are less important or are some other area's responsibility. Those activities that do not directly support the mission statement will be considered less important, and this is the time to identify them. Later in the **AAA** process, we will use additional criteria other than time to judge activities and the NWT's mission statement.

To complete this step, the NWT should post the area mission statement where everyone can see it. Then start with the first major activity on the list and ask the people to determine which of the following four statements best fits the activity:

1. It directly supports the mission statement.
2. It indirectly supports the mission statement.
3. It is an activity that is needed to run the area but does not support directly the mission statement.
4. It is an activity that is not related to the mission statement and is not needed to run the area.

Each activity should fit into one of these four classifications. If an activity is classified as a (2) or a (3), the team should question if the NWT is the best place to perform the activity. If an activity is classified as a (4), the team should either rewrite the mission statement or have management reassign the activity. Evaluate each activity in the this way until all activities on the list have been compared to the mission statement. If the vast majority of the NWT's time is not devoted to activities that directly support its mission statement, the NWT need to question if they are doing the right things.

Figure 3-4 demonstrates classification categories for a travel department and its related activities.

Step 6—Align Activities with Mission

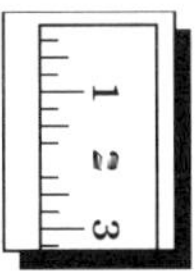

Ideally an area's major activities clearly support its mission. However, we rarely work in an ideal area. Discrepancies usually occur. It is common to find areas that are spending significant portions of their time performing activities that are outside the scope of the area's mission. In these inevitable cases, decisions have to be made to either stop doing the activity, get the activity assigned to another area, or change the mission statement. If the activity needs to be reassigned or dropped, upper management must agree and upper management should take the appropriate action. The area should never stop an activity until upper management has relieved the area of an activity that is not in alignment with the area's mission statement.

Step 7—Approval of the Area's Mission Statement and Major Activities

This step involves reviewing the results of the NWT's mission statement and major activities analysis with upper management. Upper management may have its own ideas about what your area should do and how your people should spend their time. In practice, upper management is often surprised by how the NWT invests its time.

This step should be a confirmation of what has already been discussed informally with upper management. If upper management has not been involved, then the conversation will be more difficult. It is a judgment call whether to involve the entire NWT in the meeting with upper management or have a one-on-one discussion between the NWT manager and upper management. If the NWT's manager expects upper management to be supportive of the work that the NWT has accomplished, then involve the entire team. If not, a private conversation may be more advisable.

The approval process is often an iterative process with the NWT submitting its major activity list to upper management and upper management returning the proposal along with suggestions that the NWT should consider. A word of caution: If "miscellaneous" accounts for more than 10% of the NWT's efforts, the NWT should explain what makes up this category. If upper management is in agreement, he or she should sign off on the document. This step is made much easier because upper management has already reviewed and approved the area's mission statement. However, often during this step, both the mission statement and the major activity list undergo change. Once upper management has signed off on the mission statement and major activity list, all the NWT members working in the area should also sign these documents indicating that they understand the area's role within the organization and that they will support this role.

The form shown in Figure 3-5 can facilitate this process. The circled numbers refer to the line on the form. Some line titles may not be applicable to the area using the form. Make changes as you need to. The following is a description of each line title:

1. **Function Name**. This is normally the major function in which the area is located (example: Quality Assurance).
2. **Area Name**. The name of the area if it has one (example: Magnetic Heads Quality Engineering).
3. **Area Number**. The number (perhaps alphanumeric) that designates the area.
4. **Area Mission Statement**. Describe the mission of the area. Answer the key question of why it exists.
5. **Major Activities of the Area**. Usually there will be no more than 10 major activities that the area performs. The last activity is often a miscellaneous category. It should not account for more than 25% of the total area's efforts. Most of these activities will require inputs from suppliers and must add value to these inputs. These value-added activities produce outputs. An activity that does not meet these requirements becomes highly suspect as to why it is being done at all. Define these activities well; otherwise, all that follow will be difficult to do and have very little value.
6. **Coordinated By**. This is the name of the individual who served as the leader of the **AAA** activity in the area. It may or may not be the NWT manager of the area.
7. **Date**. The date this form was completed and agreed to by the NWT.

Area Mission Statement and Major Activities	
(1.) Function Name	
(2.) Area Name	(3.) Area Name
(4.) Area Mission Statement	
(5.) List Major Activities of Area and % Total Time For Each	
1. ______	______ %
2. ______	______ %
3. ______	______ %
4. ______	______ %
5. ______	______ %
6. ______	______ %
7. ______	______ %
8. ______	______ %
9. ______	______ %
10. ______	______ %
Misc. ______	______ %
(6.) Coordinated By	(7.) Date
(8.) Approved By	(9.) Date
(10.) Understood By	
	(10.) Revision Date

FIGURE 3-5. Area Mission Statement and Major Activities Form

8. **Approved By**. This is the signature of the upper management who has the authority to delegate work to the area and who is held accountable for the performance of the area. This is the lowest-level person who can legitimize the area's mission and is responsible for funding the area's activities.
9. **Date**. The date that the form was approved by upper management.
10. **Understood By**. This is the signature of the NWT members. Each member signs the document indicating that he or she knows and understands what the area's mission is and the major activities that go on within the area. Signing the document increases the individual's personal commitment.
11. **Revision Date**. Each time the form is updated by the NWT, a new revision date should be recorded. Some organizations also record a revision level. Example: Revision 3 or Revision C.

This document replaces the mission statement document prepared in Chapter 2.

Step 8–Assign Activity Champions

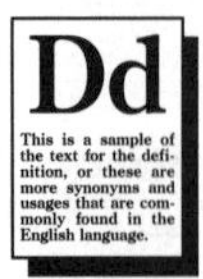

An activity champion is the member of the NWT that is assigned to lead the NWT through phases III through VII for a specific activity.

Now is the time to select an individual that will champion the improvement efforts for each activity. We call this person the "activity champion" (AC). We selected the term activity champion in place of activity owner because we want all of the people involved in the activity to feel that they own the activity. The AC should be someone that takes part in the activity and is respected by the other people that own the activity. We recommend that no one individual is assigned to be the AC for more than one activity if possible. This approach provides maximum involvement and technical growth for the individual members of the natural work team. The AC is responsible for

- coordinating and documenting the measurement system for the activity

- coordinating the definition of performance standards for the activity
- collecting and plotting the measurement data
- obtaining corrective action on customer complaints
- meeting formally and informally with customers to define potential areas for improvement
- meeting with suppliers to communicate improvement needs
- coordinating improvement efforts related to the activity
- building a consensus on challenge targets
- investigating suggestions
- defining internal weaknesses within the activity
- interfacing with supporting groups to get improvements implemented
- defining training needs and obtaining resources to fulfill these needs
- maintaining and reporting progress

Example: The natural work team that Jim Harrington is a member of at Ernst & Young is a good example. The natural work team is made up of three full-time employees and two interns from local universities. It is called the International Quality Advisory team. The following is its mission statement and activities.

Mission: To promote E&Y as a provider of quality services and to develop advanced quality methodologies that E&Y can deploy.

Service Policy: Treat all of our customers and suppliers as we would like to be treated.

Activities:

1. To service client needs and business opportunities—activity champion: H. James Harrington
2. To redesign E&Y's quality management systems (ISO 9000)—activity champion: David Farrell
3. Write and publish technical reports and books—activity champion: interns
4. Conduct external lectures—activity champion: Tia Feagai

It is important to note that the activity champion play a critical role in phases III through VII, but most of their effort takes place in phase VII—the continuous improvement phase.

Things That Can Help

- Use a computer spreadsheet to compute the time percentage.
- Use a Pareto diagram after the percentage of time has been computed.

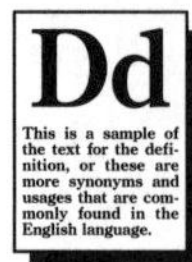

A **Pareto diagram** is a bar graph showing the frequency of occurrence of various concerns, ordered with the most frequent ones first.

- Use a nominal group technique to help identify critical activities.

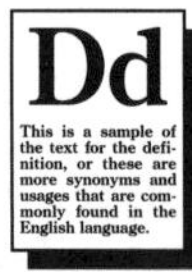

The **nominal group technique** is a structured method used to combine and prioritize a list of individual ideas by the use of a noting approach.

- Schedule your first meeting for at least two hours, depending on the complexity of the area.
- Collect the cards from everyone the day before the meeting to ensure they are ready.

Ralph Waldo Emerson provides the NWT with a good rule when he said: "Make yourself necessary to someone."[1]

Examples

The following are partial initial major activity lists by group ranked from highest to lowest by percentage of time required to complete.

Insurance Department

- Processing new policies—30%
- Researching data for salesperson before the sale—20%
- Updating policies—15%
- Preparing financial reports—15%
- Personal activities—10%
- Miscellaneous—10%

Figure 3-6 shows the completed area mission statement and major activities form for this area.

Manufacturing Line

- Inspecting incoming parts
- Kitting parts
- Scheduling work
- Processing paperwork
- Assembling parts
- Reworking parts
- Reconfiguring assembly line

Customer Service Support

- Interfacing with field service sites
- Defining how to fix the specific problem
- Training on new or current products
- Updating the database
- Working with product engineering to get corrective action documented
- Visiting customer sites
- Following up on effectiveness of corrective action

Defining major activities that the area is conducting helps the area focus on its mission. This focus provides a reason for everyone's activities. This phase begins the analysis of your area. You will use other criteria as the **AAA** process goes on.

Summary

In Phase III, the NWT should have completed the following.

- Define the activities that go on within the area.
- Quantify the resources consumed by each activity.
- Define the major activities that go on in the area.
- Relate the major activities to the area's mission statement.
- Reassign activities that are not related to the area's mission statement.

Area Mission Statement and Major Activities

Function Name Insurance Department	
Area Name Insurance Policy Processing Department	Area No. 351

Area Mission Statement

Our mission is to efficiently and effectively process insurance policies that conform to the individual requirements defined by our agents.

(5.) List Major Activities of Area and % Total Time For Each

Activity	%
1. Processing new policies	34%
2. Researching data for salesperson before sale	20%
3. Updating policies	15%
4. Preparing financial reports	15%
5. Personal activities	10%
6.	%
7.	%
8.	%
9.	%
10.	%
Misc.	6%

Coordinated By Bob Wilson	Date 5/28/97
Approved By (Upper Management)	Date 6/2/97

(10.) Understood By

(NWT members)

(11.) Revision Date

FIGURE 3-6. Filled-in Form

- Get upper management and employee support and understanding of the area's mission and activities.
- Assign an activity champion to each activity.

Notes

1. Helio Gomez, *Quality Quotes* (Milwaukee, WI: American Society for Quality Control (ASQC)-Quality Press, 1996), 207.

Putting the Puzzle of AAA Together

In this chapter we have found where "process" fits into the **AAA** puzzle.

CHAPTER 

Phase IV—Develop Customer Relationships

If You and Your Customer Have Not Agreed on What You Will Provide, You Are in No Position to Satisfy Your Customer's Needs

Chapter Purpose

Ford Motors' former chairman, Donald E. Peterson, points out: "If we are not customer-driven, our cars won't be either." Studies have shown that the cost to get a new external customer for an existing product is seven times more than to keep your current customers. As Robert W. Peach, noted quality consultant and past executive of Sears Roebuck & Co., put it: "The goods come back, but not the customer."[1]

Data also indicate that there is a 300% greater opportunity to lose an external customer over poor service than poor product quality. In most organizations there is direct positive and negative correlation between fluctuations in internal customer satisfaction and trends in external customer satisfaction.

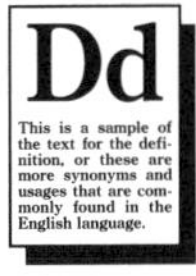

The **customer** is the person or area who receives output of the area.

It is critical that you know the wants and needs of your customers and make certain that each area has the ability to meet those needs. You must develop data systems that correctly define what the external customers want, need, and receive. It is also critical to develop methods to anticipate their future needs, not just their current needs. In addition, you must monitor the marketplace to keep track of your competition as well as changes in technology and current market pressures.

To achieve high levels of customer satisfaction and customer retention, you must understand the total needs of the external customers and consistently meet or exceed their expectations.

There are two types of customers, external and internal.

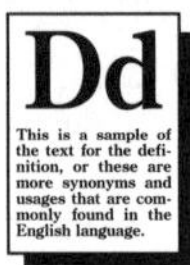

External customers are customers that are not part of the organization and usually pay for the goods and services they receive.

Internal customers are customers that are part of the organization who receive output from any other part of the organization area.

Almost every person in an organization is an internal customer for someone else in the organization.

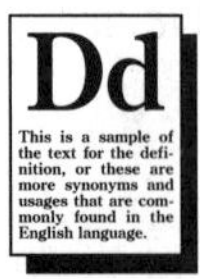

Outputs are the products and/or services provided by an activity or task that are delivered to its customer.

An **input**, on the other hand, is any product and/or service that a customer receives.

Note: A product and/or service that is output from the NWT is called input to a customer.

Retaining internal customers may not be an issue for you at this time. However, if you do not do a good job of meeting the needs of your internal customers, the needs of your external customers may not be met as well as they should be. Time after time, studies have shown that if an organization has a high level of internal customer satisfaction, it has a positive impact on the individuals who interface directly with the external customer causing them to perform better. As a result, external customer satisfaction ratings for these organizations are about 20% higher.

On the other hand, focusing on the needs of your internal customer to the point that it has a negative effect on the external customer is a sure way to lose business. Frequently, internal customers ask for things that they do not really need. Trying to meet those needs leads to waste and causes the organization to become less efficient. AAA is the process that identifies where this type of waste is generated as well as defining the area's output that is real value added.

Most NWT's do not have a direct external customer. Their major customer(s) are other areas within the organization. We will focus this chapter on analyzing the real needs of internal customers. With slight modifications, the approach provided works equally well with external customers.

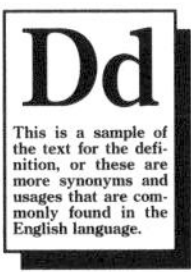

Real needs are those that must be provided to ensure that you keep your external customers and operate the organization at maximum performance.

Most organizations use different guidelines for dealing with internal and external customers. You want your internal customer to be your partner in meeting the requirements of the organization's external customer. A practice that is becoming common in many organizations is that areas are being required to pay for what they receive from other areas (profit centers). One method of accounting for these costs is called activity-based costing (ABC).

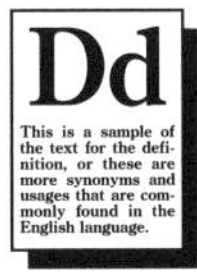

Activity-based costing (ABC) is an accounting methodology by which organizations can more realistically measure the costs and performance of activities, processes, and cost objective. To do this, actual costs are assigned to each activity within processes based on their use of such resources as people and supplies.

When areas are required to pay for what they receive, their needs often change. Instead of asking for whatever they want, they focus their requests on only things really needed.

ABC is very effective at analyzing the cost related to individual activities and then summing the task cost together with activity cost and/or process cost. At the task level, the time required to do the task can be easily measured and the cost of assets used can be determined. In most cases, ABC uses a fixed overhead cost for each area.

To offset this type of operation for internal customers, we like to have budgeted funds transferred from the internal customer's budget when an output is delivered. In addition, whenever possible, we like to give the internal customer the option of selecting who will provide this service. Activities like this have fostered a waterfall of outsourcing around the world.

There are several perceived problems with using money to justify what an NWT is doing or to justify a change to an activity. When using nonexistent money, it is easy to amplify an activity's worth. One major company that used an internal cost analysis system found that it allowed many groups to justify their existence by overstating revenue. In this case, for every dollar collected from an external customer, internal customers amplified it by five times. In other words, five different departments were able to claim the same dollar, so it looked like five dollars were collected.

For example, for a $3,000 sale, the sales, manufacturing, advertising, engineering, and distribution areas all claimed that their efforts resulted in $3,000 of revenue ($15,000 total). In truth, the value-added content of the total organization was only $1,800 because the external supplier's value-added content was $1,200. All five areas plus others need to work together to realize the $1,800 value-added content, so no one area can justify its existence on the organization's total value-added content. In reality, it is very difficult to divide the value-added content among the many areas within the organization. As a result, many organizations allow the individual areas to claim the total savings. Another approach is to divide the savings equally among the contributing departments. For example, $1,800 in savings divided by the five departments = $360 savings per department.

Through either a dialog with or surveys of its customers, the NWT should determine the customer requirements (also called "needs"). Once these requirements are agreed to, the NWT should decide how it can measure its own output to be sure that it consistently meets the customer requirements.

During the **AAA** project, the NWT will be establishing requirements, measurement systems, and performance standards for the area's major activities. We purposely started with the customer to develop these performance indicators because the activities within the area cannot be defined until the customer requirements are well defined. Likewise, the supplier's input requirements cannot be defined until the tasks that make up each major activity are well defined. Therefore, we will first develop customer partnership documents, then internal activities operations documents, and finally the supporting supplier partnership documents for each major activity. Each member of the NWT must take full responsibility for the quality of their output, as Freddy Heineken, founder of Heineken Brewers, stated: "I consider a bad bottle of Heineken a personal insult to me."[2]

Key Questions

Reaching a consensus about the following key questions about each major activity will help the NWT understand what is required to establish a good relationship with its customers.

- Who are the customers for the output of this activity?
- Does the NWT know what the activity's customer expectations are related to this activity's output?
- How does the area meet its customers' expectations?
- Do the area's customers need everything that it provides?
- How does the NWT measure the output it is providing to its customers in relationship to their requirements and expectations?
- Would the NWT's customers like it to do something different than it is doing now?
- How satisfied are the NWT's customers with its output?
- How does the NWT know that its customers are satisfied with its output?

Deliverables

At the end of Phase IV, you will be able to develop an agreed-to customer partnership document for each major activity output that will clearly define the following:

- Who the customers are for that activity's outputs.
- How the activity's output effectiveness will be measured.
- What the minimum acceptable performance level (performance standard) is for each measurement.
- How the customer will provide the area with feedback related to the performance of each activity's output.
- How and when the outputs will be delivered to the customer.

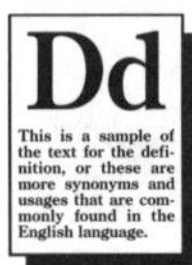

A **performance standard** is the minimum acceptable performance level that must be reached in order to meet the minimum requirements of the customer and/or management. It is the performance level that all employees (new or experienced) should meet after they have completed the defined training program.

Process Overview

So far you have defined the mission, service policy, major activities, and activity champions of your area. The NWT knows why the area exists and understands what its major activities are, but that is not enough. To do something at minimum cost and maximum outstanding quality is a total waste of effort if you don't have a customer who wants the output. It is a lot like Harrington's oil paintings. He gets a lot of satisfaction out of them and is very happy with the finished quality. However, he has no customers for them, and even his wife won't let him hang them in the house. Quality is in the eyes of the customer, not the producer.

Are you doing the right things, at the right time, in the right way for the customer? This is a question that must be answered. One way to find out is to ask questions, either face-to-face or by survey (depending on the size of your customer base). In most cases though, determining the needs and expectations of the output's customer in the **AAA** is usually done by meeting with the output's customer. The things that are agreed to with your customer continue to build the **AAA** model. They are shown in Figure 4-1.

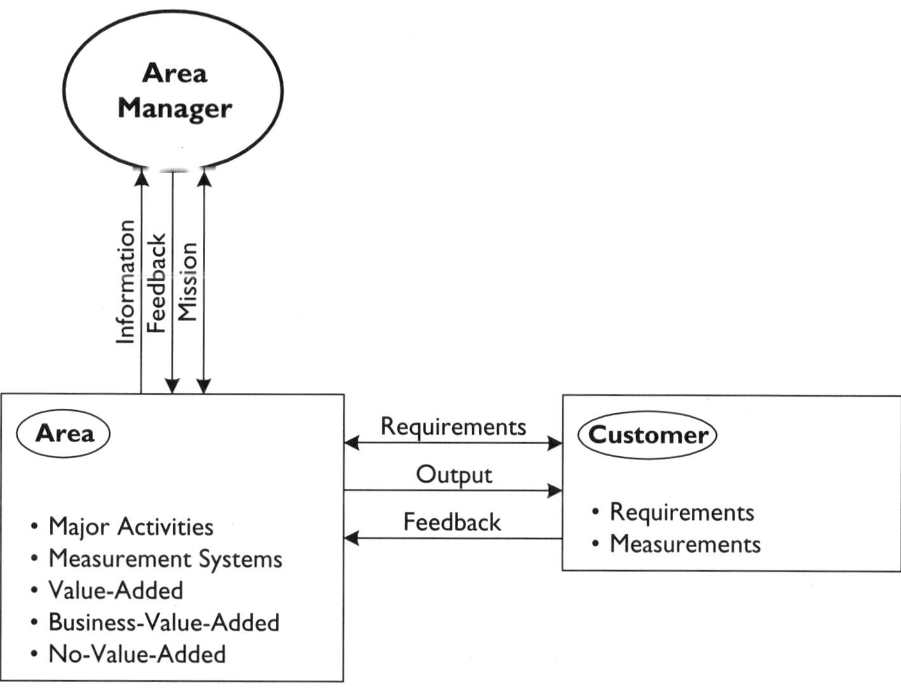

FIGURE 4-1. Customer Relationships

Customer Expectations

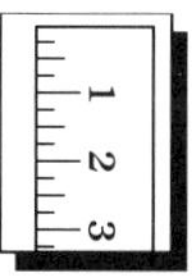

There is often a big difference between needs and expectations. Both should be defined. Needs should always be met for internal and external customers. It is important that the organization meets and exceeds the expectations for external customers. It should be the objective of every NWT to fulfill as many of the internal customer expectations as possible, as long as it does not increase the resources required to fulfill the internal customer requirements. Expectations should also be met if the internal customer can justify to management the additional resources required to meet their expectations.

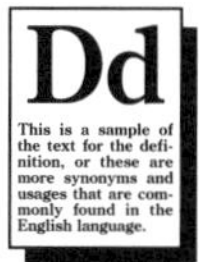

Customer requirements are the characteristics of the area's output that are important to the customer. These characteristics include cost, schedule, quantity, and quality considerations. (Customer requirements are often referred to as customer needs.)

Customer expectations are what the customer would like to have in the output that is delivered to him or her. Often, customer expectations exceed and/or are different from customer requirements. For example, the customer may *need* parts to be delivered to him or her by the 15th of the month but will *expect* them to be delivered by the 10th of the month so that there is a five-day safety factor built into the stocking plan.

The following is a list of typical customer requirements:

- Sales order input to production
  —Order form faxed to correct location.
  —Delivery date cleared with production control if parts are not in stock.
  —Financial clearance with accounting.
  —Cost quote in keeping with the latest price list.
  —All information on the sales order typed and printed.
  —The customer signed off on the order form.
  —Customer purchase order number recorded on the order form.
- Hardware (parts, subassemblies, etc.)
  —Dimensions on a blueprint for a part
  —Parts conforming to blueprint
  —When the customer expects to have a part
  —Parts not costing more than projected
  —How it should be packaged
  —Correct number of parts
- Administrative
  —Format of a report, data, letter
  —When the customer expects to have it
  —Number of copies
  —Method of receiving (network, fax, mail)
  —Readability
  —Accuracy

- Meetings
  - —Starting on time
  - —The right people in attendance
  - —The right material available
  - —Agendas revised two days in advance of the meeting
  - —Meeting ends on or ahead of scheduled time
  - —The conference room properly stocked
  - —Minutes distributed within two days after the meeting

Requirements should not be vague or general and must always be capable of being measured. How else will you and your customer know if the requirements have been met? You must also be prepared to have the customers reject your output when it does not meet their requirements. All too often when an area is driven by a schedule, it will allow output to go to the customer that is less than what the customer requires (and expects). Most of the time the customer will accept it because he or she, too, is schedule driven. The result is that the customer becomes less than satisfied with the input it receives from the NWT. This is often not communicated to the NWT because the customer does not return the unacceptable input. In reality, what the customer has done is set a new, lower-level performance standard for that input. Figure 4-2 is a picture of how an organization's marketing data for current products meets its needs. Figure 4-3 is the same data for new products.

You can tell a lot about an area by how it handles defining and documenting its output requirements. Are they firm or sloppy? How you act on this is a clear indication of how serious you are about making improvements in your area and indicates where customer satisfaction ranks in your improvement plans.

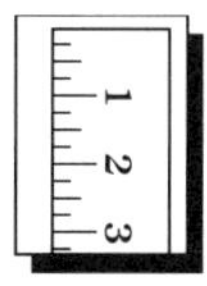

Note: The activity champion will be the catalyst that will lead the NWT through activities 2-7 in this phase and phases V, VI, and VII. The NWT's manager may serve as part of the NWT, but will not lead the analysis.

Phase IV Breakdown

The block diagram in Figure 4-4 shows the seven steps of Phase IV.

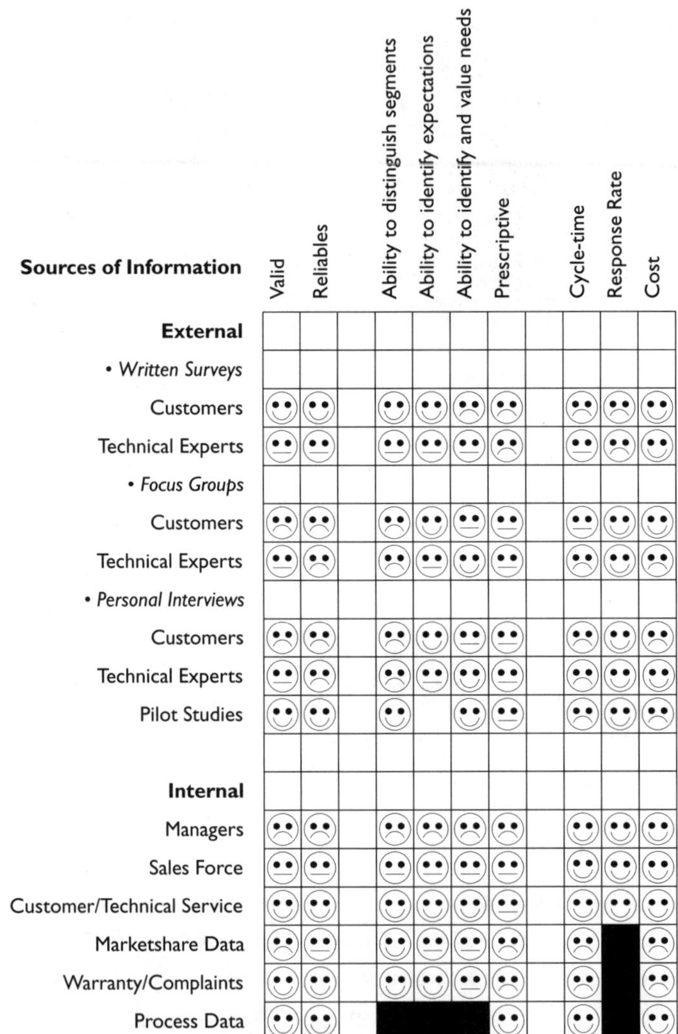

FIGURE 4-2. How Current Product Data Meets Its User's Needs

Step 1–Select Critical Activity

From the list of major activities prepared in Phase III, select one to start the analysis process. Your selection is not important because the total analysis cycle (Phases IV through VI) will be applied to each major activity before the

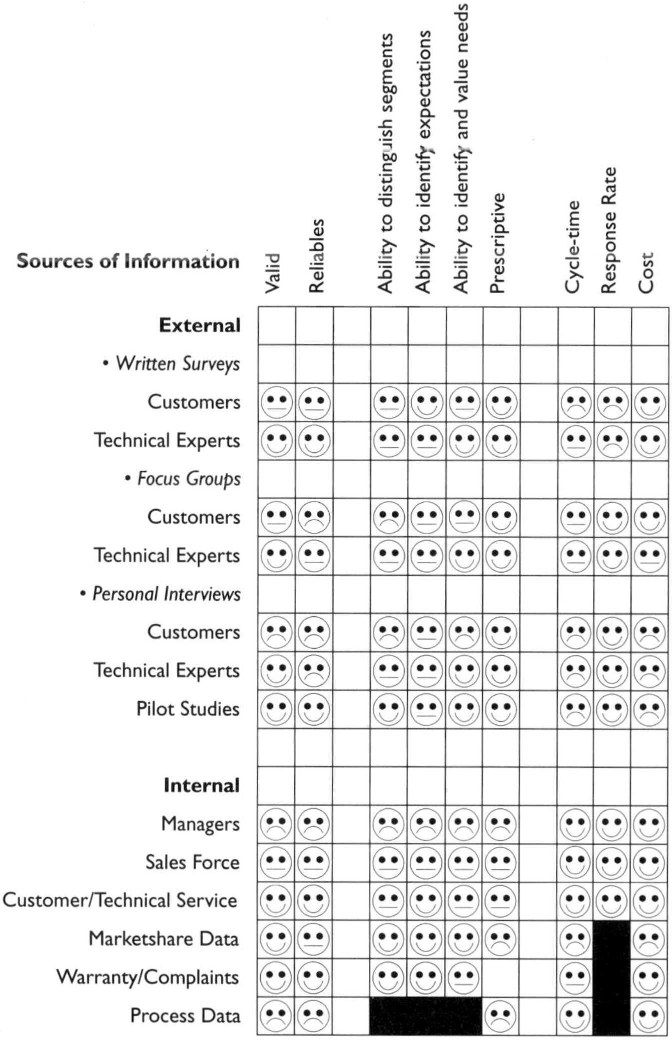

Sources of Information	Valid	Reliables		Ability to distinguish segments	Ability to identify expectations	Ability to identify and value needs	Prescriptive		Cycle-time	Response Rate	Cost
External											
• *Written Surveys*											
Customers	😐	😐		😐	☺	😐	☺		☹	☹	☺
Technical Experts	☺	☺		😐	😐	☺	☺		😐	☹	☺
• *Focus Groups*											
Customers	😐	☹		☹	😐	😐	☺		😐	☺	☺
Technical Experts	☺	😐		😐	😐	☺	☺		😐	☺	😐
• *Personal Interviews*											
Customers	☹	☹		☹	😐	☹	☺		☹	☺	☹
Technical Experts	☺	☹		😐	😐	☺	☺		☹	☺	☹
Pilot Studies	☺	☺		☺	😐	☺	☺		☹	☺	☹
Internal											
Managers	☹	☹		☹	☹	☹	☹		☺	☺	☺
Sales Force	😐	😐		😐	😐	😐	😐		☺	☺	☺
Customer/Technical Service	☺	☺		😐	☺	😐	😐		☺	☺	☺
Marketshare Data	☺	😐		☺	☺	☺	☹		☹	■	☹
Warranty/Complaints	☺	☺		☺	☺	😐			😐	■	☺
Process Data	☹	☹		■	■	■	☹		☺	■	☺

FIGURE 4-3. How New Product Market Data Meets Its User's Needs

AAA project is completed. Start the process with an activity in which the NWT has developed a close working relationship with the individuals who receive its output, allowing the team to gain customer experience in a friendly environment. Another way some NWTs start this phase is by selecting the activity that uses the highest percentage of the area's resources.

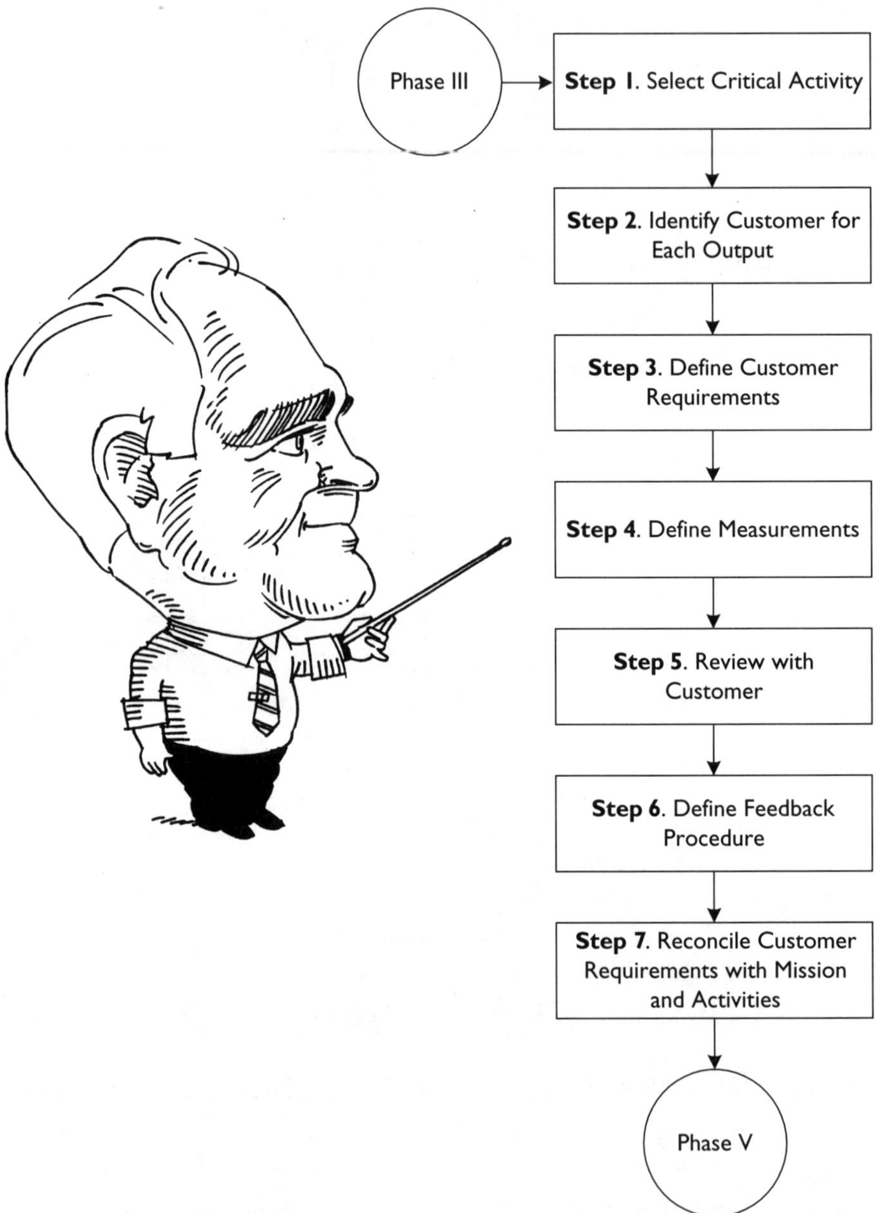

FIGURE 4-4. Phase IV. The Seven Steps That Make Up Phase IV

Step 2–Identify Customers for Each Output

For the activity that you have chosen, identify the outputs from that activity and the customers that receive each output. Frequently, an activity has only one customer. When this is the case, it is relatively easy to focus on his or her needs. When more than one customer exists for any output, their needs may conflict, requiring the NWT to negotiate to resolve the differences between the customers.

Typically, if the output is a report, the customers will be the people on the carbon copy list and the individuals to whom the report is addressed. If the output is the organization's newsletter, the customers will be everyone in the organization plus outside organizations that receive copies. Many individual activities produce numerous outputs. For example, inputting an order into the computer will trigger one output to purchasing to buy parts and a second output to production control to schedule time on the manufacturing line to assemble and test the product. In addition, many outputs have two or more different types of customers:

- Internal customers who receive the output and will use it as an input to one of their activities. In this case, their needs are very important and should be met. These are called dependent, often interchageable with primary, customers. Also, all external customers are considered dependent/primary customers.

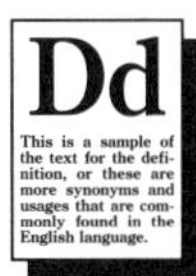

Dependent customers are customers that need the output to do their jobs and would be willing to pay for the output if they had to.

- Internal customers who receive the output to be informed about what is going on but do not take direct action based on the input each time they receive it. For example, the plant manager may receive copies of the minutes from the weekly production control status meeting. These customers are called secondary customers, and they have less influence in defining the output requirements.

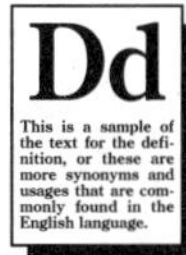

Secondary customers are customers that would not want the output if it was generated just for them and are not expected to take action as a result of the output.

Activity Name: Order Taking

Outputs	Customer	Customer Classification		Cost Per Month
		Dependent	Secondary	
Customer Order Form	• Order Entry Clerk	X		120K
	• Sales Manager		X	
	• Warehouse	X		
	• Production Control	X		
Credit Check Report	• Corp. Bank		X	95K
	• Sales Manager	X		
	• Controller		X	
	• Production Control	X		

FIGURE 4-5. Typical Customer Identification Work Sheet

Figure 4-5 is a typical customer identification work sheet for two different outputs.

The NWT should estimate what its cost is to produce the output. An estimate is acceptable at this point because we are just developing some data that we can discuss with the NWT's customer. In one of the following chapters, we will develop a more accurate database. The estimated cost is added to the customer's identification work sheet (Figure 4-5).

Step 3—Define Customer Requirements

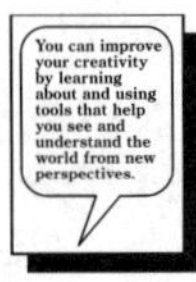

The NWT now needs to define what the customer needs and expects of each output. These needs and expectations are best defined when the NWT puts itself in the shoes of the customers who receive its output and understand how the output will be used. Once the NWT understands how the output is used, it can start to define how to measure whether the output lives up to the customer's needs and expectations. Remember that the needs and expectations of different customers can be very different for the same output. (Example: In looking at a purchase order, distribution wants to know the name and address where the items will be shipped and the date that the items are needed by the external customer. Production control wants to know how many of which part numbers need to be shipped and when they need to be shipped. The purchase order must fill the needs of both of these internal customers.)

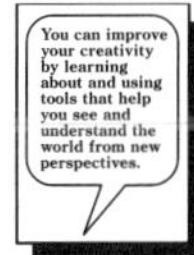

It is also important that the NWT understands the difference between needed and expected requirements. Needs set the minimum standard for the output that the customer will accept. For instance, in a hotel room you need a bed, bathroom, climate control, and phone. These are your "specifications." What you expect from a hotel room is usually very different. A typical person expects a television, some toiletries in the bathroom, a desk, and a couple of chairs. A swimming pool, a spa, an exercise room, and the newspaper in the morning would be nice too, but these fall into a third category called "desires." Desires are optional requirements that should be provided if there is no increased cost or if the customer is willing to pay for the added services.

Customer desires are the luxuries that the customer would like to have but are not expected and may or may not be used. The things that wow the customers.

Needs don't normally change, but expectations change often. Therefore, the NWT must stay very close to its customers in order for its output to meet and exceed its customers' expectations. Meeting customer expectations is often a moving target.

Developing a list of measurable customer requirements (needs and expectations) provides a means of identifying when and where an error occurs and helps the area guide its improvement process. The customer-related measurements must be detailed enough so that any person (even one not familiar with the process) can judge whether they are being met.

Requirements normally fall into three categories: *What* the output should do, *when* it should be delivered, and *how many* should be delivered. These generic categories cover all types of organizations in all types of industries including service, manufacturing, government, health care, and so forth.

- What—details of what the customer expects the activity to provide, for instance
  —A part that must meet a specification
  —A report that must be in a certain format
  —Software that will perform a specific function
  —Packaging in a certain way
- When—specify when the customer wants the output. There should be a window, for instance
  —Not after a time and date
  —Part on "A" date, the rest on "B" date
  —On "A" date plus or minus two days
- How many—defines the quantity that needs to be delivered

There are many ways that the NWT can define customer requirements. For example,

- Define the customer requirements based on what the NWT knows about the output and its customer.
- Prepare a strawman's (preliminary) version of the requirements based on the NWT's knowledge of that output and how the NWT thinks the customer will use the output. Then formalize the requirements by meeting with the customer and adjusting the preliminary requirements based on the customer's comments.
- Ask the customer to prepare the requirements and send them to the area so that the NWT can review them to determine if the area can comply with the requirements.
- The area and the customer can meet to discuss the output, then define the appropriate measurements and requirements, agreeing on what the minimum requirements are for acceptable performance.

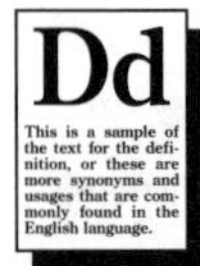

The **customer partnership specification** is a document that is signed off by the NWT and its customers that defines how an output from the NWT will be measured and what the minimum output acceptable performance level (performance standard) is for each measurement. This document also defines how the customer will provide the NWT with feedback on how well the NWT's output is performing in the customer's environment.

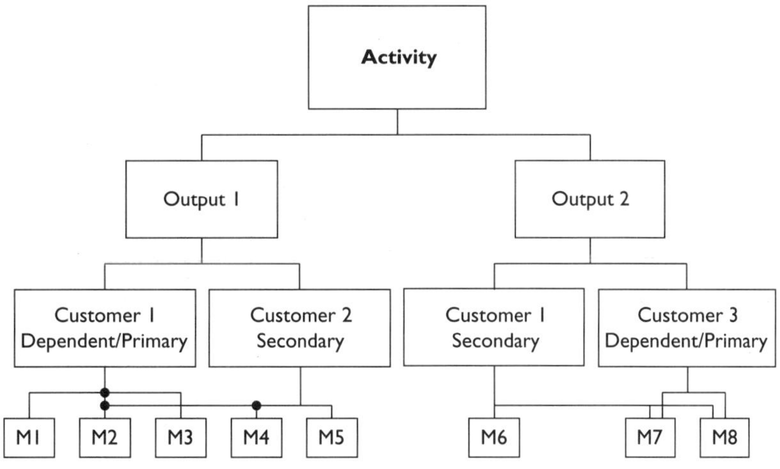

FIGURE 4-6. Customer Requirements Diagram

We like the second approach because we find that the customers are more willing to participate actively in preparing a customer partnership specification if the supplier has taken the initiative and time to prepare a working draft.

To prepare a requirements list, the NWT should review all of the outputs related to the activity being studied that go to internal or external customers. Because there is often more than one output for a single activity, each output will have its own set of customers and associated requirements (see Figure 4-6). Each requirement should then be evaluated to determine if it is a need, an expectation, or a desire, or if it is not a requirement for each customer (see Figure 4-7).

Requirement	Typed Requirement by Customer		
	P-1	S-2	P-3
Customer signed document	N	D	N
Received in mailroom by 1:00 P.M.	E	X	X
Form completely filled out	N	X	N
Printed or typed information	N	D	X

P = Dependent/Primary Customer N = Needed D = Desired
S = Secondary Customer E = Expected X = Not Required

FIGURE 4-7. Requirements Evaluation

Step 4—Define Measurements

This is one of the most difficult steps in the **AAA** methodology. In Step 3, we did a good job of defining the internal and external customer requirements, but no real progress is made until the NWT starts to measure how well it is satisfying these requirements. It is often very hard to translate customer requirements, often called "the voice of the customer," into measurements that can be used to evaluate how well the NWT's outputs are meeting these customer requirements.

The following are typical phrases that customers use to define their expectations:

- It must be user-friendly.
- It must be easy to read.
- It must be ready to use whenever I need it.
- It must arrive on time.

Typical phrases to define their requirements are:

- It should perform well.
- It should not cost too much.
- It should have a short warm-up cycle.
- It should be complete.

These are all good inputs from the customer, but none of them are measurements. The NWT needs to translate these inputs into measurements that will reflect what the customer requires. Measurements need to be developed to spell out clearly how the NWT will know if it is meeting the customer requirements. It could be anything from a visual inspection by anyone to a highly sophisticated testing device.

There are two major types of measurements that the NWT needs to understand at this time: efficiency and effectiveness.

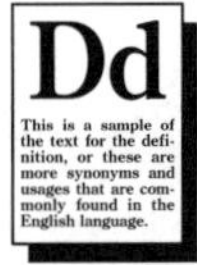

Effectiveness is the extent to which the outputs of the activity (process) meet the needs and expectations of its customers (customer-related measurements).

Effectiveness is a lot like quality, but it includes even more considerations (example: cost, schedule, easy to use, etc.). It is having the right things, at the right place, at the right time, at the right price. Effectiveness is relative to the customer's needs, expectations, and desires. Typical effectiveness measurements include:

- Accuracy
- Cost
- Performance
- Timing
- Appearance
- Reliability
- Usability
- Responsiveness

Over the past 20 years, most organizations have worked very hard on maximizing their output effectiveness for the external customer. Internal customers usually do not get the same level of consideration. Most organizations are more concerned about the second measurement, efficiency, when it comes to internal customer relationships.

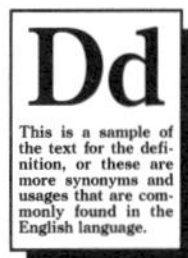

Efficiency is a measure of the resources used to produce an output.

Efficiency measurements are often similar to productivity measurements. Efficiency is an organizational measurement. As an area improves efficiency, the cost per output should decrease. Typical measurements of efficiency include:

- Resources expended per unit of output
- Value-added cost per unit of output
- Percent real-value-added time of total time
- Poor-quality costs
- Processing cycle time per item
- Processing cost per item

We will talk about developing efficiency measurements for the activities in Chapter 5. In this chapter, we will develop effectiveness measurements.

For every requirement that is classified as a need or expectation, there should be a way of measuring how well the output meets this requirement. It is not necessary to measure all requirements on each individual output all of the time, but they should be at least sampled on a scheduled basis. The measurement should be made by the NWT in most cases, but some measurements can only be made by the customer. In these cases, the NWT must rely on customer feedback to determine if it is performing well. This approach is usually acceptable for internal customers but not for external customers unless there is no other way that the data can be collected.

We find that it is sometimes hard for the NWT to define how to measure some of the customer requirements. If this is the case, don't get upset. The NWT will meet with the customer in the next step, and perhaps the customer will eliminate the requirement or have a creative way to measure it. Another book in this series will look at the subject of measurements in detail.

Figure 4-8 is a Customer Partnership Agreement form. It is a typical form that is filled out by the NWT and its customers. In this case, the NWT is the supplier to its customer. The customer indicates his or her agreement by approving the document. The NWT's manager/leader signs off on it also, indicating that the NWT can provide output that meets the defined requirements.

The form is completed as follows. The numbers in front of each title are used to designate the title description. Because some titles may not be applicable for the area/organization using **AAA**, changes are made as needed.

1. **Activity**. Use the same activity that was addressed on the Input Requirements and Measurements form (Chapter 3).
2. **Output**. The name of the output that is being analyzed.
3. **Output Performance Standard**. The minimum acceptable performance level of the total output that the customer considers to be acceptable.
4. **Requirements**. The parameters that specify what your customers expect when they receive the output, such as the time they want it, the format they want it in, the dimensions (per specification), etc.
5. **Performance Standard**. The minimum acceptable error rate that the customer will accept for the specific measurement.

Customer Partnership Agreement

Area Name and Number: ______________________

(1.) Activity: ______________________

(2.) Output: ______________________

(3.) Output Performance Standard: ______________________

- Customers:
  1. ______________________
  2. ______________________
  3. ______________________

(4.) • Requirement _____: ______________________

(5.) • Performance Standard: ______________________

(6.) • Performance as of ___/___/___: ______________________

(7.) • Measured: ____________ • Estimated: ____________

(8.) • Meets Standard: Yes: ______ No: ______

(9.) • Customer Feedback Process: ______________________

____

- Requirement _____: ______________________
  - Performance Standard: ______________________
  - Performance as of ___/___/___: ______________________
  - Measured: ____________ • Estimated: ____________
  - Meets Standard: Yes: ______ No: ______
  - Customer Feedback Process: ______________________

____

- Requirement _____: ______________________
  - Performance Standard: ______________________
  - Performance as of ___/___/___: ______________________
  - Measured: ____________ • Estimated: ____________
  - Meets Standard: Yes: ______ No: ______
  - Customer Feedback Process: ______________________

____

(10.) Prepared by: ______________ Date: ___/___/___

(11.) Supplier Approval: ______________ Date: ___/___/___

(12.) Customer Approval:

______________ Date: ___/___/___

______________ Date: ___/___/___

______________ Date: ___/___/___

FIGURE 4-8. Customer partnership agreement form

6. **Performance as of ________ / ________ / ________.** This is either the estimated or actual measured performance of the specific requirement. (These data are optional.)
7. **Measured or Estimated.** This is used to record whether the number in line 6 is a measured or estimated value.
8. **Meets Standards.** This indicates whether the output is presently meeting standard.
9. **Customer Feedback Process.** How will the customer feed back the results of the measurements to those who need to know? When will this happen?
10. **Prepared by**: The activity champion should sign here.
11. **Supplier Approval.** The manager of the NWT signs off on the document, indicating the ability of the NWT to provide the output to the parameters stated in the document.
12. **Signature.** The signature of the individual who can agree to the document for the customer.

Step 5–Review with Customer

During an interview we had with quality consultant Ken Lomax in September 1997, he stated, "I am frequently surprised at how often employees work so hard to provide their customers with output that the customers could care less about, and not provide them with what they really need."

Step 4 is one of the most difficult steps in the **AAA** methodology, but Step 5 is the most important step because the NWT is going to understand what is important to its customers and agree on what is acceptable performance. During this step, the NWT will complete the following tasks:

- Define which customers will be interviewed.
- Review outputs that the customer(s) receives.
- Verify if the customer is a dependent/primary customer.
- Verify the value of each output to the customer(s).
- Review output requirements and update as needed.
- Review measurements and update as needed.

- Define minimum acceptable outgoing performance standards.
- Define customer feedback systems.
- Discuss ways that the NWT's output could be improved from the customer's standpoint.

We often make the serious mistake of thinking we know what is best for the customer or what the customer wants. As George Bernard Shaw put it: "Do not do unto others as you would they should do unto you. Their tastes may not be the same."[3]

Define Which Customers Will Be Interviewed

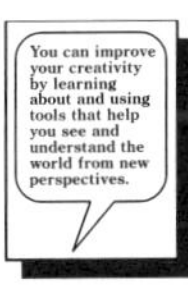

Using the customer identification work sheet (Figure 4-5), the NWT will identify the customers who receive each output. Then the NWT will determine which customers it will contact to develop agreed-to customer specifications. This is a relatively easy task if there is only one internal customer for the output, which is rarely the case.

In practice, we recommend that the NWT meets with all of the internal primary customers unless there are more than five. If there are many internal dependent (primary) customers, the NWT may need to sample the population to reduce the cost of conducting Step 5. For example, if the output was the monthly budget statement that goes to all the departments (593 departments) in the organization, it may not be practical to meet with all of the departments. In this case, a sample of the customers would be interviewed.

The sample does not have to be a completely random sample of the total population. The NWT can select specific departments that are very concerned about the output, since these areas are usually more cooperative. We like to select people who have complained about the output in the past. In addition, you would want the sample to include someone from each function within the organization. For example: when selecting the manager to represent the product engineering function, you might select Miss X because she has been very vocal about things that should be changed in the report. An effective way to get input from a large group of customers is through the use of focus groups.

All of this is fairly routine if you are interfacing with internal customers only, but how should you handle external customers? The answer is: very carefully. Often, output that goes to external customers goes to many external customers. We do not recommend that the NWT set up meetings with the external customers on its own. In most organizations there is a set protocol related to external customer contacts. Be sure that you follow this protocol. We then recommend that the NWT select customers that receive large quantities of the output, if possible. Then meet with the marketing and sales function to determine what is the best way to collect the required information. Our first preference is personal contact between the NWT and the external customer. There are five ways that this can be accomplished:

- The NWT goes to see the customer.
- The customer comes to see the NWT.
- Focus groups of customers are held at a central location.
- A conference call is placed using an audio/video conferencing center.
- A conference call is placed using regular phone systems.

All five of these approaches will work. We like use the focus group approach.

Another approach is to have the salesperson collect the data. This has a built-in problem because the salesperson usually does not understand what is required to produce the output. Because of this lack of understanding, the input collected by the salesperson is usually less complete than the previous five approaches mentioned. The other problem with this approach, is that the NWT does not get to know and understand its external customer. The major problem that most organizations have is that there is little or no personal contact between the individuals who produce the output and the individuals who use the output. It is very easy to neglect a person you have never seen and don't understand. Personal contact usually heightens the NWT's concern for the customer.

The least acceptable way of collecting the desired information from external customers is to survey them. Used as a last resort, the survey form should be designed by an expert in conducting field surveys. In addition, a very good cover letter is needed that explains how the data will be used.

At first glance, you might think that the customer requirements are already clearly defined in the product specification. This is not the case for most customer requirements. The customers, in some cases, define the requirements of the hardware they receive but very seldom define the requirements for areas like after-sales service, sales, distribution, packaging, quality assurance, accounts receivable, etc. In truth, the external customer does not define the requirements for most of the products/services that they receive that have the biggest impact on their decision to buy again from an organization or to reuse its services.

The NWT should define all of the outputs from an activity and all of the outputs' customers before the final customer interview list is completed. It is much more effective to discuss a number of outputs during one interview with a customer rather than scheduling multiple meetings about each individual output.

Once the customers have been selected, contact should be made and meeting dates established. One week prior to the meeting, agendas should be sent out to the participants. Use flip charts at the meeting to document what went on and the agreements that were reached.

Review Outputs That the Customer Receives

The meeting should start by reviewing the purpose of the meeting and the meeting agenda. The NWT should then present the outputs it provides to the customer to be sure there is complete agreement on which outputs will be discussed.

Verify If the Customer Is a Dependent/Primary Customer

The NWT should ask the customer if they require the input to perform their activities (dependent/primary customer) or if they receive the input to keep them informed but would not require it if it were going to be prepared for their use only (secondary customer). It is normally a good practice to estimate beforehand what the input cost is to generate the output. The cost often makes the customer change his or her mind about whether or not the input is needed.

Verify the Value of Each Output to the Customer

The NWT should now discuss with the customer what its costs are to provide the output. This is typically accomplished by the NWT explaining the costs to produce the output (see Figure 4-5) and how many dependent/primary customers receive the output. The equivalent cost to the individual primary customer is calculated by dividing the total cost by the number of dependent/primary customers. For example, using the data from Figure 4-5 for customer order forms, the total cost is $120,000 per month, and there are three dependent/primary customers. The cost for the input to the individual dependent/primary customer is simply calculated by diving the cost of the input ($120,000) by the number of dependent/primary customers (three), resulting in an individual cost per month per customer of $40,000.

Once this information is presented to the customer, the NWT should ask the customer if his or her share of the NWT's value-added cost would be acceptable to the customer if the customer had to pay for it. If the customer's answer is no, then the customer should be reclassified as a secondary customer, and the total cost of the output should be divided between the remaining dependent/primary customers. (Using the previous example, the total cost of the output is $120,000 per month, and it would be divided between the two remaining primary customers. Their individual costs would be $60,000 per month.) At this point in time, the NWT is not asking the dependent/primary customer to pay for the service. It is only asking the internal customer if the NWT's effort is justified. We are often surprised at the number of outputs that are not cost-justifiable and can be eliminated.

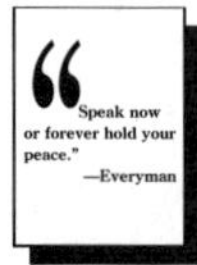

It is not enough just to give good service; the customer must perceive *the fact that he or she is getting good service.*

—ALBRECHT AND ZEMKE

Review Output Requirements and Update as Needed

The NWT should review each requirement with the help of the customer requirements diagram (Figure 4-6) and ask the customer the following about each output.

- Is each requirement something that the customer needs, expects, desires, or doesn't need?

- Are there different requirements that the customer needs or expects that are not part of the requirements defined by the NWT?

The NWT should point out that every additional requirement costs the organization money and that a way of measuring each requirement will be the next thing that will be addressed.

It is often very eye-opening to the NWT when it finds out what is really important to its customers. Sometimes many of the things that the NWT thought were important, the customer could care less about. Sometimes some of the customer's real requirements were not even considered by the NWT. If the customer adds requirements to the output that are beyond the present scope of the NWT activities, the NWT should make the customer aware of its scope limitations and commit to have the new requirement evaluated and hopefully resolved by upper management.

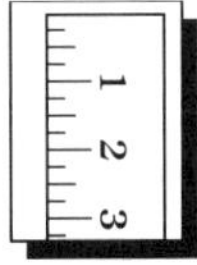

It is important that the NWT does not agree to provide output that exceeds its capabilities (for example: a specific report is prepared once a quarter, but the customer would like to have it prepared every week). The customer should be willing to help justify any additional resources that are required. The results of this task should be an agreed-to list of requirements between the NWT and its customers.

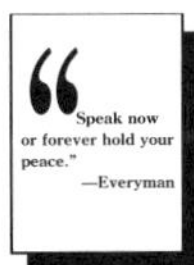

The truth of the matter is that when it comes to quality, the customer has all the votes.

—JOHN GUASPARI[5]

Review Measurements and Update as Needed

The NWT should now review, with the customers, the measurements that were developed for each of the requirements. The customers should be asked if the requirement is correct, if it is necessary to measure compliance to the requirement, and if there is a better way to measure the necessary requirements. As a result of these discussions, the output worksheet in Figure 4-9 should be updated as appropriate.

Output: Customer Order Form

Type of Requirement by Customer			Requirement	Measurement	Performance Standard	Customer Feedback System
P1	P2	P3				
N	N	N	Customer signed document	Check customer signature block	1% error rate	Return form to salesperson
E	X	X	Received in mailroom by 1:00 P.M.	Time stamp of arrival	2% error rate	Salesperson billed for overnight shipment to customer
N	X	N	Form completely filled out	Visual inspection of form	1% error rate	Phone call to salesperson to get data for monthly error report
N	N	X	Printed or typed information	Must be readable	0.5% error rate	Phone call to salesperson
Total customer order form performance standard: 2% maximum error rate						

P = Dependent/Primary Customer   N = Needed   D = Desired
S = Secondary Customer   E = Expected   X = Not Required

FIGURE 4-9. **Output Worksheet**

Define Minimum Acceptable Outgoing Performance Standards

The customer should now be asked what the minimum acceptable outgoing performance standard would be for each measurement.

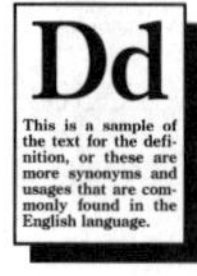

Acceptable outgoing performance standards are the minimum level that the specific output measurement must perform at so that it does not have a negative impact on the customer's performance. For example, the customer would like to have the output delivered at 11:00 A.M.

each day, but the customer does not use the output until 3:00 P.M. In this case, the acceptable performance standard is that the output must be delivered each day before 2:30 P.M.

We have had NWTs that have developed two performance standards: acceptable outgoing performance standard and preferred or targeted performance level.

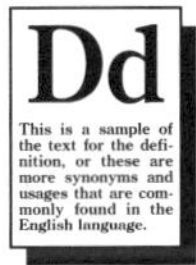

The preferred performance level is the level of performance that the customer would like the supplier to deliver most of the time, and the supplier agrees that it is a performance level that it is capable of delivering most of the time.

In the previous example, the preferred performance level would be 11:00 A.M. As a result of this task, the Performance Standard column in Figure 4-9 should be filled in.

We have often found that there is a need to define an overall performance standard that is less than the summed value of the individual performance standards. In Figure 4-9 the Total Customer Order Form Performance Standard is documented at the bottom of the work sheet.

Discuss Ways That the NWT's Output Could Be Improved from the Customer's Standpoint

The NWT should now solicit input from the customer about how the NWT's output can be improved to make it more valuable/easier to use for the customer. Some of these ideas may need to be implemented very soon in order for the customer requirements to be met. Others will relate to improvements that are not required but would have a beneficial effect on the organization if they were implemented. There may also be other ideas or concepts that will have little or no real value added to the organization. All of these ideas should be recorded at this time, but commitments should not be made to implement any of them unless the NWT's output does not meet current customer requirements. These ideas will be used to start an "idea bank," which is discussed in Chapter 8.

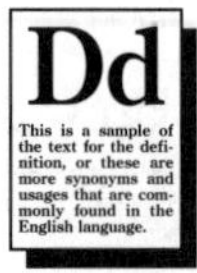

An **idea bank** is a list of ideas and concepts that may be used at a later date to improve the NWT's performance.

A word of caution: We find that it is always best to have some idea about how well the output is performing before you meet with your customers. This will greatly aid you in your discussions and minimize the amount of effort required to complete Step 5.

Step 6—Define Feedback Procedure

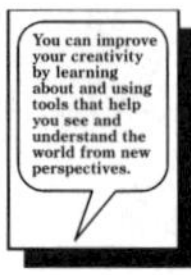

The importance of the customer providing feedback on the acceptability of the NWT's output cannot be overemphasized. The NWT should now work with the customer to define how the customer will provide feedback to the NWT related to how well the NWT's products meet the customer's requirements. The normal practice related to internal suppliers is the rule "No news is good news," but this is poor practice. The internal customer has a responsibility to its suppliers to keep them informed about the acceptability of the products/services they provide. This ongoing feedback provides a way for the suppliers to measure their performance and progress.

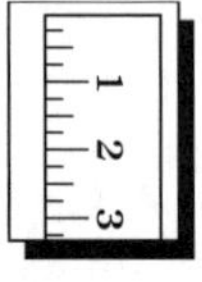

The rule we like to use is "Don't complain about poor products if you don't praise good products." With this rule in mind, the NWT and the internal customer should work together to define a feedback system that will measure changes, either positive or negative, in the NWT's products that are consumed by the customer. It may not be practical to provide this type of information on all products that the internal customer consumes. At a minimum, a system should be established to provide this type of information on all critical inputs from the NWT that are not directly measurable by the NWT.

Just as the NWT has an obligation to provide its customers with output that meets their requirements, the customers have an obligation to provide feedback to the NWT about how well the output meets their requirements. This in no way relieves the NWT from its obligation to establish in-process controls that minimize the possibilities of delivering output that does not meet customer requirements.

The purpose of the customer feedback system is to provide the NWT with regular feedback, both positive and negative, on how well its output is meeting customer requirements. Usually, internal feedback systems have only been effective at defining when the system goes out of control. It is imperative that the NWT is provided with information that allows it to evaluate both the positive and negative impact of its in-process control systems. In order for this to occur, regular feedback should be received from each customer related to the measurements that are important to that customer. As a result of this task, the Customer Feedback System column in Figure 4-9 should be filled out.

The output worksheet (Figure 4-9) is now completely filled out. This provides the NWT with the necessary information to complete the customer partnership agreement form defined in Figure 4-8. When the customer partnership agreement form is completely filled out, the customer should sign and date the document, indicating his or her acceptance of the document as defining what the customer requires for the NWT's output.

Specifying the conditions and method of feedback is one of the most overlooked items in customer/supplier relations.

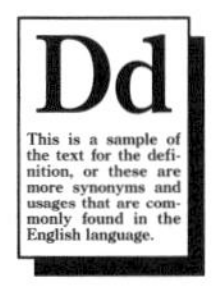

Feedback is direct input from the NWT's customer about how well the activity's outputs are performing.

There are many ways of giving and receiving feedback, including written, computer, and verbal reports. In addition, the NWT needs to know if it is meeting the customer's needs and expectations. The NWT also needs to know when the customer's requirements change.

Without proper feedback procedures, the NWT may be causing its customer unneeded difficulty or wasting resources doing something that does not need to be done. It is important to keep the lines of communication open to ensure that the NWT's activities are performing efficiently and effectively.

Step 7—Reconcile Customer Requirements with Mission and Activities

After the NWT has met with its customers and developed an agreed-to set of customer requirements and measurements, the NWT should look at its activities and mission. The NWT's customer requirements may cause the NWT to change its activities and could impact its mission. Required changes to the mission statement and/or activities should be discussed with upper management.

If upper management does not agree with adding the new requirements to the area's responsibilities, the NWT has the responsibility to get the situation resolved to the satisfaction of its customers.

Things That Can Help

The following actions can help in this step:

- Look at all of your critical activities and group their outputs by customer.
- Before meeting with your customer(s), make certain you know how to measure each output, who receives the output, and what you believe are the requirements related to each output.
- Reach agreement on a default procedure or what you will do if things do not meet your customer's requirements.
- Understand the present performance level of each output before meeting with the customer.
- Don't agree to do something that is not in line with the area's mission statement.

Examples

The following are partial lists of customer requirements by group.

Insurance Policy Processing Department/351

- Major activity
  —Policy preparation

- Customer
  - —Agent
- Needs
  - —Correct policy
  - —No errors
  - —Background check
  - —Delivered on the date the external customer requested the policy
- Expectations
  - —Quick turnaround
  - —Prompt commission posting
  - —Delivered on schedule
- Measurements
  - —Number of returned policies for wrong information
- Performance standard
  - —One nonsignificant typing error per 10,000 policies.

Figure 4-10 is the Customer Partnership Agreement Form filled in for the completed, unsigned policy.

BAK Final Assembly Area/301

- Major activity
  - —Assembling parts
- Customer
  - —Final test
- Needs
  - —Parts fit
  - —Parts function
- Expectations
  - —Do not have to wait for parts
  - —Parts at the correct engineering change level
- Measurements
  - —Zero defects on any parts
  - —Zero downtime for lack of parts

Customer Service Support Department/107

- Major activity
  - —Respond to calls

Customer Partnership Agreement

Area Name and Number: Insurance Policy Process Department/351

Activity: Policy Preparation

Output: Completed, unsigned policy

Output Performance Standard: 0.1% insignificant and 0.01% financial error rates

- Customers:
  1. Insurance agents
  2.
  3.

- Requirement 1 : Correct financial data
  - Performance Standard: One error in 10,000 policies
  - Performance as of 12 / 1 / 99 : 0.005% errors
  - Measured: X • Estimated:
  - Meets Standard: Yes: X No:
  - Customer Feedback Process: Bob Wilson notified by agent each time an error is noted.

- Requirement 2 : Correctly typed (nonfinancial)
  - Performance Standard: One error in 1,000 policies
  - Performance as of 12 / 1 / 99 : 1%
  - Measured: X • Estimated:
  - Meets Standard: Yes: No: X
  - Customer Feedback Process: Policy returned to be corrected

- Requirement 3 : Delivered on date requested
  - Performance Standard: 0.1% late
  - Performance as of 12 / 1 / 99 : 1.3%
  - Measured: • Estimated:
  - Meets Standard: Yes: No:
  - Customer Feedback Process:

Prepared by: F. Harrington Date: 12 / 1 / 99

Supplier Approval: Bob Wilson Date: 12 / 1 / 99

Customer Approval:

Agent Manager Date: 12 / 15 / 99

Date: / /

Date: / /

FIGURE 4-10. Customer Partnership Agreement Form for Completed, Unsigned Policy Output

- ▶ Customer
  - —Field customer engineer
- ▶ Needs
  - —Prompt response
  - —Correct Information
  - —Knowledgeable person
- ▶ Expectations
  - —Technical knowledge database
  - —Accurate answers
  - —Fast turnaround
- ▶ Measurements
  - —Less than one minute wait time on phone.
  - —Receive needed information 85% of the time at that time.
  - —Other 15% within two working days.
  - —No incidents of being talked down to.

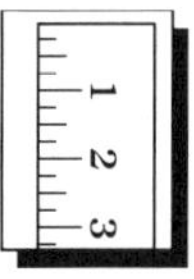

You may think that we are being picky about details, but quality demands meticulous attention to details. There is no detail too small that it cannot lose a customer for you. Careful attention to details is the way that world-class organizations do business.

Summary

During Phase IV, the NWT and its customer(s) agreed on a customer specification that defines how the effectiveness of each output will be measured, what the minimum acceptable performance level for each measurement is, and how the customer will provide feedback to the NWT related to the output's ability to meet the customer's requirements in the customer's environment. The NWT also developed an extensive list of improvement opportunities that was the start of an idea bank.

The need to establish agreed-to customer requirements is a common need in every country around the world. For example, the president of Russia stated:

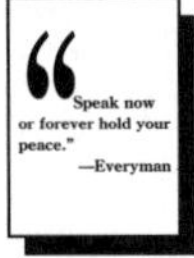

Our task is to react quickly to consumer demand . . . the quantity, range, and quality of goods, that is, just what people need, will be the main thing, and not gross output.

—MIKHAIL GORBACHEV[6]

It is essential that the NWT understands its customers and knows what they want. The biggest error NWTs can make is to think they know what their customers need without talking directly to them. As Ralph Waldo Emerson wrote: "One man's justice is another's injustice. One man's beauty another's ugliness. One man's wisdom another's folly."[7]

As a result, the NWT is now in a position to direct its attention to how the area is using its resources, which is discussed in detail in Chapter 5.

Key Principle of This Phase

The primary ingredient for the success of any organization is an excellent understanding of, and a close working relationship with, their external customer/consumer. John Young, past president of Hewlett-Packard, said: "Satisfying customers is the only reason we're in business."[8]

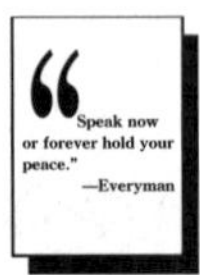

A customer is the most important person ever in this office—in person or by mail. A customer is not dependent on us, we are dependent on him. A customer is not an interruption of our work, he is the purpose of it. We are not doing him a favor by serving him, he is doing us a favor by giving us the opportunity to do so. A customer is not someone to argue or match wits with. Nobody ever won an argument with a customer. A customer is a person who brings us his wants. It is our job to handle them profitably to him and to ourselves.

—L.L. BEAN[9]

Notes

1. Helio Gomez, *Quality Quotes* (Milwaukee, WI: American Society for Quality Control (ASQC)-Quality Press, 1996), 31.
2. Ibid., 26.

3. Ibid., 6.
4. Karl Albrecht and Ron Zemke, *Service America!: Doing Business in the New Economy* (New York: Warner Books, 1990).
5. John Guaspari, *The Customer Connection: Quality for the Rest of Us* (New York: AMACON, 1988).
6. Dr. H. James Harrington, *Total Improvement Management* (New York: McGraw-Hill, 1996).
7. Helio Gomez, *Quality Quotes* (Milwaukee, WI: American Society for Quality Control (ASQC)-Quality Press, 1996), 6.
8. Dr. H. James Harrington, *The Improvement Process: How America's Leading Companies Improve Quality* (New York: McGraw-Hill, 1987), 6.
9. Helio Gomez, *Quality Quotes* (Milwaukee, WI: American Society for Quality Control (ASQC)-Quality Press, 1996), 8.

Putting the Puzzle of AAA Together

In this chapter we have found where "customer," "requirements," "output," and "feedback" fit into the **AAA** puzzle.

CHAPTER 5

Phase V—Analyze the Activity's Efficiency

Quality without Productivity Equals Bankruptcy

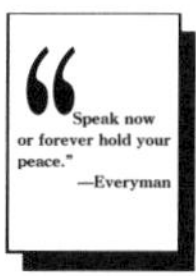

It is not enough to do a task right, you must be doing the right thing right. Doing an excellent job on something that does not need to be done wastes your skills and the organization's money.

—H. JAMES HARRINGTON

Chapter Purpose

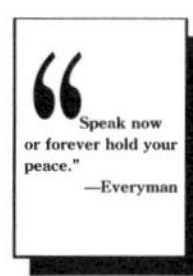

You can't drive a good work force 30 percent harder, but we've found that we could often work 30 or 50 or even 150 percent smarter.

—WALTER A. FALLON, PAST CHAIRMAN, EASTMAN-KODAK[1]

Approximately 300% more resources are wasted in the support areas than in all of the manufacturing areas put together. In management, poor-quality costs often get to be as high as 60% of the total value-added content. In the support areas, it is not uncommon to see poor-quality costs that exceed the value-added content of the total activity. Saab's vice president of engineering estimated that poor-quality cost in Development Engineering was about 78% of the total engineering budget. The president of IBM reported that poor-quality cost in their financial areas was running over 60% of the function's total costs. Organizations that are doing business process redesign activities are always surprised when they learn that the real-value-added content of their processes is usually less than 25% of the total cost of operations.

If you really want to have a high level of external customer satisfaction, you need to exceed their performance expectations but not their cost expectations. To create true customer loyalty, sell high-quality products for much less than the customer expected to pay for them. The very best way to decrease cost is by improving the efficiency of the support activities. This chapter focuses on how to identify opportunities to decrease overhead cost greatly and improve productivity.

In the previous chapter (Phase IV) we talked about defining and meeting the internal and external customers' requirements. As important as it is to meet the external requirements, you cannot forget the NWT's obligations to the organization. No organization can exist for long if all it tries to do is make the external customers happy. Even Ford, with its focus on its external customers, cannot survive without considering its other stakeholders. If the external customer was the only consideration, they would have happily sold me my new Mustang convertible for $5,000, not the over $30,000 that I paid for it. Boy, would they have had a happy customer!

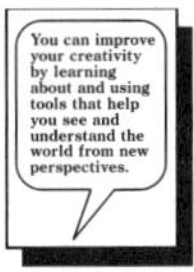

Organizations must make a profit or, at least, break even (our government excluded, since it can just print more money when it needs it). The organizations' profit doesn't just go to the rich. The lives of most people over 60 depend on how profitable the major organizations are. The biggest investor in the United States is pension funds. Profits put food on the tables of many elderly people and allow them to pay the gas bill for heating their small apartments. Yes, the nonrich depend more on organizations making a profit than do the rich. You can make customers happy and grow market share by cutting prices without cutting quality. But you make everyone happy when you reduce the cost to produce the output. David Packard, founder of Hewlett-Packard, said, "Somewhere, we got the idea that market share was an objective. I hope that is straightened out. Anyone can build market share; if you set the price low enough you can have the whole damn market. But I'll tell you it won't get you anywhere around here."[2]

During Phase V, the NWT will examine the major activities and their associated tasks to define how each activity's efficiency should be measured, performance standards, and improvement opportunities. To accomplish this, each major activity is broken down into a series of tasks. The resources that are used while performing the tasks are also defined. These tasks can then be evaluated in relation to the mission of the area and the needs of the customer. They are also usually evaluated in relation to at least two other criteria: whether the task adds value to the organization and what the consequences would be if the task was not done at all.

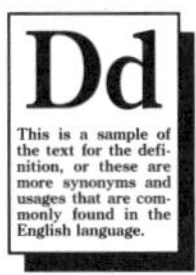

Value added is the difference between the value of an input to a task, process, or activity, and the worth of the output from that task, process, or activity as viewed by the customer of that output. The difference between the value of the input and the value of the output is the value-added content of a specific task, activity, or process.

Value-added work is that work that provides increased value to the customer. We used the word "effective" in the previous chapter to define the customer's requirements for the output from an activity. We use the word "efficient" in this chapter to describe a measure of the amount of resources to produce a specific output.

Many individuals and groups start this phase by developing flowcharts of each major activity. This approach can overwhelm less-advanced areas with detail and can make meaningful change extremely unlikely. As a result, we provide some other options that require less time and technical knowledge to use as alternatives to the flowcharting approach, giving the NWT at least two options.

Key Questions

Reaching consensus about the following key questions will help the NWT understand which activities are needed, which are being performed well, which can be eliminated, and which need to be improved.

- Why is this activity performed?
- Which parts of the activity focus on meeting the needs of the external customer?
- Which parts of the activity focus on meeting the needs of internal customers?
- Which parts of the activity are done to meet the NWT's needs only?
- What is the "cycle time" related to this activity?
- What percentage of the cycle time is wasted time?
- Which activities or tasks could be performed more efficiently?
- What tasks can be eliminated or improved?
- How often does this activity need to be done?

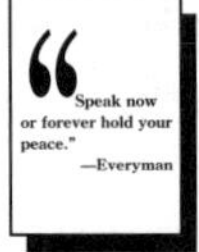

If an organization is to work effectively, the communication should be through the most effective channel regardless of the organization chart. . . . I've often thought that after you get organized, you ought to throw the chart away.

—David Packard, Hewlett-Packard[3]

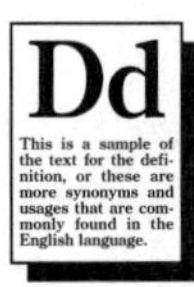

Cycle time is the elapsed time from the time that an item starts into a process, activity, or task until it is received by the customer of the process, activity, or task. For example, a purchase order leaves a manager's office on Friday at 3:00 P.M., and the information on it is put into the mainframe computer on Monday at 3:00 P.M. The cycle time would be 72 hours even though it took only three minutes to process the purchase order.)

Processing time is the amount of time that equipment or people are actually working with an item. It will typically be less than 15% of the cycle time.

Deliverables

At the end of Phase V, the NWT will have analyzed each major activity and

- Developed a flowchart of the activity
- Defined the inputs required to perform each major activity
- Prepared efficiency measurements and acceptable performance levels for each activity
- Estimated the as-is efficiency
- Established a plan to collect real data
- Identified improvement opportunities
- Identified where further training is required
- Developed a high level of commitment from the individual NWT members to improve the process
- Developed a high level of understanding about the area's operations by all of the NWT members

Process Overview

In this phase the NWT will use what it developed in the first four phases as the basis of its analysis. The purpose of this phase is to define how the efficiency of each activity should be measured and to gain a detailed understanding about how the activity is being conducted at the present time. Often, as a side effect of this phase, improvement opportunities will be identified and added to the opportunity bank that can be implemented during the continuous improvement phase.

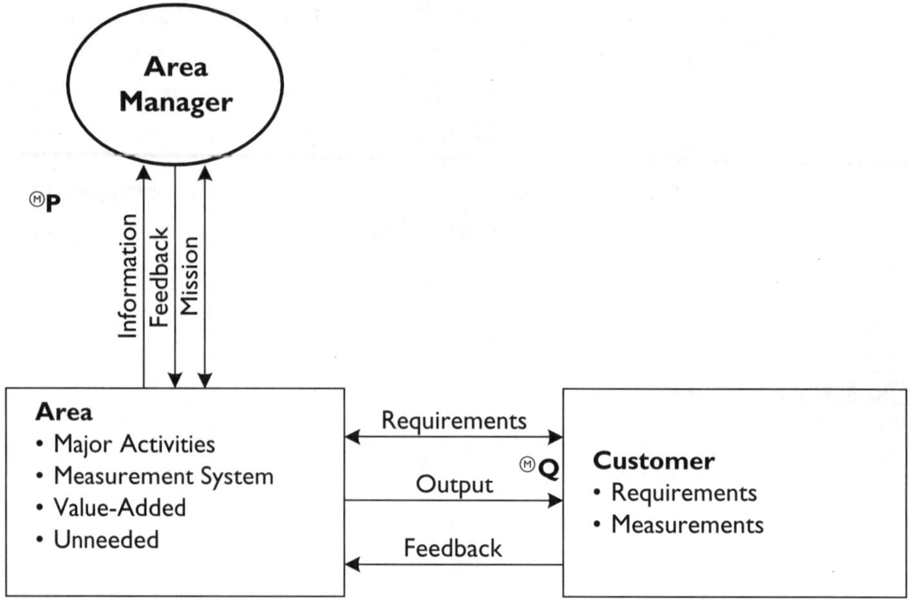

FIGURE 5-1. Activity Analysis

The NWT will need to use several criteria to evaluate what it is doing and how it relates to the area's mission and the customer's requirements. The purpose of this evaluation is to enable the NWT to define what tasks should be continued, what tasks to do away with, and what tasks need to be improved. The steps to analyzing activities are shown in Figure 5-1.

Measurement System

We will use the symbol Ⓜ to show when a measurement is critical. If the measurement is focused on effectiveness, we will follow the Ⓜ with a Q (Ⓜ Q). If it is focused on efficiency, the Ⓜ will be followed with a P (Ⓜ P). An area should be most concerned when it is not meeting its effectiveness measurements (Ⓜ Q) because it is not meeting its customer's requirements. Once the effectiveness requirements are met, the area should direct its efforts at meeting the efficiency requirements (Ⓜ P).

There is often more than one efficiency and effectiveness measurement for each activity. When doing **AAA** it is very beneficial to define the critical measurements that enable the NWT to know how it is using its resources. If the NWT can define the minimum number of measurements required to know this, it may be able to eliminate or sample many of the measurements.

Phase V Breakdown

The block diagram in Figure 5-2 shows the six steps of Phase V.

Step 1—Define Efficiency Measurements

Phase IV focused on two stakeholders—the internal and external customers. Now the NWT will develop a set of efficiency measurements designed to satisfy two other stakeholders—the investors and management, or the primary customers. Efficiency measures the resources consumed to accomplish a specific task or activity. It also often increases the external customer's satisfaction because improvements in efficiency can result in decreased product costs. Resources include things like time, people, space, money, and materials. Typical efficiency measurements are

- Cost to conduct an activity
- Process time for an activity
- Cycle time for an activity
- Poor-quality cost related to an activity
- Percentage of total resources consumed that are related to real value added
- Value-added per unit of output
- Cost per item processed

As you can see, these measurements are primarily productivity measurements. All areas that are improving should be increasing their efficiency. A typical continuous improvement process should result in a 5–15% improvement in efficiency (productivity) each year. Typical specific efficiency measurements are

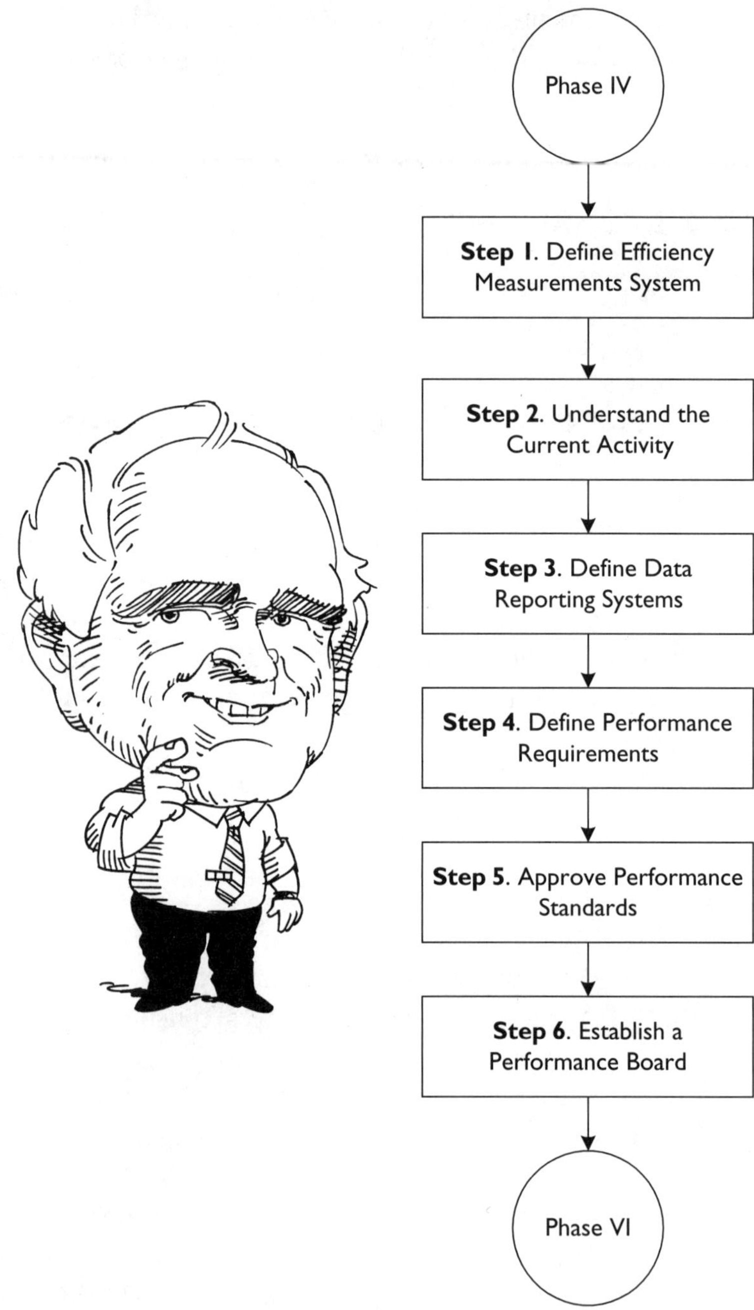

FIGURE 5-2. The Six Steps That Make Up Phase V

- Salespeople—hours to close a sale
- Order Entry Department—cycle time to process an order
- Accounting—employee hours to close the books at the end of the month
- Customer Service—cycle time to repair an item
- Product Engineering—cost to release a drawing

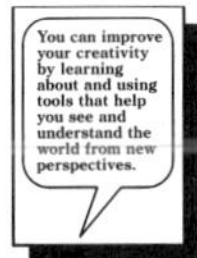

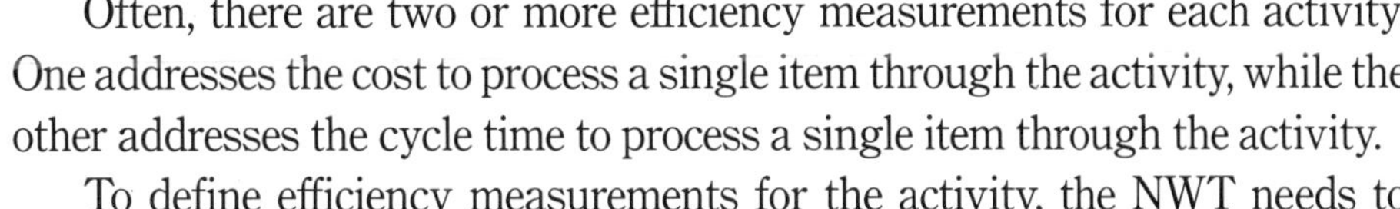

Often, there are two or more efficiency measurements for each activity. One addresses the cost to process a single item through the activity, while the other addresses the cycle time to process a single item through the activity.

To define efficiency measurements for the activity, the NWT needs to make a list of the resources that are used by the activity. Typical resources are processing time, cycle time, personnel costs, equipment (desks, computers, telephones, copiers, etc.), overhead costs, floor space, and inventory. Answering the following questions will help prepare this list:

- Is the cost to perform the activity important?
- Is the processing cost a major part of the activity's cost?
- Is there a big difference between processing time and cycle time?
- Is there a large amount of inventory involved within the activity?
- How much space is consumed by the activity?
- Is there a high poor-quality cost related to the activity?
- What percentage of the total processing cost is real value added?

The NWT should then estimate the applicable following seven items. If the data are not available to define approximate values, the NWT can rate each of the following as low, medium, or high:

- Personnel cost per unit processed
- Total cost per unit processed
- Cycle time per unit processed
- Processing time per unit processed
- Percentage of the total activity's cost that is poor-quality cost
- Square feet per item processed
- Inventory turns per month

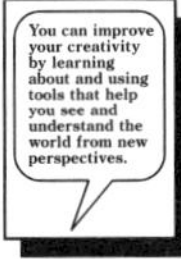

Remember that efficiency measurements are established to meet management's and the investors' needs. The NWT should define which resources management and the investors would be most interested in reducing and/or controlling. If the NWT is not sure of what that might include, it should interview the next-level manager to obtain his or her input. Typically, management wants cost, schedule, quality, and cycle time to be controlled and reduced.

There are two factors that need to be considered in defining efficiency measurements: the resources that will be evaluated and the unit that the resources will be compared to (typically items, number of employees, cost, or time).

A typical resource is money, and it could be compared to the units being processed (cost/unit). To calculate this value, the total cost of the activity over a set period of time is divided by the number of items processed during that time. With these data in hand, the NWT will have all the data required to calculate the efficiency measurements (cost/unit) for the activity.

Defining which efficiency measurement to use is only the first part of this step. The other part is defining how the efficiency measurement will be calculated. There is no use defining a measurement if the NWT cannot collect the data to report status on the measurement. We find that the NWT often defines efficiency measurements for which it cannot obtain the data that allow it to measure how well it is performing. The NWT needs to define how the proposed measurements will be calculated and how the data will be collected. All the measurements defined in Step 1 should be measurable. We will discuss the data reporting system in Step 3 of this chapter.

Step 2—Understand the Current Activity

There are many approaches to gaining understanding of the current activity. We present two approaches: a very simple one and a more comprehensive one. If a relatively low amount of resources is consumed by the activity that is being studied, we recommend the simple approach. Use the more thorough approach for those activities that consume a large amount of resources or that are performing unsatisfactorily at the present time.

Poor-Quality Cost Approach (Simple Approach)

In the U.S. about a third of what we do consists of redoing work previously 'done.'

— DR. J. M. JURAN, QUALITY EXPERT[4]

One of the approaches that is often used to measure the efficiency of an activity is called poor-quality cost. The chief advantage of poor quality cost is that it translates everything into one common term—*dollars*

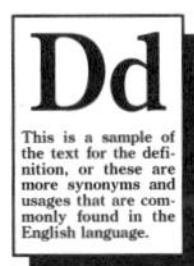

Poor-quality cost is a way of measuring the cost related to not being able to provide perfect products and/or services all the time.

It includes direct poor-quality costs that are divided into the following:

- Prevention cost
- Appraisal cost
- No-value-added cost
- Internal error cost
- External error cost
- Equipment cost

It also includes the following indirect poor-quality costs that occur because the customer is supplied less-than-perfect output:

- Customer-incurred cost
- Customer-dissatisfaction cost
- Lost opportunity cost
- Loss-of-reputation cost

Indirect poor-quality cost is a cost that is not directly reflected in the financial accounting system.

An area should always have some prevention costs; it is usually less expensive to prevent errors than to find and fix them. Prevention activities help the area do a better job for the customer and for itself. What is the best way to optimize poor-quality cost? Simple; eliminate the error costs, minimize (if not eliminate) the appraisal costs, and optimize the prevention costs. It has been shown in industry that it can be 10 to 30 times more expensive to find and fix an error than to prevent it.

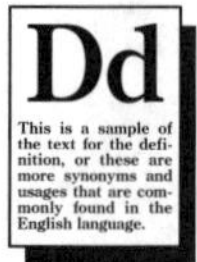

Prevention costs are all the costs expended to prevent errors from being made. To say it another way, prevention costs are all the costs involved in helping people do their job right every time. It could be considered as a cost-avoidance. These are the things you do to make sure you don't make an error. Typical prevention costs are training, error-proofing tools, maintenance, calibration equipment, process qualification, and preparing a quality manual and keeping it updated.

Appraisal costs are the costs that occur because there is a need to evaluate the output from a task, or to audit an activity or process to measure conformance to established criteria and/or procedures. To say it another way, appraisal costs are all the costs expended to determine if an activity is done right every time. Typical appraisal costs are proofreading a letter, any form of inspection, audits, reviews, approvals, tests, and so on. Appraisal activities are necessary if you cannot prevent errors from occurring.

Error costs are the costs incurred by the organization as a result of errors. There are two types of error costs: internal error cost and external error cost.

Typical error costs are rework, redo, recall, warranties, complaints, reruns, etc. Errors are a very expensive cost. Dr. Edwards W. Deming, quality guru, stated, "Defects are not free. Somebody makes them, and gets paid for making them."[5]

The NWT will have already estimated the amount of hours spent each month doing the activities. Now it will estimate how much time is spent checking to ensure the output is good (appraisal cost). It will estimate how much time is spent redoing the work when errors are detected (error cost). It

	Hrs/M	Cost/Hr	Monthly Cost
• Total hours	100 hrs.	x $65	= $6,500
• Total direct poor-quality cost hours	60 hrs.	x $65	= $3,900
• Appraisal hours	30 hrs.	x $65	XXXXXXXXX
• Error (redo) hours	25 hrs.	x $65	XXXXXXXXX
• Preventive hours	5 hrs.	x $65	XXXXXXXXX
• Productive hours	40 hrs.	x $65	= $2,600
• Percent productive hours			40%

FIGURE 5-3. Poor-Quality Cost Approach

will then estimate how much time is spent each month preventing errors from occurring (for example, training, preventive maintenance, reviewing requirements with customers, etc.). This is called prevention cost (see Figure 5-3).

The combination of the appraisal hours, error hours, and prevention hours make up the direct poor-quality hours. When the poor-quality hours are subtracted from the total hours, the difference is the productive hours. In this example, the percent productive hours is 40%.

Now the NWT needs to define what the savings would be if one hour of effort was eliminated. There are usually three options:

1. The average hourly salary of the people doing the job would be saved.
2. Option 1 plus the support overhead cost for one hour of effort.
3. Option 1 plus the overhead cost that would be eliminated if that work was not done (variables part of overhead).

Both options 1 and 3 are acceptable. Option 2 provides misleadingly high estimates of savings, and these savings will not flow down to the bottom line. In most organizations, the finance area can help the NWT define the dollar value that should be used. The **AAA** project team will often work with finance to identify a variables cost that can be added to the salary of all the employees to be used in calculating option 2. This is usually the best approach. If the activity has a lot of support costs (computer costs, subcontract costs, the cost of losing a sale, etc.), the NWT should add these costs to the hourly costs. This approach can be made a great deal more valuable if real data are collected and used to develop the poor quality and total hours rather than having the team make estimates for each category.

In addition, the NWT will probably want to collect some data to define the activity's cycle time. The total cycle time is the total elapsed hours from the time the first input comes into the area until the output is received by the area's customers.

Thorough Approach

It is often advisable to thoroughly understand the activity down to the task level in order to maximize the efficiency of the activity. In this case, the NWT will start by flowcharting the activity down to the task level. To aid in this activity, we have included a flowcharting tool in the CD-ROM that can be found in the back of this book. This flowcharting tool is provided by EDGE Software Company of Pleasanton, California, and is part of a complete process modeling software package (not supplied in this book). You will also find information on how to develop a flowchart in Appendix B. Figure 5.4 is a very simple but effective form that can be used to flowchart a simple activity. Figure 5-5 is a flowcharting form filled out for processing an order. Once the flowchart is complete, the NWT will analyze each task and classify it as being no-value-added, business-value-added, or real-value-added.

Value-Added Work

Work in any organization can be broken down into three major categories: real-value-added, business-value-added, and no-value-added (see Figure 5-6). The NWT will need to understand all three of these classifications to analyze its tasks.

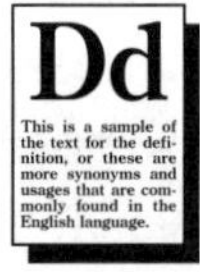

Real-value-added works are the activities or tasks that, when viewed by the external customer, are required to provide the output that the external customer is expecting. It is the work that the external customer is willing to pay for.

PROCESS FLOW CHART

Sheet No. ____ of ____

Department ______________________ Chart By ______________________

Process Name ______________________ Date ______________________

______ Proposed Method ______ Present Method

No.	Chart Symbols	Cycle Time	Process Time	Process Description
	○ □ ⇨ ◯ ◇ ⊃ ▽			
	○ □ ⇨ ◯ ◇ ⊃ ▽			
	○ □ ⇨ ◯ ◇ ⊃ ▽			
	○ □ ⇨ ◯ ◇ ⊃ ▽			
	○ □ ⇨ ◯ ◇ ⊃ ▽			
	○ □ ⇨ ◯ ◇ ⊃ ▽			
	○ □ ⇨ ◯ ◇ ⊃ ▽			
	○ □ ⇨ ◯ ◇ ⊃ ▽			
	○ □ ⇨ ◯ ◇ ⊃ ▽			
	○ □ ⇨ ◯ ◇ ⊃ ▽			
	○ □ ⇨ ◯ ◇ ⊃ ▽			
	○ □ ⇨ ◯ ◇ ⊃ ▽			
	○ □ ⇨ ◯ ◇ ⊃ ▽			
	○ □ ⇨ ◯ ◇ ⊃ ▽			
	○ □ ⇨ ◯ ◇ ⊃ ▽			
	○ □ ⇨ ◯ ◇ ⊃ ▽			
	○ □ ⇨ ◯ ◇ ⊃ ▽			
	○ □ ⇨ ◯ ◇ ⊃ ▽			
	○ □ ⇨ ◯ ◇ ⊃ ▽			

○ = Start or stop the process ◯ = Inspect ⇨ = Movement □ = Operation ◇ = Decision Point

⊃ = Delay ▽ = Storage

FIGURE 5-4. Process Mapping Form

PROCESS FLOW CHART

Sheet No. 1 of 1

Department Orders Rec — Chart By TSF

Process Name Processing an order — Date 7/02/99

_____ Proposed Method _____ Present Method

No.	Chart Symbols	Cycle Time	Process Time	Process Description
1.		12 H	4 M	Receive order by phone, fax, or mail
2.		1 H	5 M	Write phone order onto form
3.		1 H	3 M	Check fax and mail orders for errors
4.	N Y	1 H	1 M	Is the order correct?
5.		12 H	6 M	Contact customer to get required data
6.		14 H	4 M	Price order
7.		5 H	3 M	Make copy of order and price sheet
8.		16 H	2 M	File original
9.		30 H	3 M	Check credit limits with bank
10.		1 H	4 M	If credit check is good, enter order in computer
11.		1 H	2	Send order copy to warehouse
12.		1.5 H	0	Wait for return of order copy from warehouse. Hold until WH returns order copy.
13.	N Y	1 H	1 M	Check to see if the order could be filled
14.		1 H	3 M	Modify order to show back order and provide customer with a target delivery date
15.		1 H	2 M	Print out shipping documents
16.		24 H	2 M	Send shipping documents to warehouse
17.		1 H	2 M	Print out invoice
18.		24 H	2 M	File invoice in pending file to await shipment

○ = Start or stop the process ◯ = Inspect ⇨ = Movement ▭ = Operation ◇ = Decision Point ⊂⊃ = Delay ▽ = Storage

FIGURE 5-5. Process Mapping Form Filled Out for Processing an Order

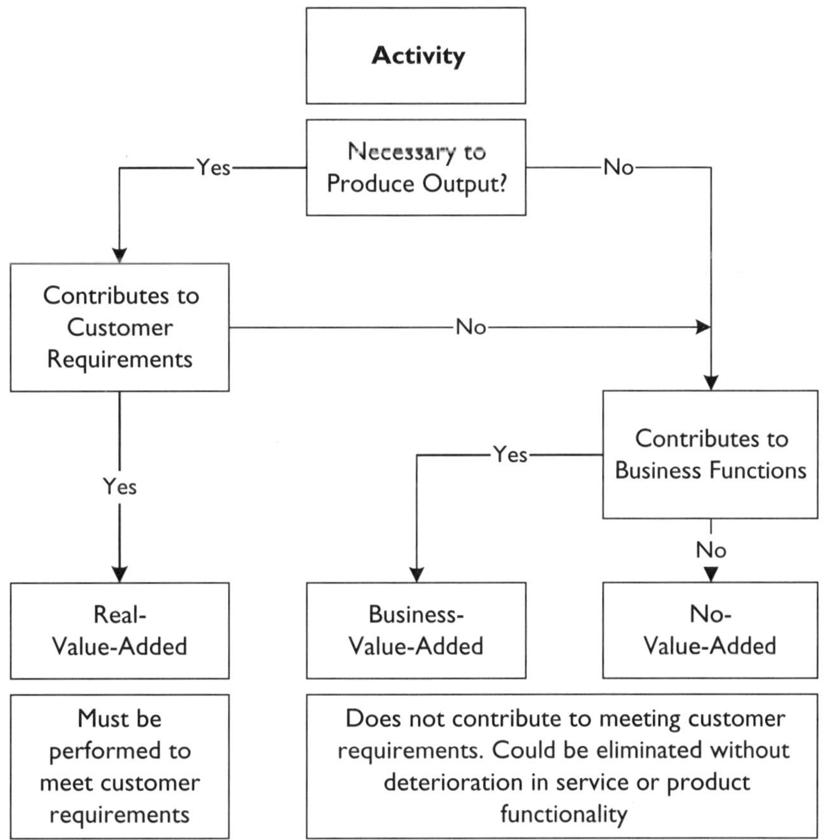

FIGURE 5-6. Types of Work That Go On within an Organization

Real-value-added activities are things like training the external customer, taking an order from a customer, assembling parts for a product, ordering parts from a supplier that will go into a customer's product, billing the external customer, and so on. The NWT needs to spend most of its time doing real-value-added work. An organization often spends as little as 20% of its efforts doing real-value-added work.

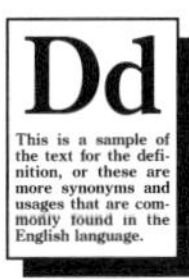

Business-value-added work includes activities or tasks like interviewing potential new employees, setting up offices, keeping business records, conducting performance evaluations, conducting customer surveys, employee training, and so on. You want to reduce business-value-added work as much as possible.

No-value-added work are activities or tasks that do not contribute to meeting customer requirements and could be eliminated without degrading the product's or service's functionality or the business. It also includes all of the inspection and checks and balances put in place to determine if work was done correctly, plus all rework activities or tasks. The customer doesn't want to pay for it, nor is it necessary for the business if everyone does their job correctly.

No-value-added activities include things like storage, moving, rework, scrap, all reviews, approvals, and many others. No-value-added work should be eliminated.

We recommend that you color the no-value-added tasks red, the business-value-added tasks yellow, and the real-value-added tasks green on the flowchart. The colored flowchart is known as a rainbow flowchart. It is used to visually demonstrate opportunities for major improvement. We have seen tasks that are part no-value-added and part business-value-added activities. This should not present the NWT with a problem, since an individual task can be classified as having a percentage of its total resources in one classification and the remainder in another. The NWT can color part of the flowchart red and the rest yellow. The NWT should then collect data that define the cost and cycle time to process one item through each task and for the total activity. This will allow the NWT to define the no-value-added cost per item processed, the business-value-added cost per item processed, the real-value-added cost per item processed, and the cycle time to process an item through the entire activity. Typical measurements that would result from this approach are

- Total cost per item processed
- Percent real-value-added cost
- Cycle time per item processed
- No-value-added cost per item processed
- Business-value-added cost per item processed
- Real-value-added cost per item processed

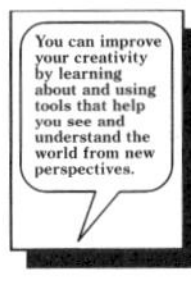

Another excellent, very effective approach to analyzing the activities from a cost standpoint that uses the flowchart as a starting point and is preferred by most financial organizations is called activity-based costing (ABC). We particularly recommend this approach if the organization has already been using ABC in doing financial analysis and has a cadre of experts that can be made available to support the individual NWTs.*

In some cases, it may be necessary to collect data that reflect the variation in the activity's measurements rather than using averages. We find that most organizations lose customers not because of the average value of the activity but because of the negative extremes of the activity's performance. If the activity has an important impact on the external customer, you probably will want to measure the variation in each key task. This is particularly true of cycle-time measurements.

For example, the phone is answered on an average of 2.3 rings, 10% of the calls are not answered and go into voice mail after 8 rings, and 15% of the calls go unanswered because the caller hangs up before the customer service representative answers the phone and before the phone goes to voice mail. In this case, it is easy to see that measuring the average number of rings can result in missing some very important data. A better measurement would be the percentage of callers that hang up and the percentage of calls that go to voice mail.

Now that the NWT has prepared a rainbow flowchart of the activity, the NWT should look at the flowchart from the poor-quality cost standpoint. This will provide the NWT with a two-dimensional view of the activity that will help define improvement opportunities.

Why go into this much detail? Most of your areas are where they are because the NWT has not paid attention to what it was doing. As a result, the NWT ends up doing a lot of things that may have been necessary at one time but are no longer needed. The NWT gets used to a certain level of performance, which soon seems normal.

This level of analysis provides a means to dissect the things the NWT does so that the waste and errors can be seen and eliminated. The goal is to

---

*For more information about ABC, we recommend *The Ernst & Young Guide to Total Cost Management* (New York: John Wiley & Sons, 1992).

Efficiency Value-Analysis Measurement Form

Area Name and Number: ______________________

Activity: ______________________

Prepared: ______________________ Date: ____/____/____

(1) How many hours per item processed? ________ Hours per item

(2) Allocate this time into three value-added categories.

- Real-Value-Added (RVA) ________
- Business-Value-Added (BVA) ________
- No-Value-Added (NVA) ________

Total ________ Hours per item processed

Percent Real-Value-Added ________

(3) Value-Added versus Poor-Quality Cost Matrix
Using the matrix below, further allocate the value-added hours to the appropriate category.

	RVA	Prevention	Appraisal	Error
RVA	________	No	No	No
BVA	________	________	________	No
NVA	No	No	________	________
Totals	________	________	________	________
Total	________	This should be equal to the hours per item processed (as above)		

FIGURE 5-7. **Efficiency Value-Analysis Measurement Form**

have an error-free, efficient process, one that your customer wants to pay for and one that you can be proud of.

To document the analysis, use the Efficiency Value-Analysis Measurement Form shown in Figure 5-7. The numbers at the start of each line refer to the line on the form. Some line names may not be applicable for the area/organization using **AAA**. The NWT should make changes as appropriate to reflect the local convention. You will normally need one of the forms depicted in Figure 5-7 for each critical activity.

1. **How many hours per item processed?** This may be for one person or for several. Make an estimate at this time, but it would be a good idea to keep a log for a period of time to obtain more accurate data.
2. **Allocate this time into the three value-added categories.** Use the definitions shown in the value-added section. The total of the three will, of course, be the hours per item processed. No time should be left over. Then calculate the percentage of the total hours that are real-value-added hours.
3. **Value-added versus poor-quality cost matrix**. Now decide how the value-added data can be allocated into the poor-quality-cost categories.

Although cost and processing time are very important measurements of efficiency, often cycle time can be even more critical. This is one area in which Asian countries are far ahead of the United States. (The new product development process for Japanese cars is a good example. It is about 60% of U.S. cycle time and about 50% of the cost.) Although some activities are repeated only infrequently (e.g., new product introduction), cycle time is very important. In such cases, some historical research may be necessary to obtain dates documenting the beginning and end of these major activities.

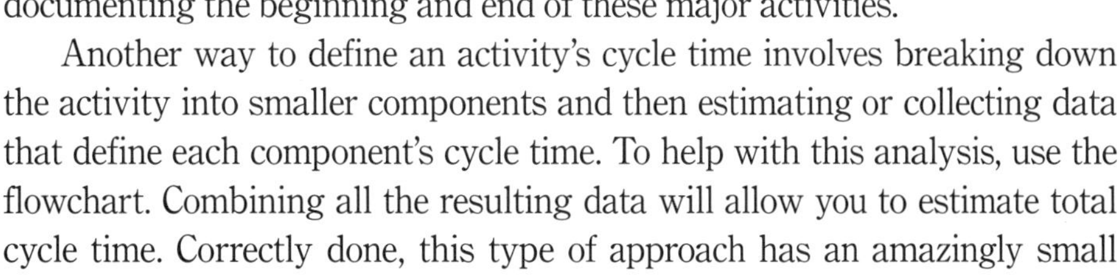
Another way to define an activity's cycle time involves breaking down the activity into smaller components and then estimating or collecting data that define each component's cycle time. To help with this analysis, use the flowchart. Combining all the resulting data will allow you to estimate total cycle time. Correctly done, this type of approach has an amazingly small error rate—frequently less than 5%.

Processing Time versus Cycle Time

Consider the cycle time of a letter-writing process shown in Figure 5-8. This scenario is closer to truth than fiction. While the process cycle time is 170.4 hours (over 7 working days, or 9 calendar days), only 2.2 hours were spent in actual work effort. The rest was wasted time. It is easy to see why we need to measure cycle time.

Activity	Process Time (hours)	Cycle Time (hours)
1. A manager estimates that it takes 12 minutes to write a one-page memo and place it in the outgoing basket.	0.2	0.2
2. The manager's secretary picks up outgoing mail twice a day, at 9 A.M. and 1 P.M. Average delay time is 12 hours.	0.1	12.0
3. The secretary assists three managers, answers phones, schedules meetings, processes incoming mail, retypes letters, and performs special assignments. All these activities have priority over typing. Average time before starting to type a letter is 26 hours.		26.0
4. The secretary types the memo and puts it into the manager's incoming mail.	0.3	0.3
5. Incoming mail and signature requests are delivered twice a day, at 9 A.M. and 1 P.M.		12.0
6. The manager reads incoming mail at 5 P.M.	0.1	17.0
7. The secretary picks up mail at 9 A.M.		16.0
8. Retyping is a priority activity and is returned in the 1 P.M. mail delivery (Note: 60% of all letters are changed by managers.)	0.2	4.0
9. The manager reads and signs letters at 5 P.M.	0.1	4.0
10. The memo is picked up by the secretary at 9 A.M.	0.1	16.0
11. The memo is put in the copy file and held for the next trip to copy center at 2 P.M.	0.1	5.0
12. The secretary walks to the copy center, makes copies, and addresses envelopes.	0.1	0.1
13. The secretary takes memo to mailbox by 5 P.M.	0.2	2.5
14. Mail is picked up at 8 A.M.		15.0
15. The memo is held in the mailroom for afternoon mail delivery at 3 P.M.	0.1	17.0
16. Secretary 2 picks up mail and sorts at 4 P.M. Secretary puts memo in manager's incoming mail.	0.1	1.0
17. Secretary delivers incoming mail to manager 2 at 9 A.M.	0.1	14.0
18. Manager 2 reads mail at 5 P.M.	0.1	8.0
19. Manager 2 drafts answer and puts it into the outgoing mailbox, telling manager 1 to supply more information. It is classified "rush" because it is now overdue.	0.3	0.3
Total	2.2	170.4

FIGURE 5–8. Cycle-Time of a Letter-Writing Process

	Cycle Time (days)			Cost ($ per purchase)		
Activity	**Processing**	**Wait**	**Total**	**Personnel**	**Other**	**Total**
1. Recognize Needs	0.1	1.0	1.1	30		30
2. Write Requisition	0.2	2.0	2.2	56		56
3. Review Requisition	0.1	5.0	5.1	28		28
4. Identify Suppliers	0.6	6.5	7.1	175		175
5. Negotiate Terms	0.2	0.5	0.7	58		58
6. Place Order	0.1	10.5	10.6	26	30	56
7. Receive Materials	0.1	7.5	7.6	26		26
8. Check with Order	0.2	1.0	1.2	54	38	92
9. Deliver to User	0.2	1.0	1.2	50		50
TOTAL	1.8	35.0	36.8	$503	$68	$571

FIGURE 5-9. **Cost and Cycle-Time Worksheet**

Typically, you will also need to understand the costs at a more detailed level. What do the major subprocesses cost? What do the key activities cost? What is the cost of each output? Make additional estimates, and complete the form shown in Figure 5-9.

Continue with the example of an office supplies purchasing process to calculate the average cost of a single purchase. We now have a good idea of what the cycle time and costs of the activities are.

You can depict this information on cost and cycle-time charts to determine problem areas on which to work. Cost and cycle-time charts (see Figure 5-10) display how a typical purchase of office supplies builds up costs over the 36.8 days that it takes from one end of the process to the other—from "recognize needs" to "deliver to user."

In this chart, the horizontal axis represents total cycle time, and the vertical axis represents costs for a single purchase. Upward sloping lines indicate processing time for the activities, while horizontal lines indicate wait time when no direct cost is incurred. If you follow the chart, you can see that

- The highest cost is incurred to "identify suppliers." Therefore, you should focus on the methods and processes used to identify suppliers.

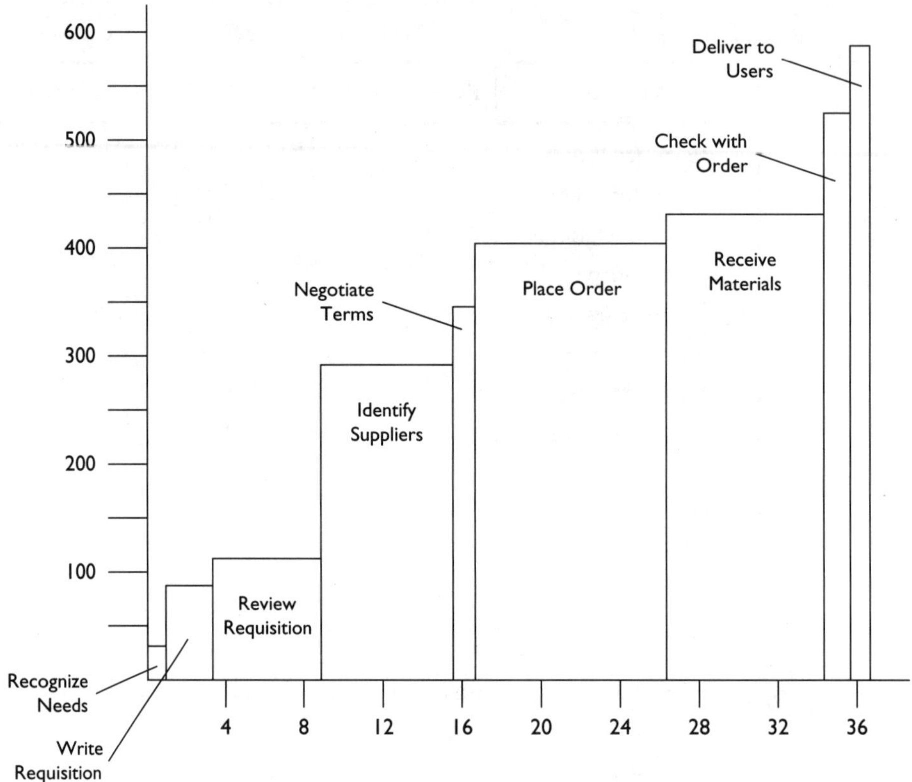

FIGURE 5-10. Cost and Cycle-Time Chart

- There are long wait times, when no activity is being performed, at the "identify suppliers" and "receive materials" stages. Expand these flowcharts to the task level to better understand why they take so much time and to determine how to improve the activity. Note in Figure 5-10 that no cost were added to the process cost during the wait periods. Although there is no direct cost added, everything that is put in a hold or wait classification costs the organization money indirectly.

At this point in the **AAA** process, the NWT should review the list of efficiency measurements that it prepared in Step 1. This list may need to be updated to reflect the additional information that was collected in this step. In addition, the data collected in this step may need to be supplemented to address the measurements selected. For example, we did not address collecting information related to support costs or floor space. It may also be necessary to translate the hours-worked figures into cost by multiplying the hours worked by the employee's hourly rate plus the variables part of overhead.

Step 3—Define Data Reporting Systems

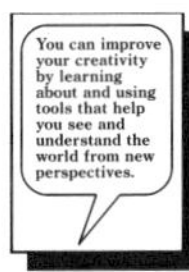

During this step, the NWT will determine how data will be collected, how often it will be collected, and how it will be reported. We find that it is often advisable to invite a representative from the Information Systems Function who understands the present data systems to sit in on these discussions.

The problem that the NWT faces is how to collect the information needed to measure the efficiency trends without adding additional business-value-added costs. We have seen some data collection systems put in place whose costs far exceed the benefits that will ever be realized by the organization from their use. For example: IBM San Jose stopped all direct labor claiming to specific jobs because the cost of the data collection process far overshadowed the cost benefits that IBM received from collecting the information.

The first thing that the NWT should look at is what data are available today that can be used without adding any additional business-value-added costs. A number of organizations today have installed process flow tracking systems. In these cases, the information that the NWT needs has already been collected, and for a small, one-time cost, a program can be prepared not only to report the data but also to present the results graphically. This is the best of all worlds because each item processed is tracked throughout the activity, allowing averages and extremes to be readily calculated.

In most cases, it is not necessary to report performance at the task level, although some task-level data are often required during the continuous improvement phase to define problems and to measure the impact of individual corrective actions. In these cases, the normal data collection system can be temporarily supplemented with a data collection process to collect the required data. We recommend that the NWT only develop reporting systems related to the total activities. This greatly simplifies the effort required to set up and maintain the reporting system.

Once the present data collection systems are understood, the NWT should again review the efficiency measurements to determine if they need to be changed in any way to make better use of the present systems (for example, change from reporting cost per month to cost per week).

The NWT should next consider how technology can help it collect the required information, minimizing the human effort required. Typical technical enablers are

- Bar coding and scanners
- Time stamps
- Computer systems
- Voice recognition systems
- Scanners

It is often advisable to contact the information technology group in your organization to obtain their insight on how technology can be used to collect and report the data. One word of caution: the information technology group usually consists of "techies," and they often come up with solutions that are far too expensive, complicated, and have long implementation cycles. Be sure to weigh their recommendations based on good, sound business judgment and the potential benefits that the organization will receive from analyzing the information.

The next thing that the NWT needs to consider is the frequency that the data will be recorded. Remember, what you are trying to do is report trends and analyze out-of-control conditions. In most activities, trends take place over long time intervals or after significant changes have been made to the tasks that make up the activity. As a result, data sampling plans can be used to measure trends. This can be supplemented with controlled experiments to measure the impact of changes within the activity. The NWT normally defines many measurements for which data will need to be collected, but it will only be actively working to improve a small percentage of them at one time. As a result, the measurements that are not being directly impacted by the improvement activities can be sampled to ensure that negative trends do not develop.

Once the information collection method is determined, the NWT should design the data collection form. Three factors should be considered at this point:

1. How the data will be used
2. How often the data will be collected and used
3. How the form will be designed to minimize the information that the individual NWT members need to record

We suggest using the following rules to guide you in developing your data collection form:

1. The form should be designed for ease of use by the person recording the data, not for the computer program that will be manipulating the data.
2. Never record any data that will not be used. For example: If you report weekly and you process the data either daily or weekly, you need not record the date. The computer program can do that job for you.

Once the data collection form is designed, the NWT needs to define how the data will be displayed graphically and reported back to the area. We suggest that a trend chart for each activity/measurement combination be generated and made available to all NWT members and appropriate upper management. This report should also include the effectiveness measurements and data defined during Phase IV.

Step 4—Define Performance Requirements

"Speak now or forever hold your peace."
—Everyman

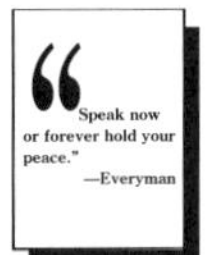

There can be no improvements where there are no standards.
—MASAAKI IMAI[6]

You can improve your creativity by learning about and using tools that help you see and understand the world from new perspectives.

Efficiency measurements all relate to how much value the employee adds to the output. Management should already have definite requirements about the minimum amount of value-added content that must be provided to justify continuing to do the job. Today's trends to outsourcing activities are driven by outside organizations that can add more value to the output at less cost than the internal organization. As a result, there is competition even when it comes to the work that is now done in the support areas. In this case, upper management is the customer and has an obligation to its investors to get the best output at the lowest possible price. Management must realize that when a new employee is assigned to a task, there is a learning curve that the employee goes through.

On the other hand, employees want to do a good job and can take a great deal of pride in being able to become more productive and, as a result, more valuable to the organization. This drive can increase an individual's earning potential. It is easy for the employees to understand that if they don't increase their value to the organization, they cannot expect to earn more money. Working with these assumptions, you can understand that management should set the minimum performance standards for the efficiency of the activities. The NWT should set the improvement targets for each measurement to demonstrate the NWT's increased value to the organization. Promotions and increased financial rewards should go to those NWT members who have the biggest improvements in their combined set of performance (effectiveness and efficiency) measurements.

The truth of the matter is that the minimum efficiency performance standards for most indirect jobs exist in the minds of the managers and have never been documented. This is really unfair to the employees and makes managing the activities much more difficult than it should be. It is difficult to address inadequate performance with an employee when a minimum standard has not been defined and documented.

If the performance standards have already been established by management, then these target performance levels should be added to the efficiency graph. If, on the other hand, the efficiency performance standards have not been defined and documented or are out of date, the NWT needs to correct this situation. Once again the NWT, as with the area mission statement, has to make up for management not providing the required direction.

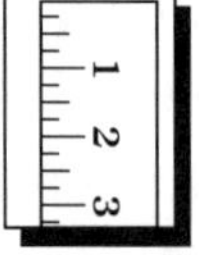

The following are some basic ground rules that can be used to aid the NWT in preparing its efficiency performance standards.

1. The standards should be defined as the level of performance a newly trained employee should meet to be performing satisfactorily. They

should be well below the productivity of an individual who is exceeding requirements.

2. The standards should be based on the tasks that make up the activity, not on past performance. The people who have been doing the job may be exceeding requirements or may not be performing all of the required tasks.
3. The standards and the budgeted staff should support the number of items that are being processed.

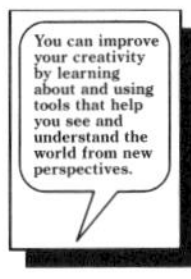

How do you go about establishing what the standards should be? In practice, there are two different approaches used: the scientific approach and the historical approach.

The scientific approach makes use of the time and motion study methodologies that were perfected in the manufacturing area. In these cases, each block on the flowchart that was constructed in Step 2 of this phase is analyzed, using time and motion studies, based on the present procedures to determine the measurement matrix for that specific task. Then the individual values related to each task are added together to define the base standard value. In addition, a 10–15% factor is added to the base value to cover outside factors (for example, going to the bathroom, getting coffee, breaks, discussions, and so forth). This can be a time-consuming and costly process and is usually only done when there is a large amount of cost involved in the activity.

The historical approach reviews what is going on today and uses this as a basis of the analysis. The NWT started collecting this type of information in Phase II in order to define which activities were the major activities within the area. During Phase V, the NWT collected more information as it performed the analysis covered in Step 2. If Step 2 was done in detail, the NWT already has the data required to define how the activity is performing today. If the database is incomplete, it may be necessary to conduct a designed experiment (for example, track 10 items through the process to measure today's cycle time). Once today's performance level is defined, the NWT needs to consider which of the following categories best describe how efficiently the activity is being performed:

1. Below requirements
2. Meets requirements
3. Exceeds requirements
4. Outstanding

Using Different Levels of Inputs

First, we like to have the NWT members, without input from the manager, quantify the activity's performance. Second, the NWT manager should quantify the activity's performance independent of the employees input. Third, the second-level manager should also quantify the activity's performance. The best case would be for all three evaluations to rate the activity a 2 (meets requirements). In this case, the activity can use the current level of performance as its minimum standard.

Because management is responsible for setting efficiency performance standards, we weight evaluations related to efficiency as follows:

Employees	1×
NWT manager	2×
Second-level manager	3×

Figure 5-11 presents a way to analyze the inputs from the three different levels. This analysis approach indicates that the present activity is performing on the high side, between "meets requirements" and "exceeds requirements" (2.833 average point score). If the present process is operating at $120 to process an item, then the efficiency performance standard for cost per item processed should be higher. For example, its standard value might be $140 per item processed. (Note: Lower performance results in increased cost per item processed. A "meets requirements" process would cost $140 to produce an item. An "exceeds requirements" process would only cost $120 to produce an item, and an "outstanding" process could produce an item for $100.)

Another approach to define how well the activity is being performed today is through analyzing the employees' performance rating. In this approach, the NWT defines the names of the people who are performing the activity. Then the manager records each individual's performance rating and

	Rating	Point Score	Opinion Weighting Score	Weighted Score
Employee	Outstanding	4	1x	4
NWT Manager	Meets Requirements	2	2x	4
Second-level Manager	Exceeds Requirements	3	3x	9
			Total weighted score (A)	**17**
			Sum of opinion weighting scores (B)	**6**
			Average point score (A÷B)	**2.833**

Legend
Below Requirements = 1 point
Meets Requirements = 2 points
Exceeds Requirements = 3 points
Outstanding = 4 points

FIGURE 5-11. Analysis of Efficiency Performance Level Using Different Levels of Input

averages out their ratings to define the overall employee performance rating for the activity. Figure 5-12 is a typical example.

In the example used in Figure 5-12, four people were working on the activity, and their average performance level was "exceeds requirements." If the cost per item processed was $120 using today's activities and the same four people, the efficiency performance standard would need to be greater than $120. For example, the efficiency performance standard for this measurement could be set at $140 per item processed.

A more accurate way to use the individual employee's performance is to weight this performance by the percentage of the total effort to perform the activity (see Figure 5-13). In this example, the present activity is performing close to outstanding (3.75 on a 4.0 scale). If the present process is operating at $120 to process an item, then the efficiency performance standard for cost per item processed should be much higher. For example, its standard value might be $170 per item processed. As you can see, this approach is much more accurate than using the average individual's performance rating alone.

People Doing the Activity	Performance Rating	Point Score
Mary T.	Exceeds Requirements	3
Jim S.	Outstanding	4
John W.	Below Requirements	1
Carrie H.	Outstanding	4
	Total	**12 points**
	Number of Employees	**4**
	Average Performance	**3 (Exceeds Requirements)**

Legend
Below Requirements = 1 point
Meets Requirements = 2 points
Exceeds Requirements = 3 points
Outstanding = 4 points

FIGURE 5-12. Analysis of Efficiency Performance Level Using Employee Performance Ratings

Once today's employee's performance level has been defined, the activity's actual performance measurements can be used to calculate the efficiency performance standards. This can be accomplished for cost per item as indicated in the following:

- Employee's current performance level is below requirements—Subtract a factor from the present activity's performance when defining

People Doing the Activity	Performance Rating	Point Score	% of Total Effort	Rating
Mary T.	Exceeds Req.	3	10%	.30
Jim S.	Outstanding	4	35%	1.40
John W.	Below Req.	1	5%	.05
Carrie H.	Outstanding	4	50%	2.00
			Total:	**3.75**

Legend
Below Requirements = 1 point
Meets Requirements = 2 points
Exceeds Requirements = 3 points
Outstanding = 4 points

FIGURE 5-13. Time-Weighted Analysis of Efficiency Performance Level Using Employee Performance Ratings

the efficiency performance standard (for example: the activity's actual cost × 80% = efficiency performance standard).

- ► Employee's current performance level meets requirements—Use the activity's actual cost.
- ► Employee's current performance level exceeds requirements—Add a factor to the present activity's actual performance value when defining the efficiency performance standard (for example, actual performance value × 120% = efficiency performance standard).
- ► Employee's current performance level is outstanding—Add a larger factor to the activity's actual performance value when defining the efficiency performance standard (for example, actual performance × 140% = efficiency performance standard).

The only time that the efficiency performance standards should be changed is when the tasks are changed or equipment is added to the activity that decreases the resources required to perform the activity. It should not change based on the people becoming more efficient in doing their assigned tasks.

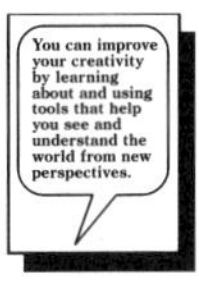

The efficiency performance standards become official when management has signed off on them. At that point in time, the standard value should be added to the reports and graphs. The form in Figure 5-14 should be prepared for each efficiency measurement in each activity. Now the NWT can combine all the data that they have collected for each activity during Phase V on a single form called "Efficiency Performance Analysis" (see Figure 5-15).

Warning

The development of efficiency performance standards seems to be an excellent application for time and motion studies. We have worked with organizations that have had the industrial engineering department help the NWT define their efficiency performance standards with little success. In one case, the industrial engineer's time and motion study indicated that there was work for only 40% of the people in the area. It takes a very sophisticated industrial engineering department to do time and motion studies, fully taking

Efficiency Measurement Specification	
Area Name and Number: ________________	
Activity: ________________	
Prepared: ________________	Date: ____/____/____
Measurement Name: ________________	
How is it measured? ________________	
________________	
How often is it measured? ________________	
________________	
How are the data recorded? ________________	
________________	
What is the performance standard? ________________	
________________	

FIGURE 5-14. Efficiency Measurement Specification

into consideration the interruptions and variations that impact the activities in support areas.

Even if the NWT does not use industrial engineering's support to prepare the efficiency performance standards, they should fully consider how the other activities that are going on in the area can impact the efficiency of the activity being studied. If the NWT flowcharts the activity and estimates the time taken to perform each task, it needs to be sure that the estimates are realistic. The NWT should double check its end results by multiplying the hours to process an item through the activity by the number of items processed per month. The NWT should then compare this number to the actual number of people performing the activity. If the two numbers are not very closely aligned, then the NWT should understand why they are different and take appropriate action to bring them in line.

Efficiency Performance Analysis

Activity: ______________________________

Area No. or Name: ______________________________

Measurement Name: ______________________________

- Performance Standard: ______________________________
- Present Value: ______________________________

(Measured ________ Estimated ________)

Met Requirements on: ____/____/____ Yes ________ No ________

Measurement Name: ______________________________

- Performance Standard: ______________________________
- Present Value: ______________________________

(Measured ________ Estimated ________)

Met Requirements on: ____/____/____ Yes ________ No ________

Measurement Name: ______________________________

- Performance Standard: ______________________________
- Present Value: ______________________________

(Measured ________ Estimated ________)

Met Requirements on: ____/____/____ Yes ________ No ________

Prepared by: ______________________ Date: ____/____/____

Approved by: ______________________ Date: ____/____/____

______________________ Date: ____/____/____

______________________ Date: ____/____/____

FIGURE 5-15. Efficiency Performance Analysis Form

We find there is often a big difference in the support areas between the time required to do a task and the actual time that is expended performing the task. Little things like stopping to answer a question or answer the phone can increase the time to perform a task by as much as 100%.

Step 5–Approve Performance Standards

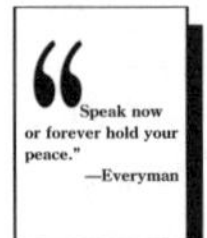

Without a standard there is no logical basis for making a decision or taking action.

—J. M. JURAN, QUALITY GURU[7]

When the NWT manager and the NWT members have completed defining the efficiency measurements and the performance standards, they should be submitted to the next higher-level manager for approval. This is usually accomplished by scheduling a meeting with the appropriate manager where the NWT presents the flowchart of the activity, the effectiveness measurements, and the performance standards. The NWT should try to relate its presentation to the higher-level manager's mission statement and to the area's budget. The measurements and the performance standards become official when the higher-level manager agrees with and signs off on the form identified in Figure 5-15.

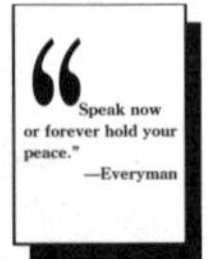

Life would be substantially more difficult without standards.

—RAFAEL AGUAYO[8]

Step 6–Establish a Performance Board

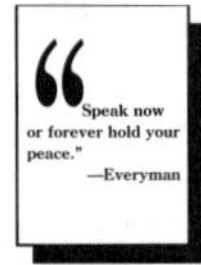

The hunger for performance is far more important to team success than team-building exercises, special incentives, or team leaders with ideal profiles.

—JON R. KATZENBACH AND DOUGLAS K. SMITH[9]

We further suggest that a four- by five-foot area performance board be set up in a very visible part of the area with the following posted on it:

1. The area mission statement
2. The area performance report
3. Improvement plans and their associated measurement charts
4. An up-to-date picture of the NWT
5. A list of the area's customers
6. Letters from customers (both positive and negative)
7. A list of the people who make up the NWT, their dates of hire, and their birthdays
8. Board posting procedure

We recommend that the area's manager encourage the NWT members to post improvement ideas and suggestions for any measurement on this board in a section of the board called "New Ideas." This eliminates the need to wait for a meeting to get actions started on good ideas. The manager in the area should review the posted ideas at least once a day and move them from the "new idea" part of the board to the "ideas in progress" part of the board (see Figure 5-16). Note that the board has many things on it similar to the area's overall improvement chart, which has not been discussed to this point but will be covered later in the book.

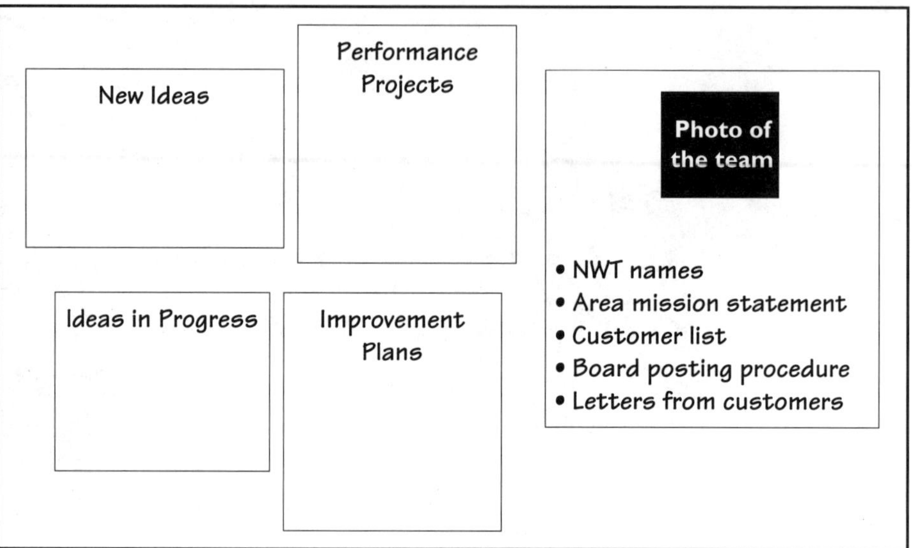

FIGURE 5-16. Performance Board

We cannot overemphasize the need to keep the performance board up to date. Nothing telegraphs management's lack of interest in performance improvement more than an outdated performance board. I have seen performance boards that have reports on them that are six months old. We like to see a statement on the board that defines when the board is updated. For example: "New reports and graphs will be posted each Tuesday that reflect the previous week's performance." If for some reason the new reports and graphs cannot be posted on schedule, an explanation of why the graphs and reports are not available and a new target date for their availability should be posted on the performance board.

We find it is good business practice to write a short document that defines what can and cannot be posted on the performance board. Some organizations will allow personal items to be posted, such as postcards from NWT members who are on vacation. We do not recommend this practice because it is hard to control. First the manager posts a postcard from an employee, then someone posts a birthday card, then someone else puts up a notice that she has a car for sale. We find it is best to clearly define what can be put on the performance board, who can put it up, where they can put it, and when it will be taken down. This type of procedure needs to be defined for each different area of the board.

Things That Can Help

- The use of dollars as a common denominator can be quite revealing since some areas carry large amounts of overhead.
- If an activity is no-value-added, do not break it down any further. Eliminate it.
- Even the most critical and real-value-added activities may contain no-value-added tasks and can often be improved.
- Don't start with a detailed flowchart.
- Make a list of all resources that the area uses.
- Define all inputs that come into the activity and evaluate how they are used.

Improving the organization's efficiency is the best way to increase the organization's performance. As Konosuke Matsushita, past CEO of Matsushita Inc., expressed it: "A business should quickly stand on its own based on the service it provides the society. Profits should not be a reflection of corporate greed but a vote of confidence from society that what is offered by the firm is valued."[10]

Examples

The following are typical efficiency analyses by each of the three industry types.

Insurance Policy Processing Department/351. The policy issuance activity was flowcharted (see Figure 5-17), and the tasks were grouped based on their value content. Four tasks were classified as

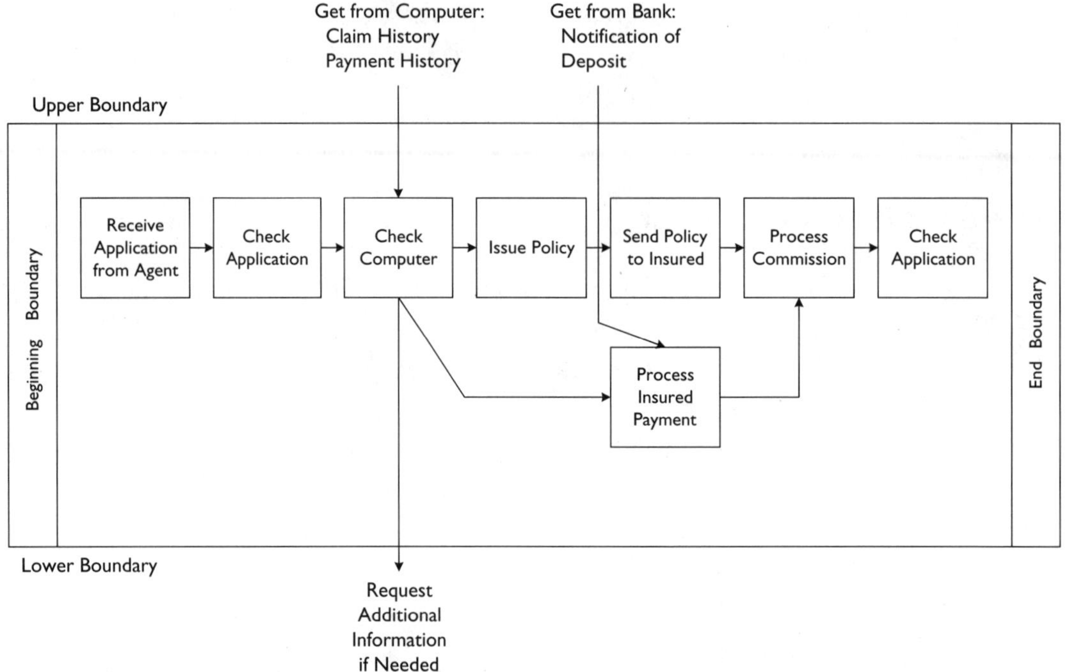

FIGURE 5-17. Policy Issuance Activity Flowchart

real-value-added work, five as business-value-added work, and four as no-value-added work (see Figure 5-18).

Even though it focuses on efficiency, it bolsters effectiveness. Agents are more effective when they are rewarded efficiently. The task of processing a commission was further analyzed using a flowchart as shown in Figure 5-19.

Each of the tasks was then analyzed using the Real-Value-Added versus Business- and No-Value-Added Costs Form shown in Figure 5-20.

The NWT should now understand that it has a lot of improvement it can do to this activity since only 12 hours out of 96 hours of effort consumed by this activity is real-value-added cost.

Figure 5-21 is the Efficiency Performance Analysis Form filled out for processing commissions. It is important to note that the NWT is not meeting the requirements in both of its efficiency measurements in Figure 5-21.

Real-Value-Added	Business-Value-Added	No-Value-Added
• Record Order • Type Policy • Research Claim • Record Claim	• Record Date Received • Order Forms • Update Personnel Records • Prepare Financial Reports • Processing Commissions	• Review/Approval • Rework • Movement • Storage

FIGURE 5-18. Policy Issuance Value Content Analysis

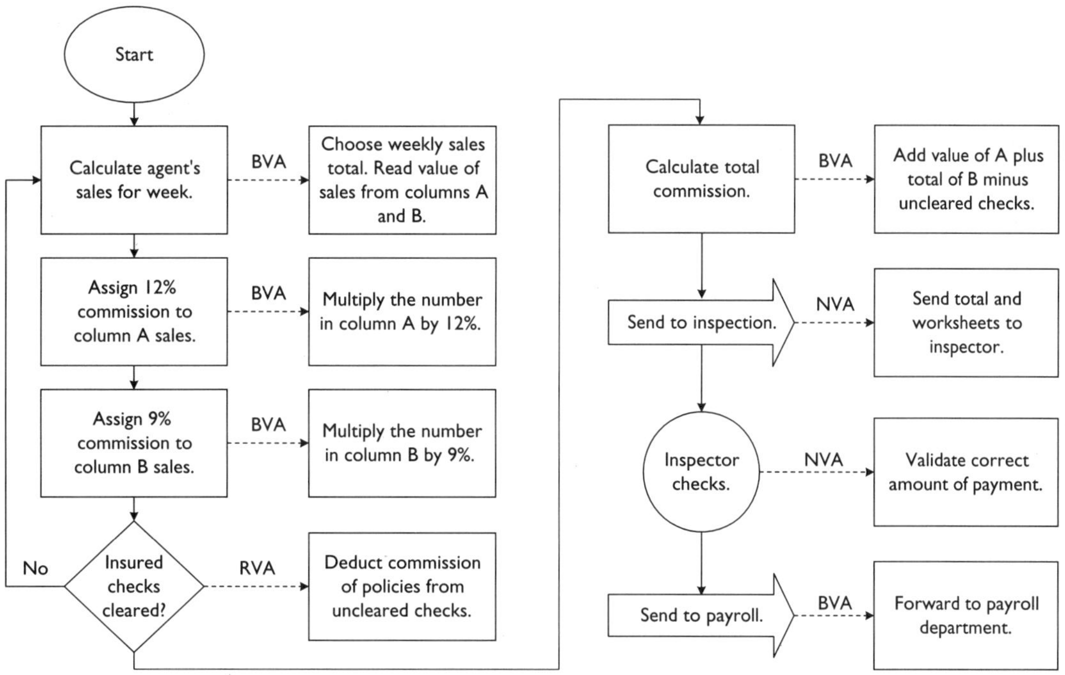

FIGURE 5-19. Processing Commissions Flowchart

Efficiency Measurement Form

Area Name and Number: Insurance Policy Processing Department/351

Activity: Processing Commissions

Prepared: Carrie Sandards Date: / /

How many hours per time processed? 96 Hours per item

Allocate this time into three value-added categories.

- Real-Value-Added (RVA) 12
- Business-Value-Added (BVA) 66
- No-Value-Added (NVA) 18

Total 96 Hours per item processed

Percent Real-Value-Added ______

Value-Added versus Poor-Quality Cost Matrix

Using the matrix below, further allocate the value-added hours to the appropriate category.

	RVA	Prevention	Appraisal	Error
RVA	12	No	No	No
BVA	38	14	14	No
NVA	No	No	6	12
Totals	50	14	20	12
Total	96			

This should be equal to the hours per item processed (as above)

FIGURE 5-20. Real-Value-Added versus Business- and No-Value-Added Cost Analysis for Processing Commissions

Efficiency Performance Analysis

Activity: Processing Commission

Area No. or Name: Insurance Policy Processing Department/351

Measurement Name: Percent real-value-added hours

- Performance Standard: 20%
- Present Value: 12.5%

(Measured X Estimated ____)

Met Requirements on: 9 / 1 / 99 Yes ____ No X

Measurement Name: Cycle time in hours

- Performance Standard: 48 hours
- Present Value: 123 hours

(Measured ____ Estimated X)

Met Requirements on: 9 / 1 / 99 Yes ____ No X

Measurement Name: ____

- Performance Standard: ____
- Present Value: ____

(Measured ____ Estimated ____)

Met Requirements on: / / Yes ____ No ____

Prepared by: Carrie Sandards Date: 9 / 1 / 99

Approved by: Second-level manager Date: 10 / 1 / 99

____ Date: / /

____ Date: / /

FIGURE 5-21. Efficiency Performance Analysis for Processing Commissions

Efficiency Performance Analysis

Activity: Inspecting incoming parts

Area No. or Name: BAK Final Assembly Area/301

Measurement Name: Percentage of storage space

- Performance Standard: 25%
- Present Value: 62%

(Measured X Estimated ____)

Met Requirements on: 9 / 1 / 99 Yes ____ No X

Measurement Name: Percent poor-quality cost

- Performance Standard: 5%
- Present Value: 23%

(Measured ____ Estimated X)

Met Requirements on: 9 / 1 / 99 Yes ____ No X

Measurement Name: Cost per item processed

- Performance Standard: $8.38
- Present Value: $7.25

(Measured ____ Estimated X)

Met Requirements on: 9 / 1 / 99 Yes X No ____

Prepared by:	NWT	Date:	9 / 1 / 99
Approved by:	Second-level manager	Date:	10 / 1 / 99
	Third-level manager	Date:	10 / 1 / 99
		Date:	/ /

FIGURE 5-22. Efficiency Performance Analysis Form for Inspecting Incoming Parts

BAK Final Assembly Area/301. The BAK Final Assembly Area defined three critical measurements that they would use to determine if the NWT's efficiency was improving:

- Poor-quality cost as a percentage of total labor cost. This was selected because the NWT was concerned about the wasted efforts that were going into inspection, rework, and scrap.
- Storage space as a percentage of total space.
- Cost per item processed.

Figure 5-22 is the Efficiency Performance Analysis Form filled out for the BAK Final Assembly Area's incoming parts inspection.

Customer Service Support Department/107. The activity the NWT members analyzed first was answering telephone calls. They found that almost 95% of the time they spent answering telephone calls related to their mission and customer needs. The NWT defined a total of three efficiency measurements:

- Percent real-value-added phone time
- Call duration in minutes
- Cost per question answered

Figure 5-23 is the Efficiency Performance Form filled out for the Customer Service Support Department's activity of answering service support phone calls. The NWT needs to complete this type of analysis for each critical activity. After it has completed analyzing each activity, it can prioritize its improvement efforts. We will discuss improvement in Chapter 7.

Summary

During this phase, the NWT gained a good understanding about the activity, how it functions, and what resources are consumed by the activity. The following should have been accomplished:

- The activity's efficiency measurements were defined.
- The activity's efficiency standards were defined and approved by the appropriate levels of management.

Efficiency Performance Analysis

Activity: Answering service support phone calls

Area No. or Name: Customer Service Support Department/107

Measurement Name: Percent real-value-added phone time

- Performance Standard: 90%
- Present Value: 95%

(Measured X Estimated ____)

Met Requirements on: 9 / 1 / 99 Yes X No ____

Measurement Name: Call duration in minutes

- Performance Standard: 3.3 minutes
- Present Value: 8.2 minutes

(Measured X Estimated ____)

Met Requirements on: 9 / 1 / 99 Yes ____ No X

Measurement Name: Cost per question answered

- Performance Standard: $23.17
- Present Value: $32.00

(Measured ____ Estimated X)

Met Requirements on: 9 / 1 / 99 Yes ____ No X

Prepared by: NWT Date: 9 / 1 / 99

Approved by: Second-level manager Date: 10 / 1 / 99

Third-level manager Date: 10 / 1 / 99

____ Date: / /

FIGURE 5-23. Efficiency Performance Analysis Form for Answering Service Support Phone Calls

- The efficiency measurement system and sampling plans were prepared.
- The activity was flowcharted.
- The activity was analyzed to determine what percentage of its resources was dedicated to real-value-added tasks.
- The NWT was trained on flowcharting, value-added analysis, and poor-quality cost.
- Area performance boards were put up.

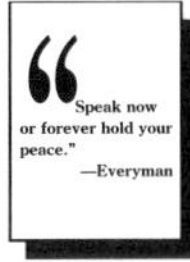

Products have limited lifespans, and even the best soon become obsolete. It is not products but the processes that create products that bring companies long-term success.

—MICHAEL HAMMER AND JAMES CHAMPY[11]

Notes

1. Helio Gomez, *Quality Quotes* (Milwaukee, WI: American Society for Quality Control (ASQC)-Quality Press, 1996), 203.
2. Ibid., 13.
3. Ibid., 13.
4. Dr. J. M. Juran, *Juran on Quality by Design: The New Steps for Planning Quality onto Goods and Services* (New York: Free Press, 1988).
5. Dr. W. Edwards Deming, *Out of the Crisis* (Cambridge, MA: MIT Center for Advanced Engineering Study, 1986).
6. Masaaki Imai, *Kaizen: The Key to Japan's Competitive Success* (New York: McGraw-Hill, 1986).
7. Dr. J. M. Juran, *Managerial Breakthrough* (New York: McGraw-Hill, 1995).
8. Rafael Aguayo, *Dr. Deming: The American Who Taught the Japanese about Quality* (New York: Fireside Books, 1991).
9. John R. Katzenbach and Douglas K. Smith, *The Wisdom of Teams: Creating the High-Performance Organization* (New York: Harper Business, 1994).
10. Helio Gomez, *Quality Quotes* (Milwaukee, WI: American Society for Quality Control (ASQC)-Quality Press, 1996), 27.
11. Michael Hammer and James Champy, *Reengineering the Corporation: A Manisfesto for Business Revolution* (New York: HarperCollins, 1994).

Putting the Puzzle of AAA Together

In this chapter we have found where value added fits into the **AAA** puzzle.

CHAPTER

Phase VI—Develop Supplier Partnerships

If Your Employees Are Your Most Valuable Asset, Your Suppliers Run a Close Second

Introduction

It is impossible to do most jobs without receiving something from someone. Just take a minute to look around where you are right now and make a list of the things you need to do your job that were supplied by another area. Our list looked like this:

- electricity
- copier
- computer and printer
- paper
- computer program
- desk
- chair
- pen
- calculator
- reference books
- office space
- telephone
- file cabinets
- fax machine
- FedEx services
- waste pick-up

There are a lot of things that we use every day that we got from a supplier. Your supplier can be either internal to your organization or external. We will use the word "supplier" to indicate both internal and external suppliers. For purposes of this chapter, we are not going to look at basic facility suppliers (for example, suppliers of electricity, office furniture, stationery, etc.). During Phase VI, the suppliers that will be discussed are suppliers that supply parts and services that are required specifically to produce the desired output (for example, suppliers of parts, data, transportation, computer output, etc.). As Harold K. Sperlich, past president of Chrysler Corporation said, "You have to work more closely with the supplier base to approach zero-defect levels; low-belt pricing won't do if the quality isn't there."

It is critical that the NWT and its supplier understand both the NWT's needs and the supplier's capabilities. Until the NWT understands its customer's needs and what it needs to do to satisfy those needs, the NWT should not try to define what it needs from its suppliers. Too often NWTs set out to help suppliers improve without really understanding what they need from the suppliers and what negative impact the NWTs' demands have on their suppliers' inputs. Once the NWT understands its activities, it can identify the input requirements that the NWT needs to receive from its suppliers. Make certain that the NWT's requirements are accurate, measurable, and reasonable and that the supplier agrees that they can provide output that meets these requirements. Then the NWT needs to insure that the supplier's output matches those requirements. Until the NWT reaches this type of understanding with its customers, it should not attempt to reach it with its suppliers. The NWT's needs often change when it understands its activities and its customers' needs.

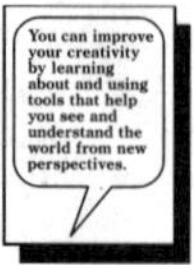

When the NWT reaches Phase VI of the **AAA** methodology, it should be ready and willing to work as a partner with its supplier. Remember, the objective is to develop win-win conditions between the NWT and its suppliers and customers. The NWT's suppliers are an invaluable part of the NWT's success. The better the supplier meets the NWT's needs, the easier it is for the NWT to meet the needs of its customer. The NWT's suppliers are often other areas within the total organization but also include suppliers who are external to the organization.

When the entire organization is using the **AAA** process, this phase is made much easier, because the NWT is a customer of its supplier. As a customer, the NWT should be approached by other internal NWTs to determine its requirements. The exception is when the activity that produces the output for the NWT is not considered a major activity by the internal supplier. If the

supplier is an external supplier, the NWT will need to follow the steps defined in Phase VI for external suppliers.

If the NWT's suppliers have not already worked with the NWT to define its input requirements, then the NWT will need to use Phase VI. Remember to carefully identify the NWT's real needs. The NWT should not become so demanding of its supplier that it receives more than it needs. Remember that there is no free lunch: Whatever the NWT orders, someone has to pay for. The supplier and the NWT are both trying to become effective at meeting the needs of the external customer as well as trying to be efficient in what they do. It should be the NWT's objective to minimize the combined resources required by the supplier and NWT and still meet the NWT's customer's requirements.

The only source of revenue is from external customers, so every extra demand on an internal supplier adds costs that must be passed along to the external customer or must be absorbed by the organization, which results in decreased profits.

Key Questions

Reaching a consensus about the following key questions will help the NWT establish a good partnership with its :

- Who are the activity's suppliers?
- What are the activity's input requirements?
- How does the area know if the supplier's inputs meet requirements?
- What happens if what the area gets is not what it expected?
- Is the area getting more than it needs or does it even need what it is getting?
- Can making changes to the area's requirements reduce the combined cost of providing the activity's output?

Deliverables

At the end of Phase VI, the NWT will

- Develop supplier specifications.
- Understand what the capabilities are of the NWT's suppliers.
- Document cost related to the inputs the NWT receives.
- Develop feedback systems that will be used to provide suppliers with performance information.
- Define acceptable input standards for all major inputs.

Process Overview

Gerard C. Hoffman, past director of Total Quality at Raytheon Company, said: "By basing relationships with suppliers on TQM principles, the DoD can keep an ethical arm's length and still work in partnership with industry."

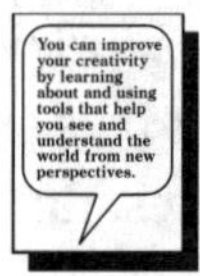

Now the NWT becomes the customer and looks to its suppliers to help it by producing the needed inputs so that the NWT can meet its customers' requirements. What should the NWT expect from its suppliers? Exactly what the NWT's customers expected from it—understanding of the NWT's needs, an awareness of what the NWT measures, and a willingness to meet the NWT's needs. In that sense then, we can repeat some of what was described in Chapter 4, but with a supplier orientation.

Is the NWT receiving the right things, at the right time, in the right way, and in the best format from its supplier? The NWT should determine its real needs (not everything it would like, but what it really needs) to do its job. Our **AAA** model continues to build in Figure 6-1. Each of the NWT's activities or tasks may have one or more inputs. Each input may come from one or more suppliers outside of the area or from other members of the NWT.

Dave Farrell, senior manager with Ernst & Young, said: "Internal customers have not met their obligation to their supplier by not defining what they expect from them and providing regular feedback related to their supplier's output." The NWT needs to identify clearly each of its input's suppliers (a company, an organization, another area in the organization, or a specific person) and specify exactly the input it requires from these suppliers. To do this, the NWT must define its requirements as accurately as possible to be

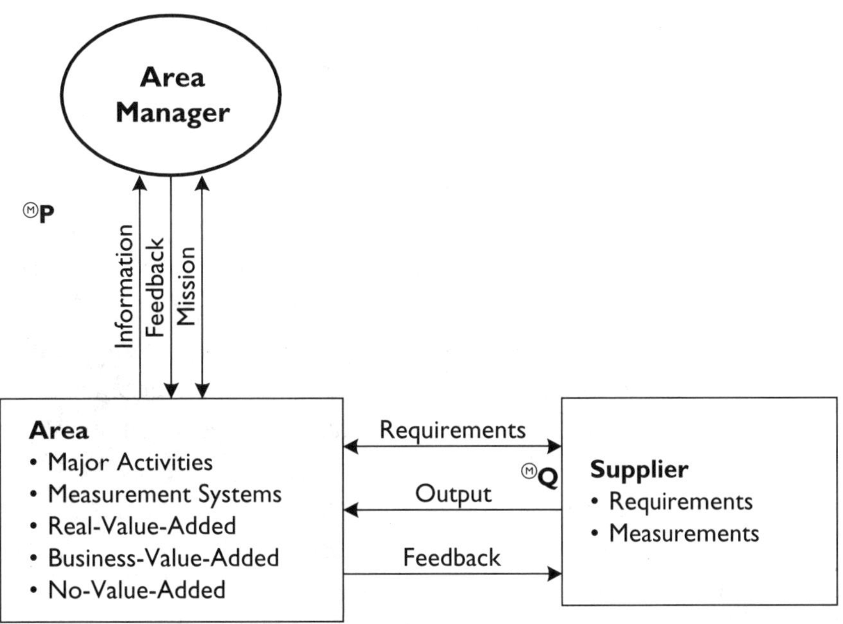

FIGURE 6-1. Supplier Partnership

sure that the suppliers of these inputs agree that they can provide output that meets these requirements. The NWT should always meet with the supplier to discuss and agree on these requirements. This is often a give-and-take discussion. Remember that the objective of the supplier/customer relationship is to maximize the combined (supplier/customer) value-added content while also minimizing the resources consumed by the combination.

Typical NWT input requirements are

- Hardware (parts, subassemblies, etc.)
  —Dimensions on a blueprint for a part
  —When the part will be delivered
  —How it should be packaged
- Administrative
  —Format of the report, data, or letter
  —When the NWT expects to receive it
  —Number of copies required
  —Method of receiving (network, fax, mail)
- Meetings
  —Starting on time
  —The right people in attendance
  —The right material available
  —The conference room properly stocked

Requirements should not be vague or general and must always be capable of being measured. If the NWT cannot measure what it receives, how will it and its supplier know if the requirements have been met?

The NWT must also have the discipline to reject input when it does not meet the agreed-to requirements. Too often organizations are driven by schedule (or cost), inputs that do not meet requirements are used because management believes that returning the inputs to the supplier will prevent the NWT from meeting its scheduled delivery dates. The result is that the supplier soon will believe that the NWT does not need the specified requirements so the suppliers relax their standards, will continue doing less than required, and the NWT has to make up for this deficiency (by doing rework, for example).

One of the book's authors was at an ASQC conference and overheard one of IBM's suppliers talking to another IBM supplier. The conversation went something like this:

> Supplier 1: You didn't reinspect and rework all those parts, did you?
>
> Supplier 2: Yes we did. IBM would have just rejected them and returned the whole lot to us anyway.
>
> Supplier 1: That must have cost a lot of bucks. What we do when we find something wrong with parts we're sending to IBM is to put a hold on the parts and send them to IBM a week or two late. By that time, IBM needs the parts on the production line and will usually off-spec them or rework them themselves. It saves us a lot of money.

You can tell right away how efficient and effective organizations (and their people) are by how they handle their input requirements. Are they firm or sloppy? Do they say, "No, that is not acceptable and we won't send it to our customers," or do they say, "Well, I guess it's good enough. I don't think the customer will have any problem using the item."?

Saying no is difficult to do, especially when the NWT is fighting a tight schedule or when it has accepted less than it needed in the past. How the NWT acts on this is a clear indication of how serious it is about making its area function effectively and efficiently. The one thing that had the biggest impact on improving supplier quality at IBM was when it embraced and enforced the slogan, *"Off-spec? No way—no how. Change the print or return the parts."*

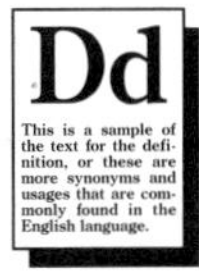

Off-spec is a document that authorizes the use of an item that does not meet requirements. For hardware, the document is normally approved by manufacturing, quality assurance, and product engineering.

For internal suppliers, this practice may be relaxed a little, allowing the NWT to rework the input and not return it to the internal suppliers, but the principle still applies. If the NWT can use discrepant inputs without increasing the resources that are required to produce the desired output, then the requirements should be relaxed. The object is to minimize the combined resources required to provide the output.

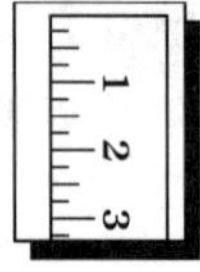

The NWT/supplier relationship can be summarized as follows:

- The NWT is responsible to
  - —Define and communicate its input requirements and how they are measured.
  - —Define the minimum performance standard for the critical measurements and the total input.
  - —Provide ongoing feedback to the suppliers related to the acceptability of the inputs they provide.
- The suppliers are responsible to
  - —Ensure they are capable of providing the input to the NWT at the minimum acceptable performance level or better.
  - —Suggest how requirements can be changed to reduce the resources required to produce the desired inputs. (Example: The requirement states that a report should be provided every Wednesday, but the same report is also run on Monday for another customer. Can both customers agree on a single day that the report is generated?)
  - —Provide inputs to the NWT that meet the requirements and continuously improve.
  - —Respond quickly to correct problems reported by the NWT and document the action taken, sending a copy to the NWT.

Phase VI Breakdown

The block diagram in Figure 6-2 shows the five steps of Phase VI.

Step 1–Identify Suppliers

Select only activities that have completed Phase V. For these activities, identify the suppliers that provide the input to each task that makes up the activity. If the activity was flowcharted in Phase V, this effort will be easy, because the flowchart will identify key inputs that come into the activity from exter-

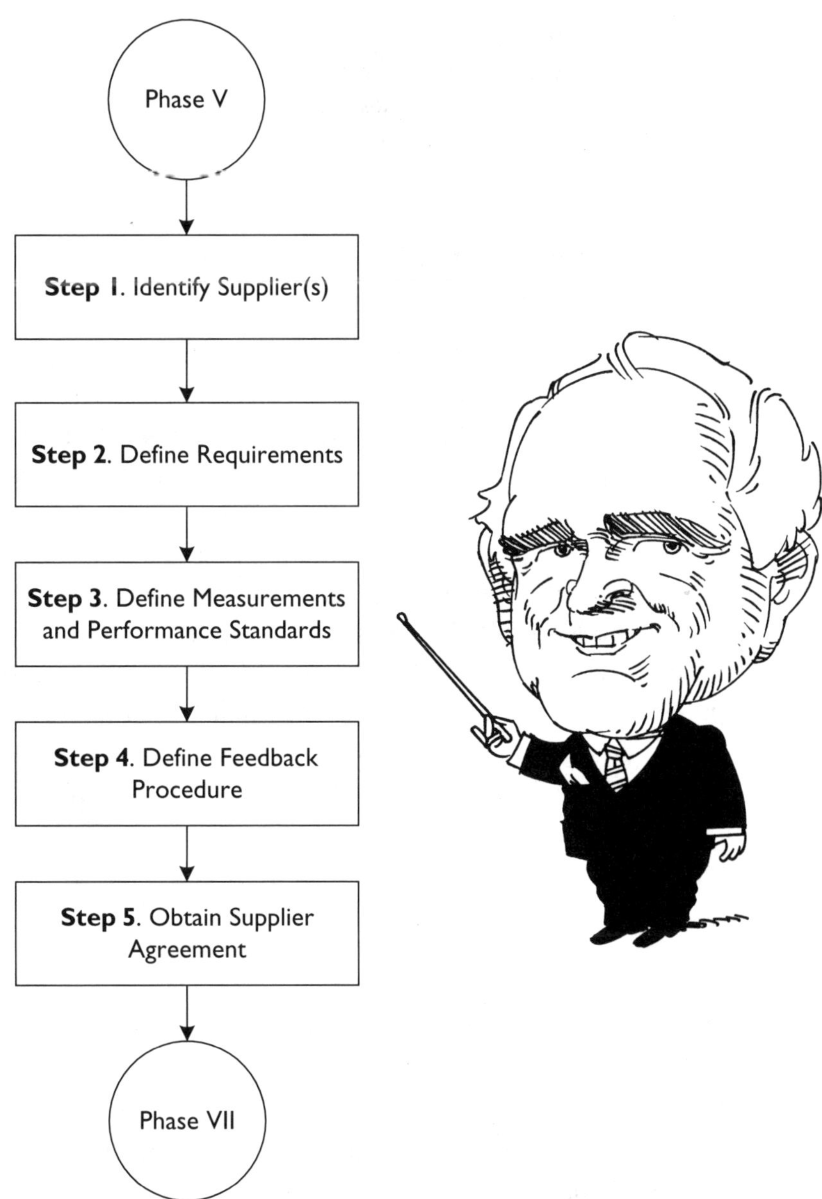

FIGURE 6-2. The Five Steps That Make Up Phase VI

nal sources. To double-check the accuracy of the flowchart, look at each task and identify what inputs are required to complete the task. Inputs can take many forms. Some of the more common are

- reports
- letters
- forms
- approvals
- materials
- phone calls
- parts
- money
- directions
- people
- equipment

Once the NWT has defined the inputs for each task, it needs to identify who supplies these inputs. During Phase VI, the NWT will only address inputs that are supplied by organizations outside of the area that is doing the AAA. Frequently, a single input to an activity has only one supplier. When more than one supplier exists for any input, the individual supplier's needs may conflict with each other. If this kind of conflict exists, the NWT will need to negotiate the differences between the suppliers so that it receives a consistent input. A complete list of suppliers and their inputs should be prepared for each activity. To simplify this process, the NWT should only analyze inputs that are unique to the area. Things like money, office space, electricity, heat, desks, phone service, utilities, and so forth, are not analyzed in most cases. (An example of an exception would be that the department responsible for acquiring phone service for the organization would consider the phone system as an input.) Filling out the form in Figure 6-3 will help with the task of identifying the NWT's suppliers and their inputs.

Step 2–Define Requirements

Use a checklist to be sure that the requirements are clearly defined. Requirements fall into the two broad categories of "needs" and "expectations." These two words have very different meanings, as we have previously discussed. The NWT must know the difference.

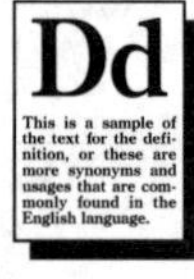

A **checklist** is a list that contains what must be done, broken into component parts that are signed off or checked off as they are completed.

Supplier Identification Work Sheet			
Activity Name:			
Task Name	**Input's Name**	**Supplier**	
		NWT	**Other**

FIGURE 6-3. **Supplier Identification Work Sheet**

Needs set the minimum standard for the input that the NWT will accept. These are the NWT's specifications. Needs don't normally change, but expectations change often. Because of this, the NWT must stay very close to its suppliers in order for the inputs to meet the NWT's needs and expectations. The NWT should examine each input by asking the following:

- How does the NWT use the input?
- Does the NWT need this input?
- What will happen if the NWT does not get the input?
- When does the NWT need the input?
- Is it coming into the area too early or too late?
- Is it coming into the area in the very best possible format or media?
- Is the NWT getting more than it needs?
- Is the NWT getting less than it needs?
- How much and what types of resources could be saved if this input is improved or changed?
- What does the NWT need from the input, and how good does it have to be?
- How much is this input worth to the NWT?

The following are typical examples of items that are found on supplier checklists. The NWT will need to modify the checklist to match its specific situation.

- ▶ What the NWT expects the supplier to provide and how it should perform.
  - —A part must meet a specification.
  - —A report must have a certain format.
  - —Software must meet a level of performance and a specific format.
  - —Packaging in a certain way.
- ▶ How much the NWT is willing to pay for the input.
- ▶ How many will be delivered.
- ▶ When the NWT expects delivery.
  - —Specify when the NWT wants the product.
  - —There should be a time window, that is, not before a time and date, and not after a time and date.
  - —This could be measured in days or in minutes.
  - —How it should be packaged.
- ▶ How the NWT will measure what it receives, and how the NWT knows it is good. If the NWT cannot define the difference between bad and good input, it can never complain to suppliers about their input.
  - —Visual inspection.
  - —Functional check.
  - —Static test.
  - —Verify supplier's supplied data.
  - —None.

In Step 2, the NWT will spell out clearly how it will measure the input. It could be anything from a visual inspection by anyone to a highly sophisticated testing device used by one person. It could be as simple as time stamping a document to record the time that it arrived.

The NWT needs to define what its requirements are for each input. To do this, it should start with the list of inputs that was developed in Step 1 (see Figure 6-3). Many NWTs try to develop requirements for all of the inputs. This is an excellent practice if the NWT receives only a few inputs. On the other hand, we have seen NWTs that have had more than 50 inputs coming into their major activities. In the case where there is a large number of inputs and suppliers involved in supporting the NWT's major activities, the NWT will need to select the inputs that it really needs to control and work with a reduced number of suppliers. Now is the time when the NWT can divide and conquer. Often, the NWT is divided into small groups of people who use a specific input that is being studied to prepare the list of requirements and to work with the related suppliers to get the suppliers' specifications completed and approved. We find that small groups of one or two people, called "NWT subgroups," can do a good job of this due to the experience that they have gained during Phases III through V of the **AAA** methodology. The supplier specification can be developed by the whole NWT or its subgroups. We use the term "NWT" to cover both approaches in the remainder of this chapter. Note: This is the only chapter in which we use NWT subgroups.

There are two approaches that are used to work with the NWT's suppliers in developing supplier specifications:

- Define all of the inputs for a specific activity that come from the same supplier, and work with that supplier to obtain agreement on the supplier specifications for all the inputs at the same time.

Supplier Specification Work Sheet				
Supplier	**Input**	**Requirements**	**Measurements**	**Performance Standards**
Purchasing Records Dept.	Approved supplier list	• Report all lots processed during the last six months. • New report out by the fifth of each month.		

FIGURE 6-4. Supplier Specification Work Sheet

- ▶ Define all of the inputs for all of the activities that come from the same supplier, and work with that supplier to get approval of all of the supplier specifications.

The advantage of the first approach is that the NWT can complete the AAA process for each individual major activity and then go on to the next activity. The disadvantage to this approach is that the NWT may meet with the same supplier on a number of occasions, one for each activity to which the supplier provides an input. The second approach requires that the NWT complete Phases I through V for all of the major activities before starting Phase VI. Although both approaches work and we have used both approaches with various clients, we prefer the first approach.

Once the inputs that need to be controlled are defined, the NWT needs to study each input to define what this input must contain (requirements) for it to meet its needs and that of the NWT's customers. The form shown in Figure 6-4 will help the NWT define input requirements.

Step 3—Define Measurements and Performance Standards

The NWT really should not have to measure or check its supplier's inputs. It is the NWT's supplier's responsibility to provide the NWT with the item that

meets its requirements without the NWT double-checking to see if it does. This double-checking was done in the past (and in some cases is still done today) because there was an adverse relationship between suppliers and customers. It was more important to get the item to the customer on time than to get the item right (the schedule-driven mentality). All of that is changing now, and the supplier is being held much more accountable for meeting quality, schedule, and cost.

The two major types of measurements, effectiveness and efficiency, are the primary measurements for any organization. If the NWT's suppliers are not using these measurements, then it is in the NWT's best interest to educate them. The NWT is directly affected by the effectiveness measurements of the input that it receives from its suppliers, but it is also impacted by the related efficiency measurements because these drive cost and schedule.

If the NWT's suppliers do not think it is necessary to measure their effectiveness and efficiency, then perhaps another supplier would be in order. Of course, when the NWT is dealing with internal suppliers, it may not have the choice of selecting a different one. This then becomes a management decision as to how to get all the suppliers and customers within an organization aligned in using the same measurement structure. If the organization is having trouble with getting internal requirements aligned, it may be time to think about outsourcing some of the problem activities.

The input's measurement system should be developed by the supplier and should reflect the NWT's requirements. In order to define how these requirements will be measured, a meeting is held between the NWT and the supplier. A sample of the input should be brought to this meeting. Approximately one week prior to the meeting, a meeting agenda and a copy of the Supplier Specification Work Sheet (sample in Figure 6-4) should be sent to all of the participants.

At this meeting, the NWT will review the inputs it receives from the supplier and discuss the NWT's requirements related to each input. It is important that the supplier understands how its inputs will be used. Often the supplier can make a slight change within his or her process and provide the NWT with input that better fulfills its expectations and uses less or the same amount of the supplier's resources.

After the supplier understands the NWT's requirements, the supplier will determine if he or she can provide the inputs that comply with these requirements. This is a give-and-take situation between the supplier and the NWT. There is little use for the NWT requiring something that the supplier cannot deliver. Often, slight changes in the NWT's requirements will result in a more cost-effective operation for the supplier. For example, the supplier could have a standard part made out of brass that will do the same job as a special part made out of plastic that the NWT requested, and the more reliable brass part costs 75% less because it is a stock part. Another example would be the NWT's requirements a report to be delivered by the fifth day of the month. Since it takes the supplier four days after the last day of the month to generate the report, the supplier would have to work his or her team on weekends whenever Saturday and Sunday fall during the first five days of the month. Changing the NWT's requirement to having the report available on the fifth working day of the month makes a big difference to the supplier. When there is a common agreement about the requirements, the Supplier Specification Work Sheet can be completed (see Figure 6-5).

Now the suppliers should explain how the agreed-to requirements will be measured. This information is recorded on the Supplier Specification Work

Supplier Specification Work Sheet				
Supplier	**Input**	**Requirements**	**Measurements**	**Performance Standards**
Purchasing Records Dept.	Approved supplier list	• Report all lots processed during the last six months.	• Number of lots that have completed receiving inspection by the 15th of the month and are not in the report	• Maximum of 2% missing • One day late, twice a year
		• New report out by the fifth of each month.	• Time stamp on the report at the NWT's location	• Five days late, once in two years

FIGURE 6-5. **Completed Supplier Specification Work Sheet**

Sheet. The NWT will then define the minimum acceptable performance standard for each of the inputs. This information will also be recorded on the Supplier Specification Work Sheet after agreement is reached between the supplier and the NWT on the absolute values.

Another consideration the NWT needs to address is what it will do if the supplier occasionally provides input that does not meet requirements.

- Does the NWT plan to correct the discrepant input provided by the supplier?
- Will the delay cost the organization money or time, or will the delay have some other negative downstream impact on the external customer?
- What is the fallback plan?

The list goes on and on about the things that happen when someone doesn't do the right job at the right time. The NWT has to be prepared for this, because it will happen. It is important that the supplier and the NWT agree on what action will be taken when the supplier input to the NWT does not meet requirements. Some typical examples of recovery plans follow:

- The supplier sends someone to work in the NWT's area to correct the problem.
- The supplier will set a higher priority for the rework of the output than for other jobs.
- The NWT will correct the problem and charge the cost of correcting it to the supplier.

Part of this preparation takes place when the NWT and its supplier(s) agree on the input requirements and measurements. Specifying the conditions and solutions for what happens when something goes wrong is one of the most overlooked items in customer/supplier relations.

Step 4–Define Feedback Procedure

Specifying the conditions and method of feedback must not be overlooked. There are many ways that the NWT can give feedback to the suppliers related to their inputs such as written, computer-generated, and verbal reports. Whichever method the NWT chooses, it should ensure that the suppliers are provided with feedback about the effectiveness of their inputs to the NWT. The suppliers need to know if what the NWT receives is what it expects and when the NWT's requirements change. Just as providing good input is a supplier's responsibility, providing feedback to its suppliers about how good the inputs are is the responsibility of the NWT. No matter how conscientious the suppliers are in evaluating their own outputs, the real measure of the outputs' worth rests in how well they satisfy their customer's needs and expectations. This means that the real worth of the supplier's outputs can only be measured in their customer's environment. In some instances, the real worth measurement takes place in the customer's (consumer's) environment. Good feedback from the customer and even the final consumer is an essential part of all supplier's continuous improvement process. No news may not be good news. It may mean that the supplier's customers have given up on them. To provide the required feedback it may be necessary for the NWT to establish an internal measurement and reporting system.

Step 5—Obtain Supplier Agreement

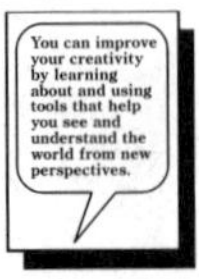

The NWT should meet with the suppliers to complete a Supplier Partnership Agreement. This agreement should be reviewed and renewed periodically. The supplier partnership agreement should be updated at least once every three years. The agreement should be in writing and signed by both parties. The NWT uses the Supplier Partnership Agreement Form (see Figure 6-6) to ensure that the NWT and its suppliers are in complete agreement about how they interface. By signing the document, both the NWT and the suppliers document their commitments to each other. Normally, the NWT manager signs for the rest of the NWT.

We like to think of these meetings between the NWT and its suppliers as two-way activities. We have often found that when the supplier understands how the input will be used, he or she can suggest ways to improve the input to make it more useful within the activity. We have also found that, in many cases, a small change in the input requirements can have a big impact on the

Supplier Partnership Agreement

Area Name and Number: ______________________________

Supplier Name and Number: ______________________________

Activity: ______________________________

Input: ______________________________

Requirements: ______________________________

____

- Performance Standard: ______________________________

  ____

- Performance as of ____/____/____: ______________________________
- Measured: ______________ Estimated: ______________
- Area's feedback process: ______________________________

  ____

  ____

- Recovery plan: ______________________________

  ____

  ____

Requirements: ______________________________

____

- Performance Standard: ______________________________

  ____

- Performance as of ____/____/____: ______________________________
- Measured: ______________ Estimated: ______________
- Area's feedback process: ______________________________

  ____

  ____

- Recovery plan: ______________________________

  ____

  ____

Prepared by: ______________________ Date: ____/____/____

Area Approval: ______________________ Date: ____/____/____

Supplier Approval: ______________________ Date: ____/____/____

Supplier Approval: ______________________ Date: ____/____/____

FIGURE 6-6. **Supplier Partnership Agreement Form**

quality and/or cost of the input. As a customer, the NWT should understand what it costs to produce the inputs it uses and be willing to work with the supplier to minimize the total cost of the combination of supplier input costs and activity costs. This approach minimizes the cost to provide the desired level of value-added content to the NWT's customers.

Things That Can Help

- The NWT should look at all of its critical inputs and group them by supplier.
- Before meeting with its suppliers, the NWT should make certain it knows how each input is used, who receives it, and the requirements related to it.
- The NWT should reach agreement on a default procedure or what it will do if the supplier's input does not meet its requirements.

Examples

The following are partial lists of NWT requirements by group.

Insurance Policy Processing Department/351

Major Activity:	Research data.
Supplier:	MIS department.
Needs:	Up-to-date, easily available data on insured.
Requirements:	Daily report delivered before 8:00 A.M.
	Data reflect the U.S. information that is complete for all but the last 20 hours.
Measurements:	Time the report arrives in the area.
	Number of hours of data not covered in the report.
	Readability of the delivered report after it is copied.

Performance Standards: No more than 95% delivered after 9:00 A.M.
No more than one report per month that does not include data for the last 20 hours.
First-generation copies should always be readable. No more than 20% of the time should second-generation copies be unreadable.

Recovery Plan: MIS will give top priority to correcting and rerunning the job. MIS will pay for the Insurance Policy Processing Department's overtime on days when the standard is not met.

Figure 6-7 is the Supplier Partnership Agreement Form filled in for the computer daily sales report.

BAK Final Assembly Area/301

Major Activity: Assembling parts.

Supplier: Preassembly.

Needs: Parts fit.
Parts function.
Proper level of stock.

Requirements: Do not have to wait for parts and no more than three boxes on hand at any time.

Measurements: Visual inspection for obvious defects before putting into the assembly.
Functional test at the assembly level.
The number of part boxes on hand.
Number of hours that the NWT is waiting for parts.

Performance Standards: Maximum of one defect per 100,000 parts.
No more than 10 minutes per month of downtime for lack of parts.
All stock can be stored in its storage bin.

Supplier Partnership Agreement

Area Name and Number: Insurance Policy Processing Department/351

Supplier Name and Number: MIS Department/901

Activity: Research Data

Input: Computer Daily Sales Report

Requirements: Delivered before 8:00 A.M.

- Performance Standard: On schedule 95%
- Performance as of 12 / 1 / 99 : 98%
- Measured: X Estimated:
- Area's feedback process: Time stamp report as it comes into the area. Corrective Action Report generated for any report more than 60 minutes late.
- Recovery plan: MIS will pay for the overtime on days that the report comes in after 9:00 A.M.

Requirements: Complete for all but the last 20 hours

- Performance Standard: Maximum of one report per month does not meet standard.
- Performance as of 12 / 1 / 99 : 3.5 reports/month
- Measured: X Estimated:
- Area's feedback process: Monthly report
- Recovery plan: MIS will pay for overtime on days that the report does not meet standard.

Prepared by: NWT Date: 12 / 1 / 99

Area Approval: Date: 12 / 10 / 99

Supplier Approval: MIS manager Date: 12 / 20 / 99

Supplier Approval: Date: / /

FIGURE 6-7. Supplier Partnership Agreement for the Computer Daily Sales Report

Recovery Plan: The preassembly department technician will be assigned to work with production control to develop a plan that will minimize the problem's impact on the manufacturing line. This plan will be submitted to the manufacturing line manager within 24 hours of the time the preassembly department was notified of the problem.

Customer Service Support Department/107

Major Activity: Answer telephone calls.

Supplier: Telecommunications department.

Needs: Working phone lines.
No busy signals.

Requirements: 24-hour availability.

Measurements: Time until the NWT gets a dial tone.
Number of busy signals per month.
Number of hours with no phone service.

Performance Standards: Less than three seconds wait time for dial tone.
Less than 0.8% busy signals for incoming calls due to internal hardware.
Less than two hours with no phone service per year.

Recovery Plan: If a monthly report indicates that the performance standards are not met for two consecutive months, additional lines will be added to provide a 25% safety factor based on the number of calls processed during those two months.

The NWT may think that it is asking a lot of its suppliers, and it is probably a lot more than it has ever asked before, but this is no more than the

NWT is expected to provide to its customers. This can only be achieved when the NWT takes every safeguard to be sure that each and every job is done the right way, at the right time, every time. In today's global competitive marketplace, everyone must pay this kind of attention to survive.

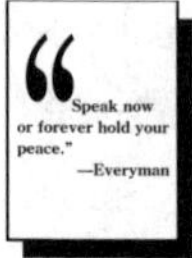

Ask yourself this question. "Do you provide your internal suppliers with as much information about requirements as you do your external suppliers?"

—KEN LOMAX, PRESIDENT OF LOMAX CONSULTING GROUP

Summary

During Phase VI, the NWT should have

- Defined all of the activities' suppliers
- Defined what the suppliers' inputs should be
- Developed and signed off on supplier partnership agreements
- Developed a balance between input cost and the cost within the activity
- Provided the supplier with information so the supplier understands how its output is used
- Established data feedback systems to the suppliers

Putting the Puzzle of AAA Together

In this chapter we have found where "input" and "supplier" fit into the **AAA** puzzle.

CHAPTER 7

Phase VII—Performance Improvement

Performance Improvement Is Not Part of the Game–It Is the Game

Introduction

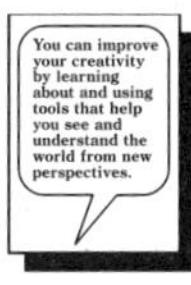

This chapter completes the AAA process and integrates it with whatever improvement process is active within the organization or prepares the NWT to start a continuous improvement effort. The NWT may begin this phase after completion of Phase V if the total organization is participating in AAA. If the NWT needs to prepare supplier specification and performance agreements, the NWT will not start this phase until phase VI is completed for the activity that is being improved. In some cases, the performance improvement activities are started as early as Phase IV when customer-related problems or performance issues are identified.

As a result of the AAA process, a list of the area's performance measurements is prepared. These performance measurements should be the activity's critical measures of effectiveness and efficiency. They will provide the NWT with insight about how well the area is performing and help the NWT identify improvement opportunities.

Improvement is a positive change in anything as viewed by one or more of its stakeholders. For this book, we will define improvement as a positive change in the effectiveness and efficiency measurements that is greater than any negative effect it has on other effectiveness and/or efficiency measurements in or outside of the area.

When the NWT reaches Phase VII, it will have completed the analysis of the area. This phase provides the integration between what the NWT found and how it will improve its performance results. **AAA** is a stand-alone process to define measurements and performance standards. It is very important that the NWT does not stop now. The real benefits of **AAA** are realized when the NWT uses these data to direct its improvement efforts. (See Figure 7-1).

The most beneficial characteristic of **AAA** is that it can integrate seamlessly with whatever improvement method the organization is using. It provides a meaningful starting point for any improvement methodology, including continuous improvement, reengineering, right-sizing, benchmarking, total quality management, creativity techniques, complexity management, and statistical process control.

If the NWT does not use the output of the **AAA** process to direct its improvement efforts, it has wasted a great deal of effort and resources. The seven steps of this phase are intentionally generic to enable the organization to modify and integrate the results of **AAA** into its culture.

Key Questions

Reaching a consensus about the following key questions will help the NWT establish what improvement actions it should take.

- What effectiveness performance standards are not being met?
- What improvement methodology should the NWT use to improve the area's performance so that all effectiveness performance standards are being met all the time?
- What efficiency performance standards are not being met?

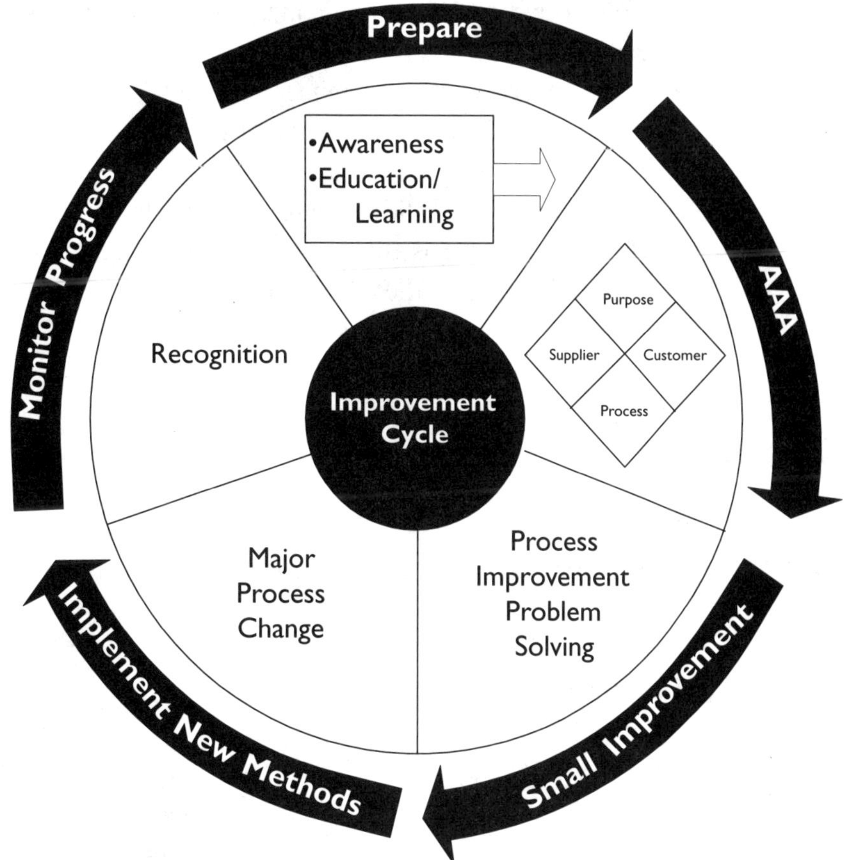

FIGURE 7-1.

- What improvement methodology should be used to improve the area's performance so that all efficiency performance standards are being met all the time?
- What are the most important measurements that should be monitored to ensure that the NWT is meeting its effectiveness and efficiency goals?
- How can the NWT challenge everyone in its area to focus on improving their efficiency and effectiveness?
- What does the NWT have to do to keep blame and shame from being placed on those who do not meet their goals?

- How does the NWT provide incentives and rewards to those who become more efficient and effective?
- Is the area content to be a meets minimum requirements performer?
- Are the people in the area content to be rated as meets minimum requirements because their output only meets the standard?
- Which outputs should be better than meets minimum requirements?
- How much better is the area performing today than it was one year ago, and how does the NWT know?
- Should the area be improving at a rate of 10% or 20% per year?

Deliverables

At the end of Phase VII, the NWT will have a clear picture of how to integrate the results of **AAA** with its current improvement methodology.

Process Overview

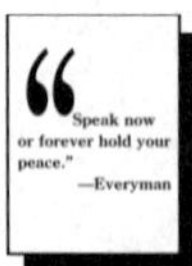

Our business world has accepted errors as a way of life. We live with them, we plan for them, and we make excuses for them. They have become part of the personality of our business. Our employees quickly recognize our standards and create errors so that they will not disappoint us.

—*The Improvement Process*[1]

The **AAA** model is complete at this time (see Figure 7-2). Effectiveness measurements and standards are in place for the NWT's output to its customers. The way the NWT uses its resources (efficiency) is measured, standards have been developed, and supplier specifications have been defined and agreed to. In addition, upper management is receiving information on the NWT's efficiency and on its effectiveness.

It is upper management's responsibility to focus the organization on becoming more efficient and effective. They need to establish an environment within the organization that fosters teamwork, encourages risk taking, keeps internal customers from making unnecessary demands on their internal sup-

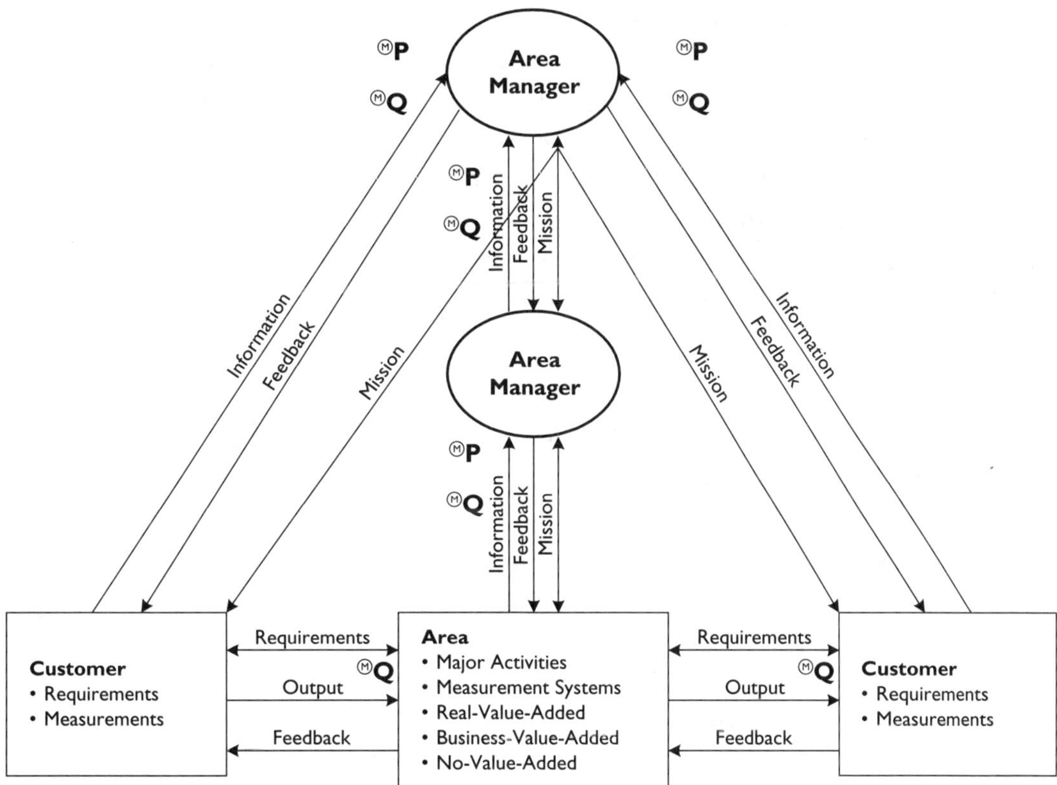

FIGURE 7-2. **AAA Model**

pliers, and provides a vision that requires everyone to continuously improve and to be uncomfortable when things are not changing. Lack of upper management's full support of the internal customer satisfaction concept can lead to waste and loss of focus that will result in a negative impact on the external customer. It is for this very reason that we encourage top management to be the first area to use the **AAA** methodology. Our data indicate that a typical executive makes between 50 and 80 behavioral errors per week, yet they require their employees to work at the PPM (parts per mission) level. All TQM or other improvement projects should start with the executive team using the **AAA** process. Then focus on reducing their error rates.

What if you do not get top management's full support? We do not recommend that any area that reaches this point in the **AAA** process holds back by waiting for any other area to catch up with it, not even upper management. Often the line areas don't have a good view of what top management is working on. As a result, the line areas may falsely believe that they are not fully supported by top management when, in reality, they do have top management's full support. Remember, top management's role is not to fight today's fires but to develop the strategic direction and focus for the organization over the next 5 to 20 years. We believe that the best leaders in the twenty-first century will do three things well:

1. Provide a clear vision.
2. Ask the right questions.
3. Communicate appropriate war stories (case studies).

All else will be secondary.

Don't wait for any other organization. Jump right in and begin to improve the way the NWT is performing. If every area just started to improve the measurements that were developed as a result of the **AAA** process by implementing corrections that they can accomplish by themselves, it would revitalize the total organization.

The NWT should first direct its improvement activities at measurements that are not performing at an acceptable level as defined by the performance standards. The following improvement priority order is usually the correct way to bring about improvement within an activity.

- Priority 1—Effectiveness measurements that are not meeting the agreed-to external customer specifications (performance standards).
- Priority 2—Effectiveness and efficiency measurements that relate to the external customer and would give the organization a significant competitive advantage if they were improved.
- Priority 3—Effectiveness measurements that are not meeting the agreed-to internal customer specifications (performance standards).
- Priority 4—Efficiency measurements that are not meeting agreed-to performance standards.
- Priority 5—Measurements that can be improved with the resources within the NWT and are easy to improve.
- Priority 6—Efficiency measurements that account for large amounts of resources and are meeting agreed-to performance standards.

- Priority 7—Effectiveness measurements that will exceed the customer's expectations without increasing the cost of the output.

Once specific improvement opportunities are defined, it is time to start training the area's personnel on how to solve problems. There are literally hundreds of improvement tools available today. It always amazes us when an organization trains everyone on how to use an improvement tool and then tells them to go out and find a place to use it. This results in billions of dollars of wasted training costs every year. The result is that some very effective tools are misapplied, causing the organization to believe the tools do not function well, and discourages the workforce. For example, billions of dollars were spent reengineering processes in the last 10 years that produced little or no results. The problem was not that the reengineering methodology did not work, because it does. The root cause of reengineering's poor results was because it was applied to processes that should have been redesigned, not reengineered. The employees were trained to reengineer processes and not trained on how to redesign processes. As a result, they applied a sledge hammer (process reengineering) when they should have been using a tack hammer (process redesign), resulting in poor overall results. We estimate that about 80% of the processes that had process reengineering applied to them should have used process redesign methodologies instead, thereby producing exceptional results.

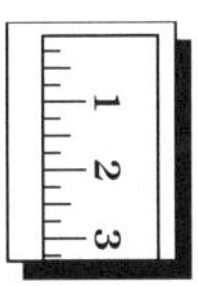

Rule Number 1 in continuous improvement is to define the improvement opportunity first, then train the employees on how to use the correct tools to take advantage of the specific opportunity.

The Opportunity Cycle

Henry J. Kaiser, an industrialist, said: "Problems are only opportunities in work clothes."[2] Let's change the way we look at problems. Let's think about each problem we face each day as an opportunity to contribute to making the organization more successful. As these opportunities arise, we need to have a systematic way of addressing them so that they are not just put to bed, but buried. If you put a problem to bed, it can and will get up some time in the future to cause the organization more disruptions. It may be next week or next month or next year, or perhaps in five years, but it will come back until the

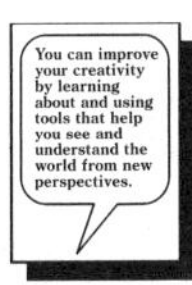

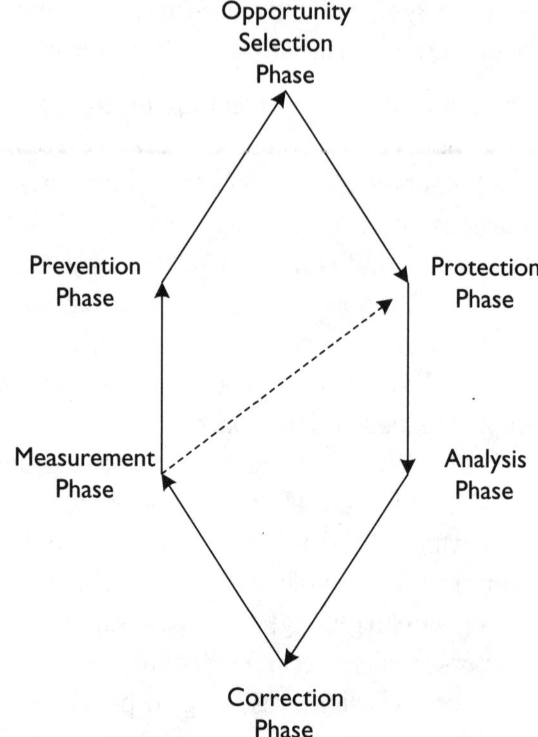

FIGURE 7-3. The Opportunity Cycle

process that allowed the problem to occur initially is error-proofed. When you have error-proofed the process that allowed the problem to occur, then and only then have you buried the problem so that it will not come back. That's what the "opportunity cycle" is all about (see Figure 7-3).

Maslow wrote in *The Farther Reaches of Human Nature:* "The best way to view a present problem is to give **it** all you've got, to study it and its nature, to perceive **within** it the intrinsic interrelationships, to discover (rather than to invent) the answer to the problem within the problem itself."[3] When you investigate each problem, go through the six distinct phases indicated in Figure 7-3. Each phase contains a number of individual activities. The total cycle consists of 25 different activities.

- Phase 1: Opportunity Selection Phase
  - —Activity 1: Listing the problems

—Activity 2: Collecting data
—Activity 3: Verifying the problems
—Activity 4: Prioritizing the problems
—Activity 5: Selecting the problems
—Activity 6: Defining the problems

- Phase 2: Protection Phase
  —Activity 7: Taking action to protect the customer
  —Activity 8: Verifying the effectiveness of the action taken
- Phase 3: Analysis Phase
  —Activity 9: Collecting problem symptoms
  —Activity 10: Validating the problem
  —Activity 11: Separating the cause and effect
  —Activity 12: Defining the root cause
- Phase 4: Correction Phase
  —Activity 13: Developing alternative solutions
  —Activity 14: Selecting the best possible solution
  —Activity 15: Developing an implementation plan
  —Activity 16: Conducting a pilot run
  —Activity 17: Presenting the solution for approval
- Phase 5: Measurement Phase
  —Activity 18: Implementing the approved plan
  —Activity 19: Measuring cost and impact
  —Activity 20: Removing the protective action (installed in Phase 2)
- Phase 6: Prevention Phase
  —Activity 21: Applying action taken to similar activities
  —Activity 22: Defining and correcting the basic process problem
  —Activity 23: Changing the process documentation to prevent recurrence
  —Activity 24: Providing proper training
  —Activity 25: Returning to Phase 1, Activity 1

When NWTs follow these six phases (or a similar process), their lives become much easier. Unfortunately, the more experienced the NWT becomes, the more likely it is to take shortcuts. Process shortcuts have probably led to the demise of more NWTs than can be counted. Sir Arthur Conan Doyle stated: "It is a capital mistake to theorize before you have all the evidence. It biases the judgment."[4] When the NWT elects to circumvent the correct problem-solving process, it automatically reduces its ability to function in a continuous improvement environment. The NWT may ultimately be successful, but it will be by accident, not by design.

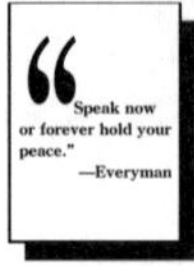

Problems breed problems, and the lack of a disciplined method of openly attacking them breeds more problems.

—PHILIP CROSBY, *QUALITY IS FREE*[5]

Performance Index

Determining how much, or even if, an area is improving is very difficult due to the many different measurements that are involved. As a result, we suggest that the NWT develop a performance index for the area. To accomplish this, each measurement within the area should be weighted based on its contribution to the total organization's performance. The total of the individual weighting should add up to 100%. Then by calculating the change in a specific measurement over a set period of time and multiplying it by the appropriate weighting factors, a change-weighted value can be calculated for each measurement. Adding up the change-weighted value calculation for each measurement provides a total change figure for the entire organization. There are measurements that improve when they get smaller (for example, cost per unit processed) and other measurements that improve when they get bigger (for example, percentage of units that go directly to stock). The following formulas are used to calculate change-weighted value.

- V_S = change-weighted value when a smaller number signifies improvement.
- V_B = change-weighted value when a bigger number signifies improvement.
- S_V = starting value.
- C_V = comparison value.
- W = weighting factor.

- $V_S = (S_V/C_V)(W)(100)$.
- $V_B = (C_V/S_V)(W)(100)$.

In Figure 7-4, the yearly improvement for the inventory management area is calculated. Note that five measurements are weighted. The measurement for percent rush orders improved from 13.6% in year 1 to 13.4% in year 2. The year 2 performance level is 101.5% of year 1's performance (13.4 divided into 13.6). This is a positive improvement because the goal was to reduce the percentage of rush orders. Percent rush orders are weighted at 20% of the total organization's priorities. By multiplying the weighting factor (20%) by the improvement percentage (101.5%), the total weighted performance can be calculated (20.3%). When the totals are summarized, we find that there has been an improvement of 7.8% in the area's performance over a one-year period. It is important to note that in some cases improvement is indicated by higher values. (Example: Percent direct to stock in year 1 was 18% and 20% in year 2. In this case, the best practice would be to have good enough inputs coming into the activity so that 100% of them could be shipped directly to stock.) In other cases, improvement is represented by a decrease or lower value. (Example: Percent unlocated stock was 3.4% in year 1 and 2.5% in year 2. It should be the objective of the area to have zero unlocated stock.) Also note in Figure 7-4 that the cost per $1,000 processed increased when the objective was to decrease cost. As a result, the delta performance level—year 2 cost (0.38) divided into year 1 cost (0.34)—is less than 1.00.

	Year 2 (c)	Year 1 (s)	△	Weight (w)	Total
• % rush orders	13.40	13.60	1.015	20%	0.203
• Days of inventory	93.00	105.00	1.130	30%	0.338
• % direct to stock	20.00	18.00	1.110	20%	0.222
• % unlocated stock	2.50	3.40	1.360	10%	0.136
• Cost/$1,000 processed	0.38	0.34	0.894	20%	0.179
					1.078

FIGURE 7-4. **Combined Total Performance Index for an Area**

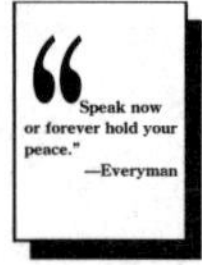

Problems should be viewed as stepping stones to improved performance, not as stumbling blocks.

—ANONYMOUS

Performance Improvement Weapons and Methods

Our research shows that there are more than 400 different improvement weapons and methods that exist today, and these data probably are not complete. Each of these tools works under the right conditions. Many solve the same types of problems. Some of them are the same approach that has just been modified in a small way and called a different name. There are many things that need to be considered in selecting the tools that the NWT will use to drive its improvement effort. NWTs are made up of different individuals with different personalities (see Figure 7-5). Just as individuals differ, organizations differ in many ways (see Figure 7-6).

Add to this complexity the fact that winning, surviving, and losing organizations have to do very different sets of things to improve. Considering

Everyone Is Different

- Some are big, others are small.
- Some are thin, others are tall.
- Some can run, others must crawl.
- Some are strong, others are weak.
- Some are loud, others are meek.
- Some are men, and some are boys.
- And some still like to play with toys.
- Some are women, and others are girls.
- Some are bald, and some have curls.
- While some struggle, others are blessed.
- There's just no one right way to dress.

FIGURE 7-5. **How Individuals Differ**

Organizations Differ Also

- Management personality
- Customers
- Products
- Culture
- Location
- Profit
- Environment
- Quality levels
- Productivity
- Technology
- Core Competencies

FIGURE 7-6. The Ways Organizations Differ

these differences, it becomes readily apparent that there is no one approach to improvement that is correct for all organizations and their NWTs. Keeping this in mind, the following is a list of some of the tools and methods that we have found used effectively by NWTs:

- ▶ Benchmarking
- ▶ Best-value-future-state solution
- ▶ Brainstorming
- ▶ Cause-and-effect diagrams
- ▶ Check sheets
- ▶ Control charts
- ▶ Cycle-time reduction methods
- ▶ Design of experiments
- ▶ Error-proofing
- ▶ Failure mode and effect analysis
- ▶ Flowcharting
- ▶ Force-field analysis
- ▶ Kaizen
- ▶ Management's seven tools
- ▶ No-value-added analysis
- ▶ Pareto diagrams
- ▶ PERT
- ▶ Plan-do-check-act cycle
- ▶ Precontrol
- ▶ Process capability studies
- ▶ Process redesign
- ▶ Process reengineering
- ▶ Quality-control circles
- ▶ Regression analysis
- ▶ Scatter diagrams
- ▶ Storyboard
- ▶ Taguchi techniques
- ▶ Test of hypothesis

- Mind maps
- Nominal group techniques
- Value engineering
- Work simplification

This is not a complete list, as there are many more tools and methods that work equally well. It is not our intent to tell you which tools and/or approaches you should be using to improve your area's performance. The selection of the specific tool to meet the NWT's challenges will have to be made by the NWT after considering the challenges it faces, the NWT makeup, the organization's culture, and the condition that needs to be improved. As a result, the process that we define in this phase will be very general in nature.

It is very important that each member of the NWT is trained to understand how to use the selected improvement tools and even more important to do his or her work assignment correctly. In a study of young medical doctors, only 20% of them use the most basic of all medical tools—a stethoscope—correctly.

Phase VII Breakdown

The block diagram in Figure 7-7 shows the eight steps that make up Phase VII.

Step 1–Set Up the Reporting Systems

During Phases IV through VI, the NWT defined and documented a data collection system that was designed to support the area's performance improvement efforts. It is important that this system is installed effectively and that the reports generated from the system are accurate. A great deal of effort can be wasted when the area reacts to bad data. It is beyond the scope of this book to define in detail how the NWT should set up its performance reporting system, but we provide the NWT with some key points to consider:

- Define how the data will be used and what format it will be reported in.
- Define how the data will be processed.
- Define the amount and the frequency that data should be collected.

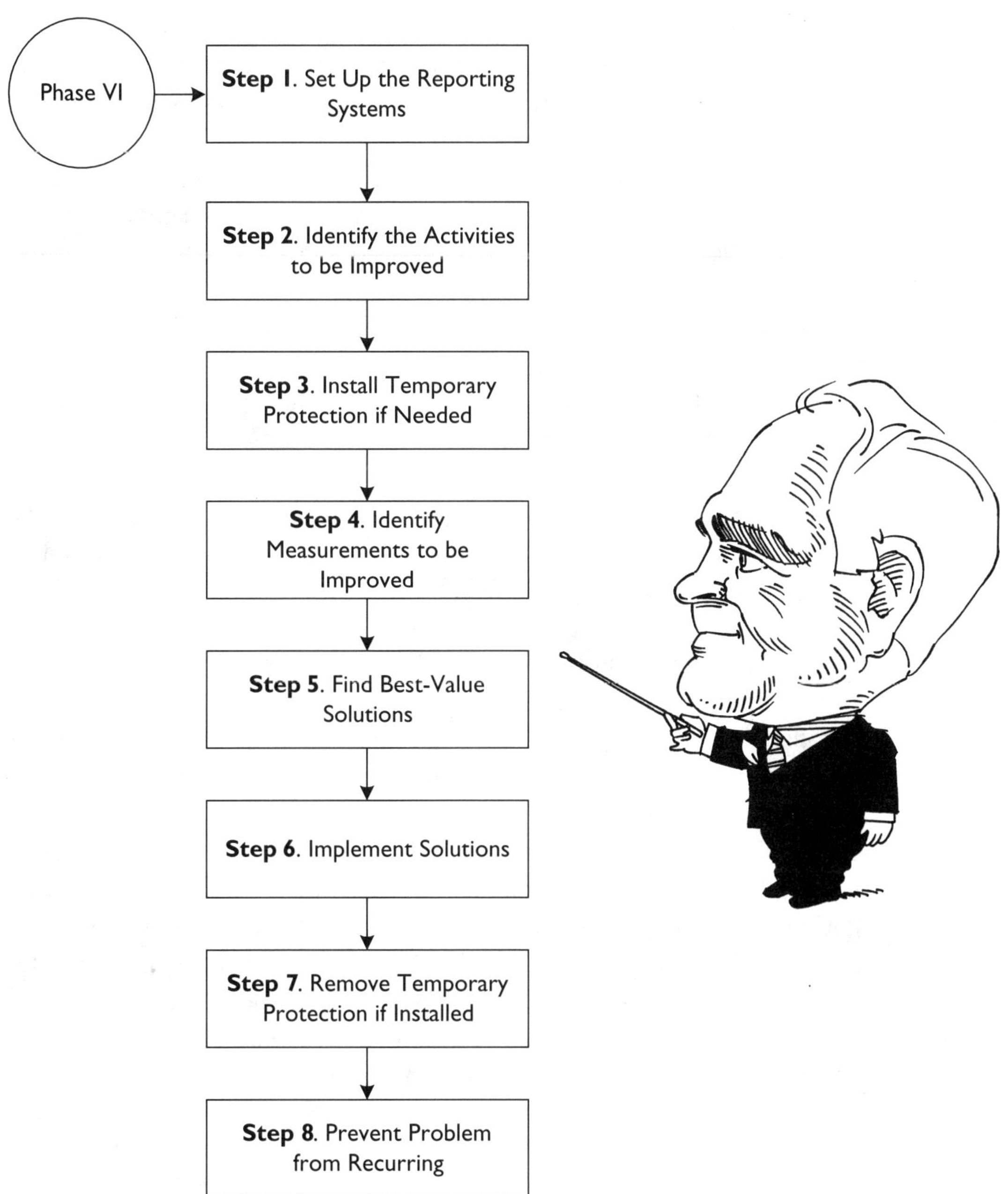

FIGURE 7-7. The Eight Steps That Make Up Phase VII

- Design the input format that will be used to collect the data so that it is user-friendly. Be sure that the form is designed so that it is easy to use by the person recording the data. The form should not be designed with the computer application as the primary objective. Of course it is important that the computer application is considered in the form design, but it should not be the prime consideration.
- Develop the supporting computer programs and debug them using real data.
- Train the people who will be recording the data on how to fill out the form and how the data will be used.
- Conduct a pilot run where the validity of the input data and the output reports can be evaluated.
- Implement the reporting system.
- Copies of the report should go to appropriate suppliers, customers, and upper management. A copy of the report should also be posted on the area performance bulletin board.

We strongly recommend that the NWT solicit the support of the organization's information systems group in designing the data collection and reporting system. This group should have a great deal of experience in using information technology to minimize the resources required to collect and process the data.

The NWT often finds it difficult to implement the total reporting system all at one time. In these cases, we recommend that the design of the total reporting system be done first. This is necessary because there is often interaction between activities and their associated measurement systems. As a result, it is usually most effective if the NWT first identifies all of the input data required and the output requirements, and then develops a data system design so that it will meet the needs of the total data collection system. The NWT should then prioritize the implementation activities to meet the unique needs of the NWT and the other data collection system work that is already underway or planned for within the organization.

Having real data that define how well the NWT is performing and are capable of measuring changes in the NWT's performance is a key milestone in any performance improvement effort. All too often, NWTs that do not have the direction that a good measurement system provides do a good job of solving problems that have only minimal impact on the NWT's performance. This is one of the reasons that the quality circle movement was not more successful in North America and Europe. The quality circle programs focused on the problem-solving process and not on the results that they achieved. This is a good training approach, but is not an effective way to run a results-oriented organization.

Step 2–Identify the Activities to Be Improved

If during the interviews with the NWT's external customers, the external customers expressed dissatisfaction with the inputs provided by the NWT, these activities should become the priority improvement projects for the NWT. We would hope that the NWT would have established a corrective action plan as soon as these problems were identified by the external customers. We are going to assume that these problems are already being addressed. (If not already corrected, the NWT should get to work on them fast.)

The NWT now needs to look at the data being collected and define which activities and associated measurements are the primary candidates to be improved. We recommend that the NWT consider using the seven improvement priorities listed earlier in this chapter in the Process Overview section. This prioritization system places first priority on meeting external customer's specifications and then on improvement opportunities that give the organization a competitive advantage. The remainder of the priorities are based on other internal business considerations.

The NWT should use the performance reports and the suggested prioritization rules to define a small group of 5 to 10 measurements that the NWT wants to improve. The NWT should then analyze these measurements to define if the required changes can be made by the NWT or if the changes are outside its scope of operation. All of the critical external customer improvement opportunities should be addressed, but the NWT should give primary priority to the improvement efforts that it can totally control. A lower priority should be given to those improvement opportunities that can be changed by the NWT with the additional support of a small number of other people.

Those opportunities that are outside the scope of the NWT and a small group of other individuals to correct should be submitted to upper management so that they can take action to capitalize on these opportunities.

After three to four of these opportunities have been corrected, the NWT should repeat this step to develop a new list of improvement opportunities. The opportunities that are on the first list may or may not be on the second list because of changes in the business environment, the NWT's internal operating environment, and improvements that the NWT or others have implemented.

Step 3—Install Temporary Protection If Needed

Temporary protection is required when the external customer's specifications are not met. It is also required when major effectiveness problems occur. A temporary protection should be robust enough to temporarily resolve the situation but should not be considered a long-term resolution.

If the protection addresses an effectiveness issue, the protection activity may be expensive and require a great deal of extra effort on the part of the area. Typical protection activities would be the addition of 100% inspection for a specified problem, sending a technician along with the product to help with the installation, or having the product recalled from the customer's locations. This is preferable to losing a valuable customer or suffering negative publicity, but it should not be sustained for the long term. It is easy to see that all protection action is no-value-added cost even though it may be necessary.

Key questions to be answered in Step 3 include

- What impact does the situation have on the customer?
- What is the impact on customers if bad outputs get to the customers?
- How complex is the situation?
- Is there a way to contain the situation within the area and still make the NWT's commitments to its customers?
- How long will the protection need to be in place?

Step 4—Identify Measurements or Task to Be Improved

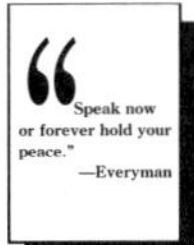

Standards must be observed, but they are only the starting points for further improvements.

—SHIGERU NAKAMURA[6]

Develop charts for the selected improvement activity measurements and post them on the performance bulletin board. Make these activity team improvement charts (TICs) large enough so they can be read from a distance. TICs should show at least six months of data and should contain the standard performance levels. For measurements that are meeting standard performance levels, the NWT should develop challenge targets for them. The challenge target level should be above the current level of performance and above the standard performance target. Each indicator that has met its target for three consecutive months should have its target reset. Remember, there is no shame associated with not meeting a target as long as the target is better than the performance standard (see Figure 7-8).

Two types of targets are used. The first type is the "performance standard target" that meets the customer's and management's requirements. The second is a tighter target called a "challenge target." Challenge targets provide the NWT with interim goals between the customer's and management's required performance level and the ultimate performance of error-free performance. The challenge targets are set by the NWT.

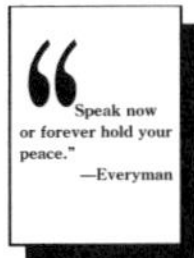

The more [a guy] feels he has set his own goals, the more likely it is that he'll go right through a brick wall in order to reach them.

—LEE IACOCCA[7]

This scheme eliminates the tendency of most organizations to stop all efforts to improve an activity just because the target has been met. It also means that management must look at targets in a new way. Management should expect all performance standard targets to be met 100% of the time, but they should not expect the challenge targets to be met most of the time.

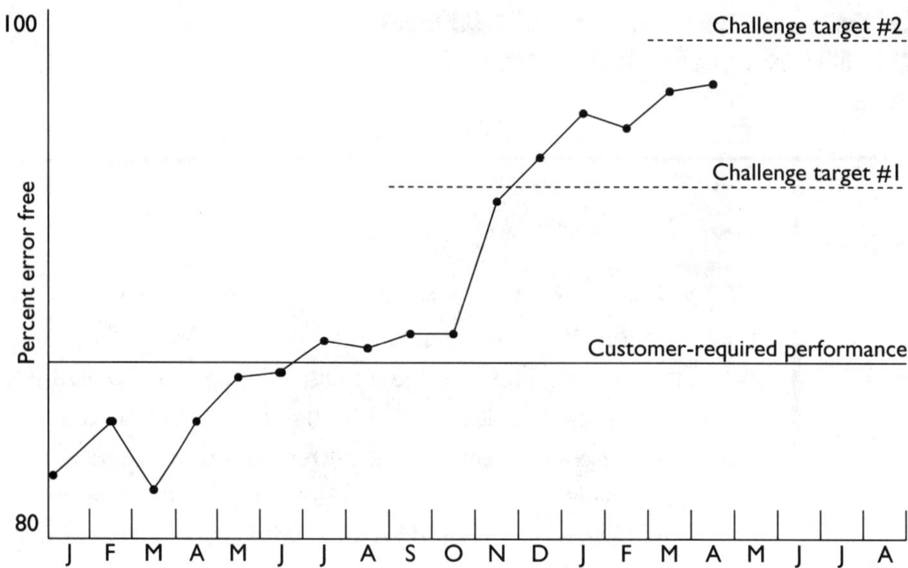

FIGURE 7-8. Team Improvement Chart (TIC) Indicators

This process is designed so that 90% of the time, 90% of the challenge targets will not be met, thereby driving a continuous improvement cycle. When used correctly, these measurement indicators can have a major impact on improving performance, increasing creativity, and increasing productivity of everyone in the organization.

Now the NWT is ready to start into the most productive phase of the improvement process. It has selected challenge targets for a group of performance measurement indicators. It will then use problem-solving techniques to develop a time-line plan designed to allow the area to meet and/or exceed the new challenge targets. Rudyard Kipling documented the key guidelines for correcting problems:

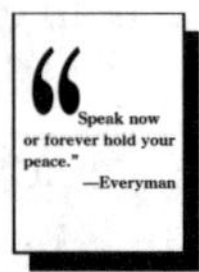

I keep six honest serving men (They taught me all I knew);
Their names are What and Why and When and How and Where and Who.[8]

It then implements the plan, adjusting it as necessary to meet the challenge targets. When the targets have been reached, the NWT receives proper recognition from management for the efforts. Then, it sets new improvement tar-

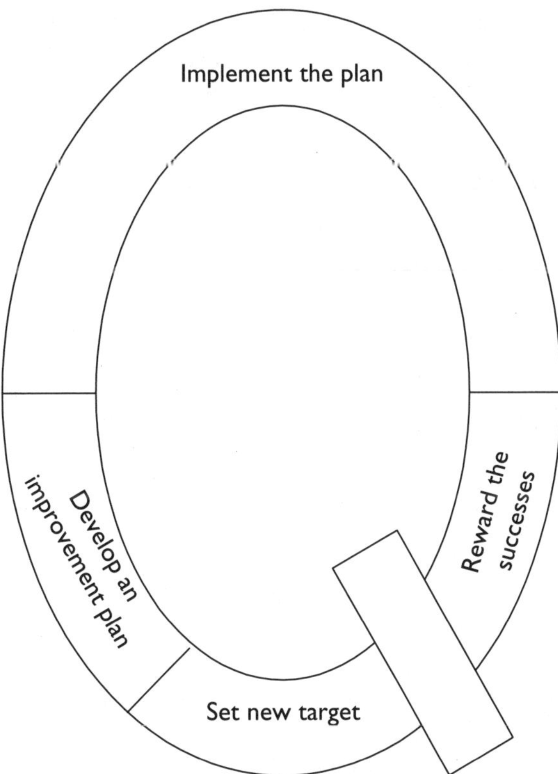

FIGURE 7-9. **The Quality Ring**

gets, and the cycle starts all over again. This cycle is called "The Quality Ring" (Figure 7-9).

Each time a change is implemented or a problem is solved, the NWT should prepare an analysis that records how the change improved performance. This report should be submitted to upper management.

Step 5–Find Best-Value Solutions

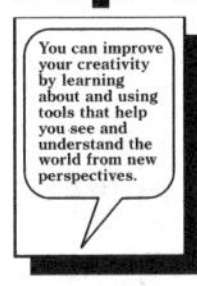

Once the NWT has selected a measurement to improve, the next task is to select the tools that will be used to develop a solution. Most NWTs should be trained on how to use the following tools:

- Brainstorming
- Cause-and-effect diagrams
- Check sheets
- Data stratification
- Histograms
- Pareto diagrams
- Scatter diagrams
- Mind maps
- Nominal group techniques
- Plan-do-check-act cycle
- Storyboard
- Flowcharting
- Control charts
- Force-field analysis

Appendix D provides more information on tools that will help the NWT solve problems. Training on other more complex improvement tools and methods should be given based on the opportunity that the NWT is trying to take advantage of. Often the NWT will not be working on solving problems, but instead it will be working on efficiency of the activity.

Often organizations that are just starting to develop their NWTs will have facilitators work with the teams during the problem-solving sessions to provide training and to keep the team meetings functioning effectively. A facilitated meeting usually runs faster and accomplishes more than a meeting left on its own. We find that using a facilitator for the first 8 to 10 meetings have a very positive impact on the NWT's ability to quickly produce effective solutions to their problems.

The NWT should review the idea bank that was created in an earlier phase to see if it contains any suggestions that will have a positive impact upon the measurement. The idea bank is an excellent source of good ideas that have not been implemented.

Being more effective and efficient does not mean just working harder. It means finding better ways to use the NWT's limited resources. To make significant improvements, the NWT will need to break the mold of what it is currently doing. Having completed the earlier phases of **AAA** has enabled the NWT to understand the needs of its external customer(s) and the needs of its organization. These two needs are often in conflict with each other. Just making simple improvements to what the NWT is doing may meet the needs of both the customer and organization.

The NWT needs to become more creative in its approach to what it does and how it does it. Another book in this series—*The Creativity Toolkit* (McGraw-Hill, 1998)—that focuses on how to become more creative, enabling individuals and groups to break out of the mold that they are in, will help in this area. If what you are doing just needs incremental improvement, another book in this series provides an incremental approach. (*Performance Improvement Methods*)

You may be using a totally different approach to improvement than either of these two methods. More advanced approaches include process reengineering, process redesign, benchmarking, total preventive maintenance, FAST, or HIT. There is no one right way to improve any task, process, activity, area, or organization. Whatever way the NWT chooses to improve, it must match the organization's culture, resolve, resources, needs, and desires. Remember to keep the solution mission focused.

This is the part in every book that is quickly glossed over: Typically, a book will tell the reader to collect information, analyze the data, brainstorm for a solution, and implement the solution. Well, we all know it is not that easy.

It is our experience that NWTs tend to latch onto one solution and then spend most of their time trying to cost justify that solution. We are going to recommend a different, more challenging approach. It is called Best-Value-Solution Analysis. With this analysis, the NWT will develop three or more potential solutions to each opportunity. Then it will evaluate each of them to determine which is the best-value solution for the organization. Often, different solutions are developed to meet different ground rules. For example:

1. What can be done at a cost that is no greater than *X* dollars?
2. What can be done and implemented in the next 30 days without disrupting the work flow within the area?
3. What can be done if the NWT did not have to consider implementation costs and implementation cycle time to implement the solution?

There are a number of factors that need to be evaluated to determine which solution provides the best value to the organization. For example, is it better to implement Solution A that reduces the per-unit cost from $10 to $8 or Solution B that reduces the per-unit cost to $6.50? Both Solution A and Solution B produce the same outgoing quality. The answer should be Solution B if that is all the information we have. But let's look at Figure 7-10. With these additional data, we find that the additional cost to implement Solution B is $1,499,000,

	Per-Unit Cost	Time to Install	Cost to Install	Units Process/ Month
Solution A	$8.00	10 days	$1,000	1,000
Solution B	$6.50	18 months	$1.5 million	1,000

FIGURE 7-10. Solution A & B Estimates

and it will take an additional seven years to break even, compared with implementing Solution A. The best-value solution in this case is Solution A.

There are a number of things that must be taken into consideration when defining best-value solutions. Some of the more common ones are

1. Amount of improvement
2. Cost to implement the improvement
3. Cycle time to implement the improvement
4. Impact on other measurements
5. Risk involved in making the change

In most cases there are many different measurements impacted by a single change. Look at Figure 7-11 and define which solution is the best-value solution. For more information on best-value solutions, read the *Complete Benchmarking Implementation Guide,* by H. James Harrington (McGraw-Hill, 1996).

The NWT may need to change tasks, processes, methodologies, and technologies. All of these are doable if the NWT maintains its focus on its customer's requirements. Remember the NWT's mission. It must be its guide. Key questions that should be answered in Step 5 include

- How will the NWT know when it has the best solution?
- Does the NWT have a theory or model as to how the new process will work?
- What risks are involved in implementing the solution?
- What overriding reason is there to implement this new process?

Measurements	Org. Perf.	Best-Value Solutions		
		1	2	3
• Cycle time (days)	35.0	16.2	19.5	17.5
• Processing time (hours)	10.0	6.5	8.3	7.5
• Errors/1,000	25.1	12.3	9.2	3.0
• Cost/Cycle	$950	$631	$789	$712
• Service response time (hours)	120	65	30	8
Implementation				
• Cost in $1,000		$1,000	$100	$423.50
• Cycle time (months)		29	6	18
• Risk		35%	10%	12%

FIGURE 7-11. Benefits/Cost/Risk Analysis Chart for Three Alternative Best-Value Solutions

- Will Organizational Change Management concepts need to be used to ensure the change is accepted?
- How long will the solution be effective?

Step 6—Implement Solutions

Successfully implementing a solution requires that the NWT develop a specific plan for each change. Many improvement efforts stop at this point or fail when changes are made without a well-developed implementation plan. Many times people believe that the situation is obvious and everyone should know what to do. This is a recipe for disaster. Even when changes appear small and simple, the timing of actual changes should be planned, time lines followed, responsibilities assigned, and measurements of implementation developed. Without a written and agreed-upon plan, the NWT is setting itself up for failure. Questions that should be answered in Step 6 include

- Should Organizational Change Management activities be part of the plan?

- Does the NWT have a step-by-step action plan for implementing the solution?
- Are the people who are affected by the change going to support the change?
- Does everyone in the process know what the implementation team is going to do and when?
- Does the NWT have a fallback strategy if the new method does not work as planned?
- Has the required training been defined to support the plan, and are resources committed to provide the training?

For more information on Organizational Change Management, we suggest you read *Managing at the Speed of Change,* by Daryl Conner (Random House, 1994), or *Total Improvement Management,* by H. James Harrington (McGraw-Hill, 1995). One of the books in this series will also address how to manage change.

Step 7—Remove Temporary Protection If Installed

The removal of the temporary protection installed during Step 3 should be a part of the implementation plan, since the new method should not rely on this protection. Protection activities usually waste time and resources but are often necessary. In our experience, it is not the protection activities that are bad but the failure to remove them when they are no longer needed. Protective activities often result in the establishment of bureaucracy that remains in place when the protection is no longer needed. Of course, the protection activities should not be removed until the major activity can perform at an acceptable level without the protective activities in place. This is often determined when the protection activities stop finding errors. Questions that should be answered in Step 7 include

- Was there a protection activity put into place?
- What new processes, tasks, or bureaucracies did the protective activity put into place?

- What critical effectiveness or efficiency criteria did the protective activity impact?
- Did the corrective action eliminate the need to continue the protective activity? If not, what additional corrective action needs to be taken so that the protective action can be eliminated?

Step 8–Prevent Problem from Recurring

During this step the NWT should check to see if the new method is producing the intended effectiveness or efficiency results. The NWT may need to put in place a number of improvements before the desired results are obtained. When the new method is able to consistently meet the targeted performance, it is time to develop a way to keep this kind of situation from recurring in this area or any other area within the organization. During this step, the NWT reviews the knowledge gained about the problem and then applies it to the rest of the product lines and/or organization's activities with similar conditions.

This final step in Phase VII allows the experience gained on a single problem to be applied to a global solution. The object of this step is to alter the systems so that the problem can be permanently eliminated from future activities. This probably will be the most difficult step in Phase VII, but it is the step that could have the most important consequences. Figure 7-12 illustrates how an NWT attacks a problem using the eight steps in Phase VII. The first part of the prevention activities should be focused on the procedures that control the problem (engineering specs, manufacturing operating procedures, management procedures, and so on). These procedures should be modified to reflect the solution as appropriate.

Frequently, the NWT does not have a good overview of the organization's activities so it cannot define all other potential applications for the solution. For this reason, management should identify solutions that could have further applications and publish them regularly in an "opportunity newsletter" that is sent to all managers. This provides management with a list of new, good ideas.

The eight steps in this phase provide a systematic way to solve problems and prevent them from recurring. All too often, people will select a problem,

Problem Phase:	A small wire breaks at a printed circuit board connection, causing an open circuit.
Analysis Phase:	The heat required to melt the solder caused embrittlement to take place in the wire in some cases, depending on how long the soldering iron is left on the connection or if the solder joint is reworked.
Corrective Action Phase:	The solder pad size was increased to allow the heat to be more evenly dissipated.
Measurement Phase:	Broken wire failure rates in the manufacturing cycle decreased from 0.01 to 0.005 percent. In the customer's application, wire failure rates decreased from 100 parts per million to 0.5 parts per million per 10,000 hours of use.
Prevention Activities Phase:	The team found four other printed circuit boards in two other product lines that had the potential for the same problem, so the design was changed on all four part numbers. In addition, the engineering standards manual was changed to define the minimum solder pad versus wire size.

FIGURE 7-12. **Action Taken to Eliminate a Problem and Prevent Its Recurrence**

analyze its root cause, implement action to correct it, and then go on to the next problem, failing to measure how effective the action was and never applying the knowledge they have gained to other situations. Prevention occurs through the application of knowledge learned, not by solving individual problems.

One of the best methods of prevention is to make the **AAA** process part of the annual budgeting process. While the NWT is developing its fiscal budget, it also needs to develop its effectiveness and efficiency plans. Questions that need to be answered in Step 8 include

- What has the NWT learned that it can use elsewhere?
- Did the NWT get support and resources from the process owner and/or any other key decision makers?

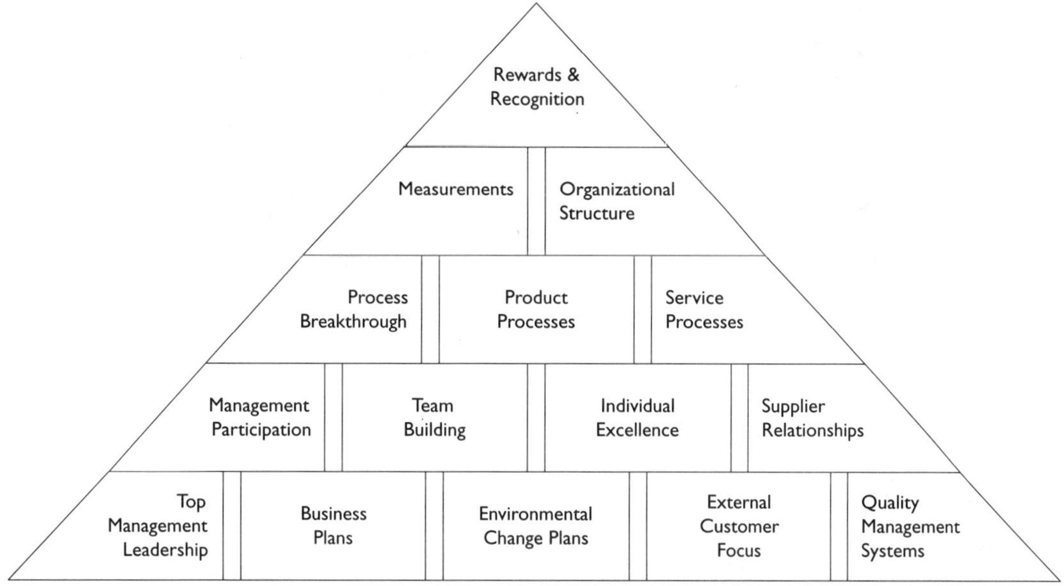

FIGURE 7-13. The Tasks That Make Up the Total Improvement Pyramid

- Did the NWT members get support, encouragement, and recognition from each other?

It is important to realize that the **AAA** approach to continuous improvement is not a complete process for a total organization. This approach was designed to help an area improve its performance. A total improvement process is much more complex and involves many other considerations. Figure 7-13 is the total improvement management pyramid. It is a model that has been effectively used by many organizations to implement their performance improvement initiatives. For more details about this approach, we suggest the book *Total Improvement Management,* by H. James Harrington and James S. Harrington (McGraw-Hill, 1996).

Things That Can Help

The following are some thoughts that can help the NWT implement its continuous improvement activities.

- Use a consistent approach to improving performance.
- Implement the solution that results in the best value to the organization, not the best performance solution.
- Make the AAA process part of the annual budgeting cycle.
- Keep track of the performance improvement results and their ROI.
- The NWT should keep its mission in mind when it is examining solutions.
- Remember that if the NWT continues to do what it has always done, the best it can hope for is the same results that the NWT have always gotten.

Does It Work?

Does the improvement process work? You can bet on it. Let's look at the results from two different case studies.

Scunciti Manufacturing Ltd. in Hong Kong provides an excellent example of a white-collar team's corrective action. In June, a team from the personnel department set out to reduce errors in wage computation. Error rates were running at about 6% when they set a challenge target to reduce it to 1%. The team established a data system and developed a Pareto diagram that showed

Cause of Errors	*Percentage*
Carelessness	52.4
Insufficient rechecking	23.8
Time clock	15.8
Supervisor's remarks	8.0

Once the problem was understood, improvement came quickly. By September, wage error rates dropped to 0.4% and have not gone up.

At IBM, Information Systems Support had a significant number of reruns each month in support of a major design area. By systematically analyzing the problem, new process requirements were prepared and a feedback system established. As a result, reruns dropped 50% at a savings of $70,000 per year. CPU time was decreased 30%, and one man-year of effort was saved annually.

Examples

The following examples do not go into great detail about the actual improvements made since each organization's improvement methodology is different. We identify the processes or tasks focused on for improvement by each area.

Insurance Policy Processing Department/351. Since this area is being effective in meeting its customers' needs, it decided to focus on an efficiency process. It decided to focus on the inspection process and associated tasks since they were no-value-added tasks.

By identifying the need to have information available from MIS on a timely basis, the area reached an agreement with MIS to provide the information on-line. When the information is available on-line, there is no more need for inspection. The money budgeted for inspection will be provided to the MIS department to enable it to make the changes. In the meantime, overtime will be authorized for a three-month time frame to enable the changes to be made to the MIS department.

BAK Final Assembly Area/301. This area focused on the bad parts it was receiving from its internal suppliers. It raised its issues to upper management because it was not able to reach an agreement directly with its suppliers. The whole organization was not participating in the AAA process, so the NWT's suppliers did not consider it a customer.

Upper management set a standard for the internal suppliers and asked the managers to develop a corrective action plan that would improve supplier output to the point that the standard was met. The supplier team all pitched in and, after studying the problem, discovered that the buildup of tolerances sometimes causes the pin holes to be out of line, causing the assembly to bend when the pins were pressed into place. They then found that the problem could be eliminated if one dimension was held to ±0.002 in place of the specification tolerance of ±0.005. The also discovered that the equipment they were using could produce parts to ±0.002 tolerance without any difficulty. The supplier immediately started to produce parts to ±0.002. They also sent in a request to engineering to change the tolerance on the part drawing to ±0.002 to prevent the problem from recurring. As a result, the NWT's problems were eliminated in 30 days, and it was able to stop, doing 100% at final test. This reduced the NWT's cost for the assembly by 24%. The supplier's costs were also reduced by 18% (the scrap cost of the returned parts).

Customer Service Support Department/107. This area found that it needed to focus its efforts on providing additional training to its support personnel. It found that the information that was passed on to the field and then to the external customer was incorrect 15% of the time.

The area instituted a daily meeting to provide the latest information to all of the support personnel and an on-line question-and-answer database. This resulted in the area's answers being right 98% of the time.

Summary

During this phase, the NWT built upon all of the work that was done during the other six phases. As a result, it was able to accomplish the following:

- Implemented a data collection and reporting system.
- Established a performance bulletin board and kept it updated.
- Prioritized the improvement opportunities.
- Learned how to use the appropriate problem-solving tools.
- Used some of the ideas that had been previously stored in the idea bank and added new ideas to it.
- Developed potential solutions and defined which ones were the best-value solutions.
- Performed a risk analysis related to each best-value solution.
- Developed Organizational Change Management plans for selected solutions.

Conclusion

This completes the seven phases of **AAA**. **AAA** is the tool that an organization should use to help get all NWTs started on a productive performance improvement process. **AAA** helps an organization accomplish the most basic of all management tasks: defining the mission of the NWT, defining what must be done to satisfy the mission statement, defining both internal and external customer requirements, defining what acceptable performance is and how it should be measured, and setting minimum performance standards. **AAA** is not another technique for improving processes, lowering cycle time, or reducing costs. Simply stated, **AAA** helps the NWT clarify what is expected of it, define key measurements, set performance standards, and focus the NWT's efforts on the organization's objectives. It also ensures that the area's improvement efforts are directed at improvement activities that have a real impact on the organization's performance.

AAA is the foundation tool that should be used before other improvement methodologies are undertaken. Whether an area is being newly created, combined, or has existed for a number of years, **AAA** is the tool for ensuring that everyone understands their area's function and how its performance is measured.

The next step is up to you. The sooner you begin the **AAA** process, the sooner you will know where to focus your improvement efforts. **AAA** should be the first step that every NWT takes to transform it from a group of people to an effective operating team.

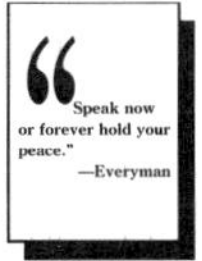

Every organization must improve. When it stops improving, it is not standing still, but slipping backward, because the competition is improving.

—H. James Harrington

We would like to end this book with a poem written by Edgar A. Guest in 1928. We hope you like it as much as we do.

Good Enough

With "good enough" ships have been wrecked,
The forward march of armies checked,
Great buildings burned and fortunes lost;
Nor can the world compute the cost
In life and money it has paid
Because at "good enough" we stayed.

Who stops at "good enough" shall find
Success has left them far behind.
With "good enough" the shirkers stop
In every factory and shop;
With "good enough" the failures rest
And lose to those who give their best;
With "good enough" the car breaks down
And those of high renown fall down.
My son, remember, and be wise
In "good enough" disaster lies.
My son, beware of "good enough,"
It isn't made of sterling stuff;
It's something anyone can do,
It marked the many from the few,
It has no merit to the eye,
It is something anyone can buy,
Its name is but a sham and bluff,
For it is never "good enough."
There is no "good enough" that's short
Of what you can do and ought.
The flaw which may escape the eye
And temporarily get by,
Shall weaken underneath the strain
And wreck the ship or car or train,
For this is true of men and stuff—
Only the best is "good enough."

Notes

1. Dr. H. James Harrington, *The Improvement Process: How America's Leading Companies Improve Quality* (New York: McGraw-Hill, 1987).
2. Helio Gomez, *Quality Quotes* (Milwaukee, WI: American Society for Quality Control (ASQC)-Quality Press, 1996), 83.
3. Abraham Maslow, *The Farther Reaches of Human Nature* (New York: Viking Press, 1975).

4. Helio Gomez, *Quality Quotes* (Milwaukee, WI: American Society for Quality Control (ASQC)-Quality Press, 1996), 97.
5. Philip Crosby, *Quality is Free: The Art of Making Quality Certain* (New York: Mentor, 1980).
6. Shigeru Nakamura, *The New Standardization Keystone of Continuous Improvement in Manufacturing* (Portland, OR: Productivity Press, 1993).
7. Lee Iacocca and William Novak, *Iacocca: An Autobiography* (New York: Bantam Books, 1984).
8. Helio Gomez, *Quality Quotes* (Milwaukee, WI: American Society for Quality Control (ASQC)-Quality Press, 1996), 94.

Putting the Puzzle of AAA Together

In this chapter we have found where "improvement" fits into the **AAA** puzzle. The puzzle is now complete.

APPENDIX  Glossary

AAA Methodology A proven approach used by each natural work team (area) to establish efficiency and effectiveness measurement systems, performance standards, improvement goals, and feedback systems that are aligned with the organization's objectives and understood by the employees involved.

AAA Process The activities required to implement the AAA methodology within an organization.

AAA Project The combination of resources, planning, and commitment required to implement the AAA methodology within a specific organization. It usually will include a project plan and the follow-up activities to execute the project plan.

AAA Project Team The group of individuals assigned to develop the AAA project plan and coordinate its implementation throughout the organization.

AAA Project Team Leader The individual who will act as the AAA champion throughout the organization.

AAA Team The members of an NWT who have undertaken the project of applying the AAA methodology to their area.

Acceptable Outgoing Performance Standard The minimum level that the specific output measurement must perform at so that it does not have a negative impact on the customer's performance.

Activities Subsets of a process or subprocess. Activities that are connected together are often referred to as a process. An activity will normally take place in a single area. Each activity can be further divided into tasks that are performed by individuals.

Activity Model A flowchart that pictorially presents the relationships of the tasks that are included in the activity.

Activity-Based Costing (ABC) An accounting methodology by which organizations can more realistically measure the costs and performance of activities, processes, and cost objective. To do this, actual costs are assigned to each activity within processes based on their use of such resources as people and supplies.

Analysis Analysis is a way to look at a situation and remove the irrelevant factors so that the true situation can be clearly defined. As used in **AAA**, this analysis means that the members of the **AAA** team are able to clarify what is expected of their area, define key measurements, set performance standards, and focus their efforts on the area's mission.

Appraisal Cost These are the costs that occur because there is a need to evaluate the output from a task or to audit an activity or process to measure conformance to established criteria and/or procedures. That is, appraisal costs are all the costs expended to determine if an activity is done right every time. Typical appraisal costs are proofreading a letter, any form of inspection, audits, reviews, approvals, tests, and so on. Appraisal activities are necessary if you cannot prevent errors from occurring.

Area An area is any NWT that is organized to work together for an extended period. For example, it can be the organization's president and all the vice presidents and staff reporting to him or her. It can also be the maintenance foreperson and all the maintenance workers reporting to him or her.

Business-Value-Added These are the activities or tasks that need to be performed in order to manage the organization but are of no value to the external customer. The external customers would not be willing to pay for your business-value-added work if they had the option.

Checklist A checklist is a list that contains what must be done, broken into component parts that are signed off or checked off as they are completed.

Customer Expectations Customer expectations are what the customer would like to have in the output that is delivered to him or her. Often, customer expectations exceed and/or are different from customer requirements. For example, the customer may *need* the parts to be delivered to him or her by the 15th of the month, but will *expect* the parts to be delivered to him or her by the 10th of the month so that the customer has a five-day safety factor built into the stocking plan.

Customer Partnership Specification A document that is signed off by the NWT and its customers that defines how an output from a supplier will be measured and what the minimum output acceptable performance level (performance standard) is for each measurement. This document also defines how the customer will provide the NWT with feedback on how well the NWT's output is performing in the customer's environment

Customer Requirements The characteristics of the area's output that are important to the customer including cost, schedule, quantity, and quality considerations. (Customer requirements are often referred to as customer needs.)

Customer The person or area who receives output of the area.

Cycle Time The elapsed time from the time that an item starts into a process, activity, or task until it is received by the customer of the process, activity, or task. (Example: A purchase order leaves a manager's office on Friday at 3:00 P.M., and the information on it is put into the mainframe computer on Monday at 3:00 P.M. The cycle time would be 72 hours, even though it took only three minutes to process the purchase order.)

Dependent Customers Customers that need the output to do their job and would be willing to pay for it if they had to.

Effectiveness The extent to which the outputs of the activity (process) meet the needs and expectations of its customers (customer-related measurements).

Efficiency A measure of the resources used to produce an output.

Error Cost Costs incurred by the organization as a result of errors. There are two types of error costs.

External Customers External customers are not part of the organization and usually pay for the goods and services they receive from the organization.

External Supplier Suppliers that are not part of the customer's organizational structure.

Feedback Direct input from your customer about how well your activity's processes are performing.

Force-Field Analysis A tool that looks at the positive and negative forces that cause a situation to exist. These two forces are called "driving or facilitating forces" and "restricting or inhibiting forces." The two force fields push in opposite directions. While the stronger of the two will tend to characterize the situation, a point of balance is usually achieved that gives the appearance of a steady-state condition. The force-field approach allows the individuals to analyze the negative and positive forces that cause the situation to exist. This allows them to establish action plans that reinforce the positive forces and minimize the negative forces, thereby bringing about improvements in the situation.

Idea Bank A list of ideas and concepts that may be used to improve the NWT's performance.

Improvement This is a positive change in any thing as viewed by one or more of its stakeholders. For this book, we define improvement as a positive change in the effectiveness and efficiency measurements that is greater than any negative effect it has on other effectiveness and/or efficiency measurements in or outside of the area.

Input Any product and/or service that a customer or the NWT receives is referred to as input in this book.

Internal Customers Internal customers are part of the organization who receive output from any area. Almost every person in an organization is an internal customer for someone else in the organization.

Internal Supplier Areas within an organizational structure that provide input into other areas within the same organizational structure.

Mission Statement Used to document the reasons for the organization's or area's existence. It is usually prepared prior to the organization or area being formed and is changed only when the organization or area decides to pursue a new or different set of activities. For the **AAA** methodology, a mission statement is a short paragraph, no more than two or three sentences, that defines the area's role and its relationships with the rest of the organization and/or the external customer.

Natural Work Team (NWT) or Natural Work Group (NWG) A group of people who are assigned to work together and report to the same manager or supervisor. **AAA** projects are implemented by NWT.

Nominal Group Technique This is a structured method used to combine and prioritize a list of individual ideas by the use of a noting approach.

No-Value-Added These are activities or tasks that do not contribute to meeting customer requirements and could be eliminated without degrading the product's or service's functionality or the business. It also includes all of the inspection and checks and balances put in place to determine if work was done correctly, plus all rework activities or tasks. The customer doesn't want to pay for it, nor is it necessary for the business if everyone does their job correctly.

Off-Spec A document that authorizes the use of an item that does not meet requirements. For hardware, the document is normally approved by manufacturing, quality assurance, and product engineering.

Organization A company, corporation, firm, enterprise, or association or any part thereof, whether incorporated or not, public or private, that has its own functions and administration (source: ISO 8402: 1994).

Output The products and/or services provided by an activity or task that are delivered to its customer.

Pareto Diagram A "bar graph" showing the frequency of occurrence of various concerns, ordered with the most frequent ones first.

Parking Board A list of subjects or ideas that will be addressed later. Usually these subjects or ideas are not relevant to the meeting's agenda but warrant discussion at a later time.

Performance Standard The minimum acceptable performance level that must be reached in order to meet the minimum requirements of the customer and/or management. It is the performance level that all employees (new or experienced) should meet after they have completed the defined training program.

Poor-Quality Cost A way of measuring the cost related to not being able to provide perfect products and/or services all the time. It includes direct and indirect poor-quality costs.

Preferred Performance Level The level of performance that the customer would like the supplier to deliver most of the time, and the supplier agrees that it is a performance level that it is capable of delivering most of the time.

Preparation The things that a manager needs to do to ensure that a project will succeed in his or her organization.

Prevention Cost These are all the costs expended to prevent errors from being made. That is, prevention costs are all the costs involved in helping people do their job right every time. It could be considered as a cost avoidance. These are the things you do to make sure you don't make an error. Typical prevention costs are training, error-proofing tools, maintenance, calibration equipment, process qualification, and preparing a quality manual and keeping it updated.

Primary Customers The person(s) in upper-level management who legalizes the activity that an individual or group performs.

Process An activity or interrelated series of activities that takes an input, adds value to it, and produces an output. A process can be as small as a single activity or it can include many activities and subprocesses. A process usually involves more than one NWT. Processes are usually subdivided into activities.

Processing Time The amount of time that equipment or people are actually working with an item. It will typically be less than 15% of the cycle time.

Project Plan A formal, approved document used to guide project execution and project control. The primary uses of the project plan are to document planning assumptions and decisions, to facilitate communication among stakeholders, and to document approved scope, cost, and schedule baselines. A project plan may be summarized or detailed (source: Project Management Body of Knowledge, PMBOK).

Project Team Groups of people who are temporarily assigned or volunteer to work together to accomplish a short-term objective or to solve a specific problem. These teams may be made up of individuals from different NWTs or from one NWT. Project teams are often called problem-solving teams or cross-functional teams. They have a specific goal to accomplish and are disbanded when this goal is accomplished (For example, release a new product, make a sale, solve a problem, install new equipment, complete a study, and so on).

Project A temporary endeavor undertaken to create a unique product or service (source: Project Management Body of Knowledge, PMBOK).

Real-Value-Added The activities or tasks that, when viewed by the external customer, are required to provide the output that the external customer is expecting. It is the work that the external customer is willing to pay for.

Secondary Customers Customers that would not want the output if it was generated just for them and are not expected to take action as a result of the output.

Supplier An organization that provides a product (input) to the customer (source: ISO 8402).

Task An individual element that is a subset of an activity. Normally, tasks relate to how an individual performs a specific assignment.

Team (1) Two or more draft animals harnessed to a vehicle or farm implement. (Note: This sounds like the way we worked at the beginning of the 1900s.) (2) A vehicle along with the animal or animals harnessed to it. (Note: People are animals and most of us are harnessed to our work, so we must be a team.) (3) A group of players on the same side in a game. (4) Any group organized to work together.

Teamster A person who drives a team. (Note: In a team environment, should all of our managers be called "teamsters" instead of "managers" or "coaches.")

Teamwork The cooperative effort by the members of a team to achieve a common goal.

Upper Management Any level of management that can delegate an activity and its associated responsibility and/or accountability to the specific individual. Upper management to the vice president of R&D would be the president of the organization. Upper management to an accountant would be his or her department manager.

Value Added The difference between the value of an input to a task, process, or activity, and the worth of the output from that task, process, or activity as viewed by the customer of that output. The difference between the value of the input and the value of the output is the value-added content of a specific task, activity, or process.

APPENDIX 

Standard Forms

The following appendix provides the various forms we discussed throughout this book. The figure number and caption remains so you can refer back to the chapter if necessary to understand how to use the form.

Area Name: ______________________________

Area No.: ______________ Revision Date: ______________

Area Mission Statement: ______________________________

____

____

____

____

____

____

____

____

____

Prepared by:

______________	______________	______________
______________	______________	______________
______________	______________	______________
______________	______________	______________
______________	______________	______________
______________	______________	______________

Date Prepared: ______________

Approved By: ______________________

NWT Manager: ______________________ Date: ______________

Next-Level Manager: ______________________ Date: ______________

FIGURE B-1. A Typical Mission Statement Form

ACTIVITY	HOURS PER DAY						
	Mon.	**Tues.**	**Wed.**	**Thurs.**	**Fri.**	**Sat.**	**Total**
1.							
2.							
3.							
4.							
5.							
6.							
7.							
8.							
9.							
10. Misc.							
Total							

FIGURE B-2. Data Collection Form

Area Mission Statement and Major Activities	
Function Name	
Area Name	Area Name
Area Mission Statement	
List Major Activities of Area and % Total Time For Each	
1. ______	______ %
2. ______	______ %
3. ______	______ %
4. ______	______ %
5. ______	______ %
6. ______	______ %
7. ______	______ %
8. ______	______ %
9. ______	______ %
10. ______	______ %
Misc. ______	______ %
Coordinated By	Date
Approved By	Date
Understood By	
	Revision Date

FIGURE B-3. Area Mission Statement and Major Activities Form

Customer Partnership Agreement

Area Name and Number: ______________________

Activity: ______________________

Output: ______________________

Output Performance Standard: ______________________

- Customers:
  1. ______________________
  2. ______________________
  3. ______________________

- Requirement ____: ______________________
  - Performance Standard: ______________________
  - Performance as of ___/___/___: ______________________
  - Measured: ______________ • Estimated: ______________
  - Meets Standard: Yes: ________ No: ________
  - Customer Feedback Process: ______________________

- Requirement ____: ______________________
  - Performance Standard: ______________________
  - Performance as of ___/___/___: ______________________
  - Measured: ______________ • Estimated: ______________
  - Meets Standard: Yes: ________ No: ________
  - Customer Feedback Process: ______________________

- Requirement ____: ______________________
  - Performance Standard: ______________________
  - Performance as of ___/___/___: ______________________
  - Measured: ______________ • Estimated: ______________
  - Meets Standard: Yes: ________ No: ________
  - Customer Feedback Process: ______________________

Prepared by: ______________ Date: ___/___/___

Supplier Approval: ______________ Date: ___/___/___

Customer Approval:

______________ Date: ___/___/___

______________ Date: ___/___/___

______________ Date: ___/___/___

FIGURE B-4. Customer Partnership Agreement Form

PROCESS FLOW CHART

Sheet No.____ of____

Department________________________ Chart By ________________________

Process Name________________________ Date ________________________

______ Proposed Method ______ Present Method

No.	Chart Symbols	Cycle Time	Process Time	Process Description
	○ ▭ ⇨ ◯ ◇ ⊃ ▽			
	○ ▭ ⇨ ◯ ◇ ⊃ ▽			
	○ ▭ ⇨ ◯ ◇ ⊃ ▽			
	○ ▭ ⇨ ◯ ◇ ⊃ ▽			
	○ ▭ ⇨ ◯ ◇ ⊃ ▽			
	○ ▭ ⇨ ◯ ◇ ⊃ ▽			
	○ ▭ ⇨ ◯ ◇ ⊃ ▽			
	○ ▭ ⇨ ◯ ◇ ⊃ ▽			
	○ ▭ ⇨ ◯ ◇ ⊃ ▽			
	○ ▭ ⇨ ◯ ◇ ⊃ ▽			
	○ ▭ ⇨ ◯ ◇ ⊃ ▽			
	○ ▭ ⇨ ◯ ◇ ⊃ ▽			
	○ ▭ ⇨ ◯ ◇ ⊃ ▽			
	○ ▭ ⇨ ◯ ◇ ⊃ ▽			
	○ ▭ ⇨ ◯ ◇ ⊃ ▽			
	○ ▭ ⇨ ◯ ◇ ⊃ ▽			
	○ ▭ ⇨ ◯ ◇ ⊃ ▽			
	○ ▭ ⇨ ◯ ◇ ⊃ ▽			
	○ ▭ ⇨ ◯ ◇ ⊃ ▽			

○ = Start or stop the process ◯ = Inspect ⇨ = Movement ▭ = Operation ◇ = Decision Point

⊃ = Delay ▽ = Storage

FIGURE B-5. Process Mapping Form

Efficiency Value-Analysis Measurement Form

Area Name and Number: ______________________________

Activity: ______________________________

Prepared: ____________________ Date: ____/____/____

How many hours per item processed? __________ Hours per item

Allocate this time into three value-added categories.

- Real-Value-Added (RVA) __________
- Business-Value-Added (BVA) __________
- No-Value-Added (NVA) __________

Total __________ Hours per item processed

Percent Real-Value-Added __________

Value-Added versus Poor-Quality Cost Matrix

Using the matrix below, further allocate the value-added hours to the appropriate category.

	RVA	**Prevention**	**Appraisal**	**Error**
RVA	______	No	No	No
BVA	______	______	______	No
NVA	No	No	______	______
Totals	______	______	______	______
Total	______	This should be equal to the hours per item processed (as above)		

FIGURE B-6. **Efficiency Measurement Form**

Efficiency Measurement Specification

Area Name and Number: ______________________

Activity: ______________________

Prepared: ______________________ Date: ____/____/____

Measurement Name: ______________________

How is it measured? ______________________

____

How often is it measured? ______________________

____

How are the data recorded? ______________________

____

What is the performance standard? ______________________

____

FIGURE B-7. Efficiency Measurement Specification

Efficiency Performance Analysis

Activity: ____________________

Area No. or Name: ____________________

Measurement Name: ____________________

- Performance Standard: ____________________
- Present Value: ____________________

(Measured ________ Estimated ________)

Met Requirements on: ____/____/____ Yes ________ No ________

Measurement Name: ____________________

- Performance Standard: ____________________
- Present Value: ____________________

(Measured ________ Estimated ________)

Met Requirements on: ____/____/____ Yes ________ No ________

Measurement Name: ____________________

- Performance Standard: ____________________
- Present Value: ____________________

(Measured ________ Estimated ________)

Met Requirements on: ____/____/____ Yes ________ No ________

Prepared by: ____________________ Date: ____/____/____

Approved by: ____________________ Date: ____/____/____

____________________ Date: ____/____/____

____________________ Date: ____/____/____

FIGURE B-8. **Efficiency Performance Analysis Form**

Supplier Identification Work Sheet			
Activity Name:			
Task Name	**Input's Name**	**Supplier**	
		NWT	**Other**

FIGURE B-9. Supplier Identification Work Sheet

Supplier Partnership Agreement

Area Name and Number: ______________________

Supplier Name and Number: ______________________

Activity: ______________________

Input: ______________________

Requirements: ______________________

____

- Performance Standard: ______________________

  ____

- Performance as of ____/____/____: ______________________
- Measured: ____________ Estimated: ____________
- Area's feedback process: ______________________

  ____

  ____

- Recovery plan: ______________________

  ____

  ____

Requirements: ______________________

____

- Performance Standard: ______________________

  ____

- Performance as of ____/____/____: ______________________
- Measured: ____________ Estimated: ____________
- Area's feedback process: ______________________

  ____

  ____

- Recovery plan: ______________________

  ____

  ____

Prepared by: ______________________ Date: ____/____/____

Area Approval: ______________________ Date: ____/____/____

Supplier Approval: ______________________ Date: ____/____/____

Supplier Approval: ______________________ Date: ____/____/____

FIGURE B-10. Supplier Partnership Agreement Form

APPENDIX **C**

Flowcharting: Drawing a Process Picture

Flowcharting, over the years, has provided a useful way of analyzing many different types of manufacturing and business processes. This appendix looks at some of the more useful flowcharting methods and shows how to effectively use them alone or in combination.

Introduction

"A picture is worth a thousand words." If we may modify this age-old proverb and expand it a little to cover your business processes, it might read, "A flowchart is worth a thousand procedures." Flowcharting, also known as logic diagramming or flow diagramming, is an invaluable tool for understanding the inner workings of, and relationships between, business processes. This appendix is designed to help the AAA team member accomplish the twofold task of

1. Understanding some of the available flowcharting techniques.
2. Applying these techniques to understand activities.

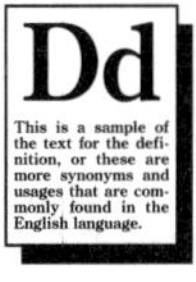

Flowcharting is defined as a method of graphically describing an existing process or a proposed new process by using simple symbols, lines, and words to display pictorially the tasks and sequence in the activity.

What Are Flowcharts?

Flowcharts graphically represent the activities that make up a process or the tasks that make an activity in much the same way that a map represents a

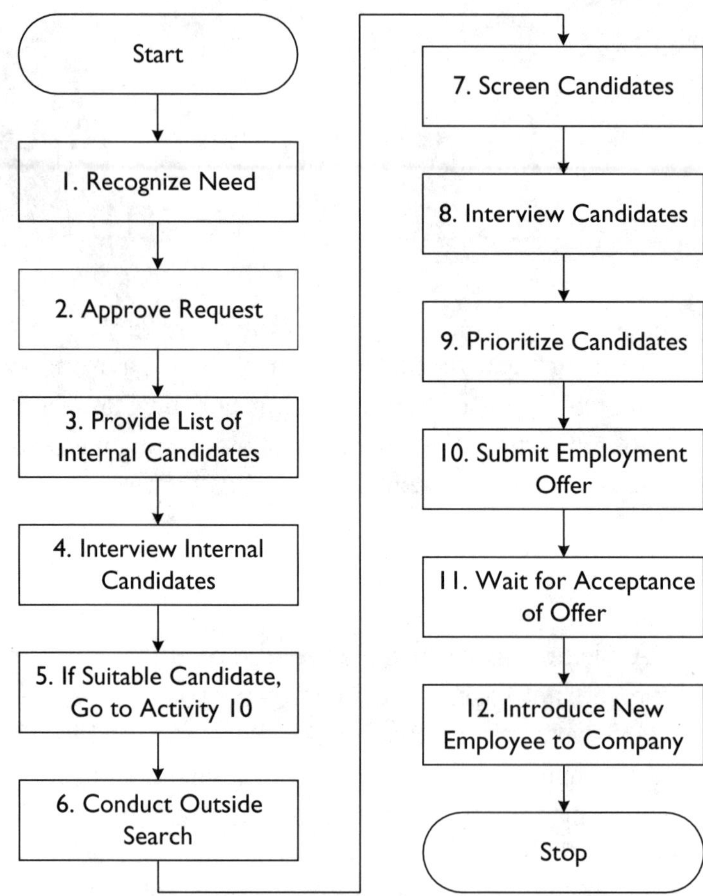

FIGURE C-1. **Hiring Process at HJH Company**

particular area. Some of the advantages of using flowcharts are similar to those of using maps. For example, both flowcharts and maps illustrate how the different elements fit together.

Consider Figure C-1, a flowchart of the process for hiring a new employee in the fictitious HJH Company. The process begins with recognition of the need to hire someone and ends with the employee reporting to work. This brief overview of the major activities in the process enables those who understand how to read this story to compare quickly the ways in which HJH's hiring process resembles and differs from that of other companies. For example, you easily can see that HJH emphasizes hiring from inside the organization.

Another advantage is that constructing flowcharts disciplines our thinking. Comparing a flowchart to the actual process activities will highlight the areas in which rules or policies are unclear, or are even being violated. Differences between the way an activity is supposed to be conducted and the way it is actually conducted will emerge. Then, with just a few short steps, you and your colleagues will be able to determine how to improve the activity. Flowcharts are a key element in business process improvement. Good flowcharts highlight the areas in which fuzzy procedures disrupt quality and productivity. Then, because of their ability to clarify complex processes, flowcharts facilitate communication about these problem areas.

Flowcharting Overview

Flowcharting an entire process down to the task level is the basis for analyzing and improving the process. Assigning portions of the process to specific team members will speed up what can be a time-consuming task.

Every situation and/or process will present unique charting problems. The team will have to deal with them as they arise. For instance, existing documentation seldom is sufficient to allow flowcharting of every task and activity without talking to the people performing the tasks. Be careful to distinguish between what the documentation says should be done and what actually is done.

There are many different types of flowcharts, each with its own use. You must understand at least four of these techniques to be effective in the AAA team. They are

1. Block diagrams, which provide a quick overview of a process
2. American National Standards Institute (ANSI) standard flowcharts, which analyze the detailed interrelationships of a process
3. Functional flowcharts, which depict the process flow between organizations or areas
4. Geographic flowcharts, which illustrate the process flow between locations

Figure C-2 presents examples of these four techniques.

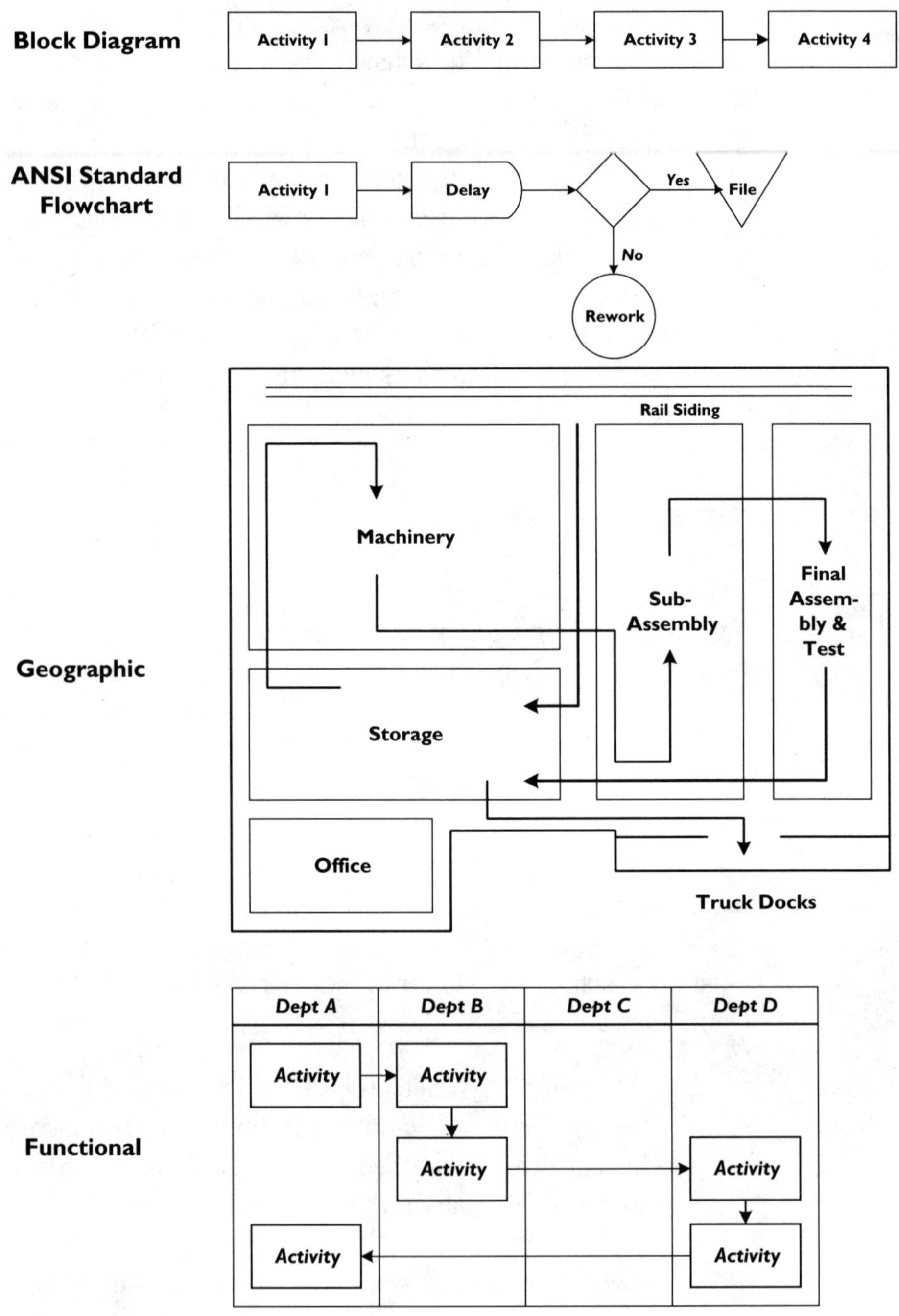

FIGURE C-2. Types of Flowcharts

Block Diagrams

A block diagram, also known as a block flow diagram, is the simplest and most prevalent type of flowchart. It provides a quick, uncomplicated view of the process. Figure C-1 is a block flow diagram that provides an overview of the hiring process. Rectangles and lines with arrows are the major symbols in a block flow diagram. The rectangles represent activities, and the lines with arrows connect the rectangles to show the direction of information flow and/or the relationships among the activities. Some block flow diagrams also include elongated circle start and stop symbols, to indicate where the flowchart begins and where it ends. Figure C-3 shows some of the symbols typically used in block diagrams.

Use block diagrams to simplify large, complex processes or to document individual tasks. Include a short phrase within each rectangle describing the activity being performed. Keep these descriptive phrases (activity names) short.

Let's decode the story told in Figure C-1.

Activity 1—A manager recognizes a need for another employee because of high overtime, an employee leaving, and so forth. To fill this need, he or she must complete the required forms and get the proper approvals.

Activity 2—The appropriate people review the request for a new employee and approve or reject it. This approval may result in a budget

Symbol	Name	Purpose
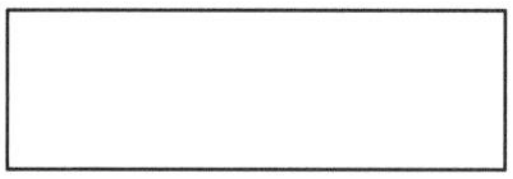	Activity	Indicates that some change has occurred
	Direction of flow	Denotes the direction and order of the operation
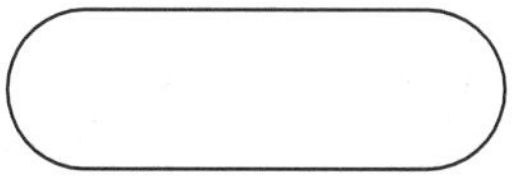	Boundaries or Start/Stop Symbols	Indicates the beginning or end of the block diagram

FIGURE C-3. **Some Typical Symbols Used in Block Diagrams**

increase. After the necessary approvals are obtained, the approved request is sent to personnel.

Activity 3—Personnel looks for internal candidates who have been recommended for promotion or transfer who also meet the needs of the job. The HJH Company does not post jobs. A list of candidates, along with their personnel files, is sent to the requesting manager.

Activity 4—The manager reviews the files and arranges to interview suitable candidates. Then he or she notifies personnel of the results of the review and the interviews.

Activity 5—If one of the candidates is acceptable, go to activity 10. If not, continue to activity 6.

Activity 6—Personnel conducts an outside search for candidates by running ads in newspapers, reviewing on-file applications, hiring a search firm, and so on.

Activity 7—Personnel reviews potential candidates' applications and conducts screening interviews with the best candidates. Then interviews are set up between the manager and the most promising candidates.

Activity 8—The manager interviews the candidates.

Activity 9—The manager prioritizes the acceptable candidates and sends this list to personnel.

Activity 10—Personnel submits an employment offer to the best candidate.

Activity 11—The company waits for the candidate's response. If the offer is rejected, activities 10 and 11 are repeated for the next candidates on the priority list. Once the offer is accepted, go to activity 12.

Activity 12—Personnel arranges for the employee to report to work, familiarizes him or her with company procedures, and presents the employee to the manager.

As you can see, many activities are performed within each rectangle. If desired, each rectangle can be expanded into a block diagram of its own. Figure C-4 takes the first activity in Figure C-1 and explodes it into a more detailed block diagram comprising the following tasks.

Task 1—The manager analyzes the amount of overtime to determine if a new employee could reduce it sufficiently to offset the cost of his or her salary and benefits.

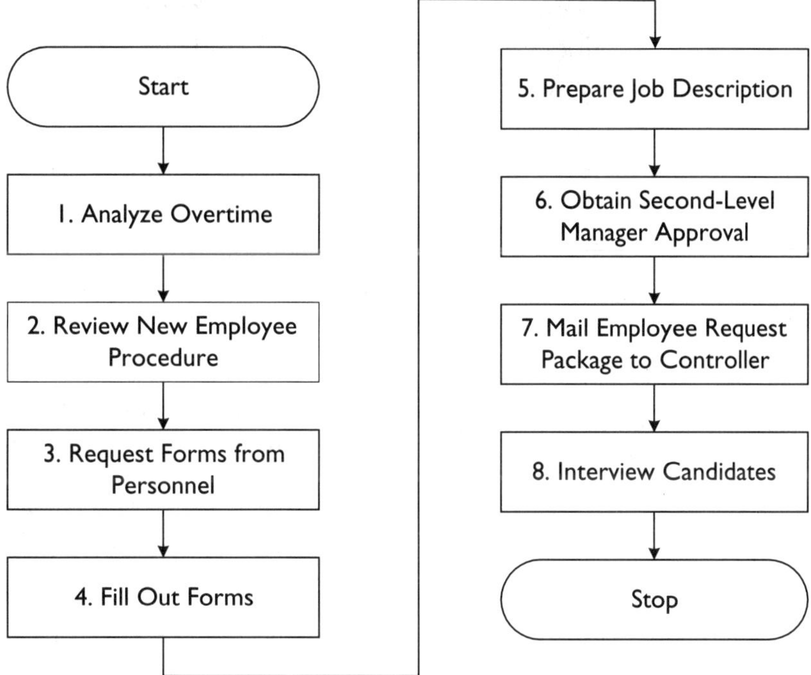

FIGURE C-4. Management Action Required to Obtain New Employee Approval

Task 2—He or she reviews the procedure for acquiring a new employee.
Task 3—The manager asks personnel to send blank personnel requisition forms and budget variation forms.
Task 4—He or she fills out forms.
Task 5—He or she prepares a job description for the new job.
Task 6—He or she reviews with the second-level manager and gets a sign-off.
Task 7—The manager mails the job description, budget change request, and employee requisition form to the controller for approval.

Even in Figure C-4, some of the tasks could be broken down into individual sub-task flowcharts. For example, how to write a job description could easily be a separate block diagram.

Notice that the label description of each activity or task begins with a verb. Although not mandatory, following this practice is a good general rule.

Standard phrasing speeds understanding for the reader. In addition, all business activities can be described by a verb. Thus, by starting each block label with a verb, you ensure that the label does, in fact, describe a true business activity.

If there are conditional statements in your flowchart, you may not be able to begin every label with a verb. For instance, in Figure C-1, activity 5 begins with a conditional statement, "If suitable candidate, *go* to activity 10." The rule of using a starting verb is still followed—immediately after the conditional statement.

Block diagrams can flow horizontally or vertically. Figures C-1 and C-4 flow vertically. Figure C-5 is a block diagram of a barbecue that is plotted horizontally to the page. Despite the change, the diagram still leads you through the process in a logical way.

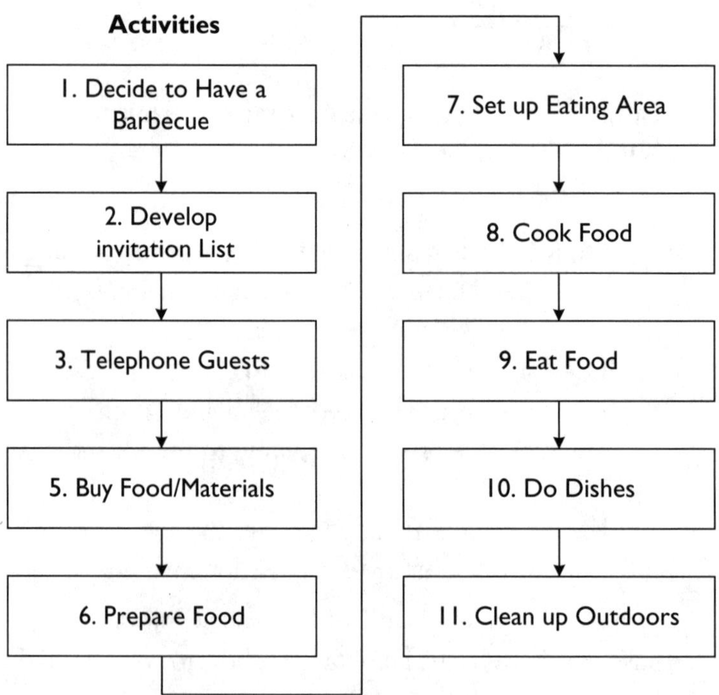

FIGURE C-5. Block Flow Diagram for Conducting a Barbecue

Block diagrams provide a quick overview of a process, not a detailed analysis. Normally, they are prepared first to document the magnitude of the process; then another type of flowchart is used to analyze the process in detail.

Typically, many activities and inputs are intentionally not detailed in a block diagram, so that a very simple picture of the total process can be drawn. Consider activity 4 in Figure C-5: Develop menu. Many activities and inputs must go into developing a menu for the barbecue. The typical inputs required are

1. The amount of money to be spent
2. Guests' preferences
3. What we prepare well

The typical activities include:

1. Listing the items to be served
2. Listing the materials needed for the menu
3. Getting money to pay for the food and condiments

It's easy to see how each of the blocks in the block diagram can be exploded to provide a detailed picture of how the activity or task is performed. Don't worry if all the process details are not documented in the block diagram. The detailed activities will come later in the flowchart process.

Figure C-6 takes Figure C-5 and plots it vertically, adding a new dimension to block diagramming. Here, responsibility for each activity has been assigned to a specific person or persons. The name or title of the person responsible for the activity is indicated in the open-ended rectangle. This symbol is called an "annotation symbol," since it is used to provide additional information about the activity. A broken line leads away from the activity to the annotation symbol. The broken line is used so that the reader will not mistake it for a direction flow line. The arrow leads away from the block diagram activity and points to the person or persons responsible for that activity. When your organization uses block flow diagrams to chart a set of business activities, you may indicate responsibilities differently. You may use the name of a department, the job titles of employees and managers, or the actual names of the individuals in denoting responsibilities.

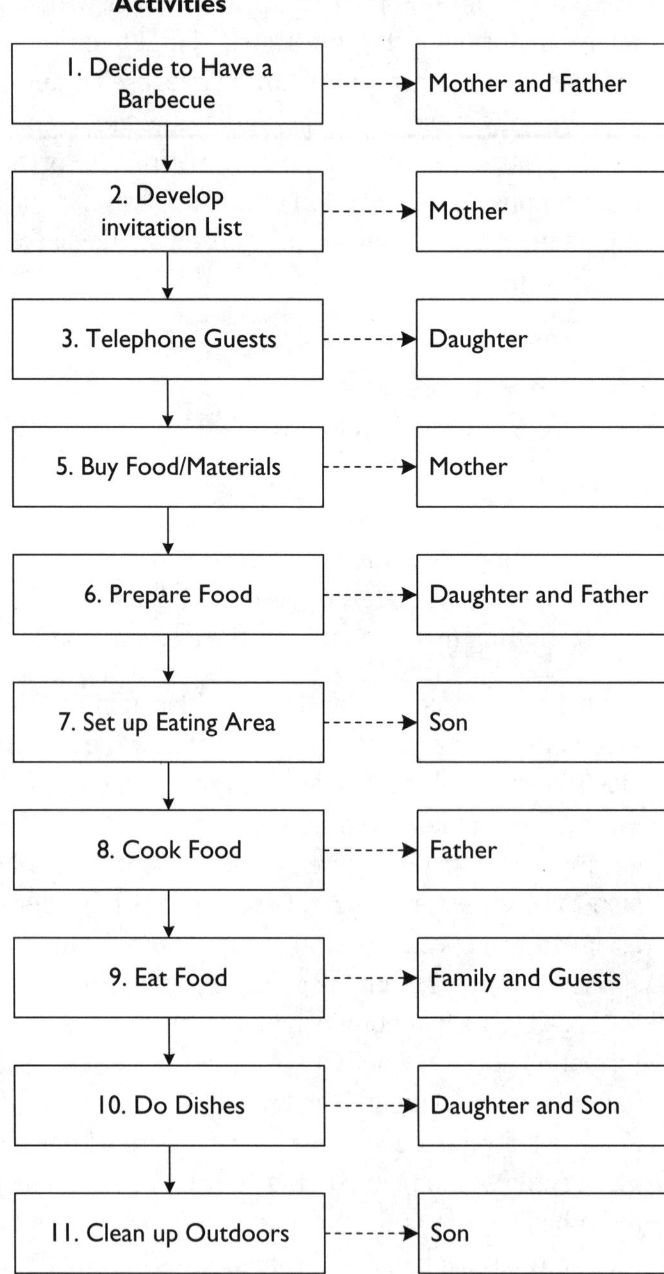

FIGURE C-6. Block Flow Diagram with Assignment of Responsibilities

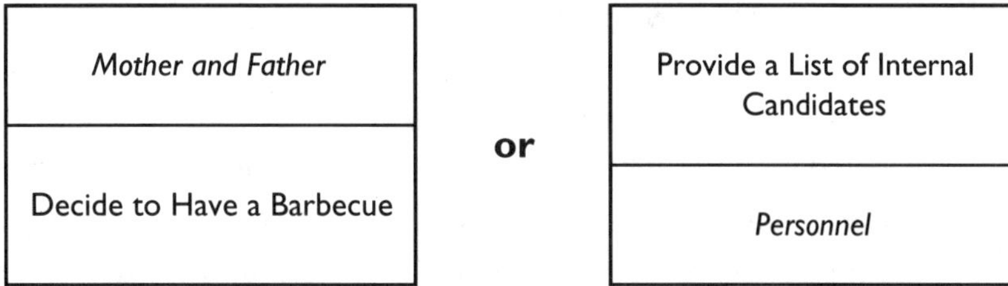

FIGURE C-7. **Another Way to Denote Ownership of an Activity**

Although not considered proper procedure by flowcharting experts, Figure C-7 presents another way of connecting an activity with the person(s) or area(s) responsible for performing that activity.

The purpose of flowcharting is to paint a picture that is easy for your team to understand and use. You can modify rules, such as starting each activity name with a verb or using annotation symbols in place of the activity owner's name within the activity rectangle, if doing so significantly improves the understanding and use of the flowchart.

However, given that any nonstandard deviation may confuse other people within the organization using the flowchart at a later date, it is a good idea to have the NWT establish a complete list of symbols at the beginning of the **AAA** to minimize deviations.

It is good practice to start your business process flowcharting by block diagramming the process. The block diagram can be used to help define which of the other flowcharts best provides a detailed understanding of the tasks within the process.

Standard Flowchart Symbols

Before examining the remaining three types of flowcharts, we should define some additional symbols. The most effective flowcharts use only widely known, standard symbols. Think about how much easier it is to read a road map when you are familiar with the meaning of each symbol, and what a nuisance it is to have some strange, unfamiliar shape in the area of the map you are using to make a decision about your travel plans.

The flowchart is one of the oldest of all the design aids available. For simplicity, we will review only 12 of the most common symbols, most of which are published by the American National Standards Institute (ANSI) (see Figure C-8).

Let's examine the symbols summarized in Figure C-9. The 12 symbols listed here are not meant to be a complete list of flowchart symbols, but they are the minimum you will need to adequately flowchart your business process. As you learn more about flowcharting, you can expand the number of symbols you use to cover your specific field and needs.

ANSI Standard Flowchart

An ANSI standard flowchart provides a detailed understanding of a process that greatly exceeds that of a block diagram. In fact, a block diagram often is the starting point, and a standard flowchart is used to expand the activities within each block to the desired level of detail. Each task in the process under study can be detailed to the point that the standard flowchart can be used as part of the training manual for a new employee. For most BPI activities, this type of detail is done on an exception-only basis during the improvement phase. The detailed flowcharting is done only when the process nears world-class quality, to ensure that the improvements are not lost over time.

People follow many different processes throughout their daily lives. As an example, a person takes on a particular routine for such simple tasks as eating breakfast, taking a shower, or enjoying a Saturday morning. Most of these processes are not even thought about. Some processes involve other people to such a degree that we don't think about our own involvement, such as getting a haircut from the friendly corner barber and/or going fishing (which, generally, the man really wants to do). This process is flowcharted in Figures C-10 and C-11.

The standard flowchart in Figure C-10 shows diamonds as decision symbols representing points at which different paths may be taken. Notice that the words "yes" and "no" are used to clarify alternatives. The small circles are connector symbols leading you to the second page of the chart (Figure C-11).

A Simple Business Process Flowchart

While the flowcharts in Figures C-9 and C-10 are very simple, charting a business process requires careful attention. Consider a manager of a large retail store in a big city. The procedures he or she must follow can become

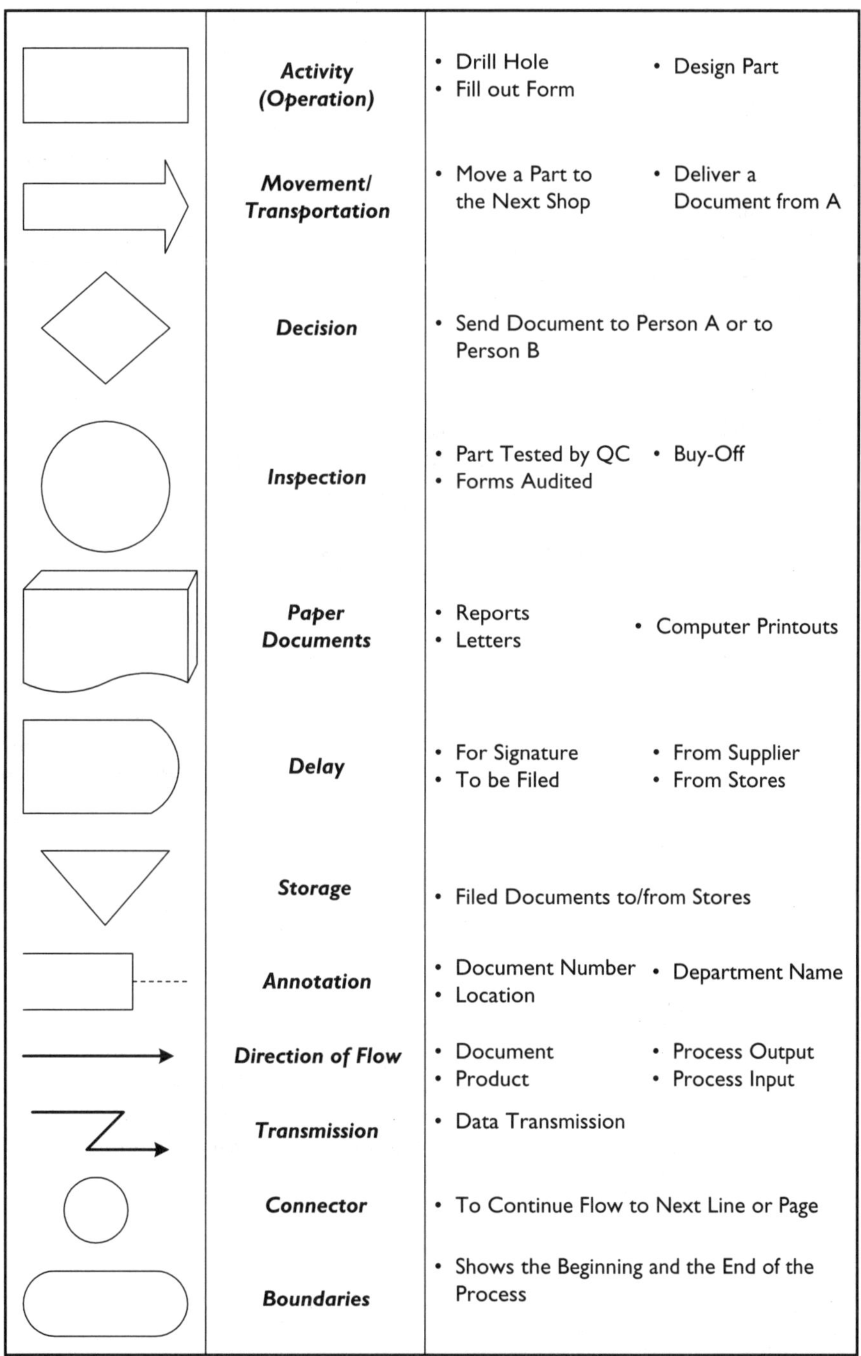

Symbol	Name	Examples	
	Activity (Operation)	• Drill Hole • Fill out Form	• Design Part
	Movement/ Transportation	• Move a Part to the Next Shop	• Deliver a Document from A
	Decision	• Send Document to Person A or to Person B	
	Inspection	• Part Tested by QC • Forms Audited	• Buy-Off
	Paper Documents	• Reports • Letters	• Computer Printouts
	Delay	• For Signature • To be Filed	• From Supplier • From Stores
	Storage	• Filed Documents to/from Stores	
	Annotation	• Document Number • Location	• Department Name
	Direction of Flow	• Document • Product	• Process Output • Process Input
	Transmission	• Data Transmission	
	Connector	• To Continue Flow to Next Line or Page	
	Boundaries	• Shows the Beginning and the End of the Process	

FIGURE C-8. The Most Common Flowchart Symbols

Activity (Operation): Rectangle
Use this symbol whenever a change in an item occurs. The change may result from the expenditure of labor, a machine activity, or a combination of both. It is used to denote activity of any kind, from drilling a hole to computer data processing. It is the correct symbol to use when no other one is appropriate. Normally, you should include a short description of the activity in the rectangle.

Movement/Transportation: Fat Arrow
Use a fat arrow to indicate movement of the output between locations (e.g., sending parts to stock, mailing a letter, etc.).

Decision Point: Diamond
Put a diamond at the point in the process where a decision must be made. The next series of activities will vary based on this decision. For example, "If the letter is correct, it will be signed. If it is incorrect, it will be retyped." Typically, the output from the diamond are marked with the options (e.g., Yes-No, True-False, etc.).

Inspection: Big Circle
Use a big circle to signify that the process has stopped to evaluate the quality of the output. It typically involves an inspection conducted by someone other than the person who performed the previous activity. It also can represent the point where an approval signature is required.

Paper Documents:
Wiggle-Bottomed Rectangle
Use this symbol to show when the output from an activity included information recorded on paper (e.g., written reports, letters, or computer printouts).

Delay: Blunted Rectangle
Use this symbol, sometimes called a bullet, when an item or person must wait, or an item is placed in temporary storage before performing the next scheduled activity (e.g., waiting for an airplane, waiting for a signature, etc.).

Boundaries: Elongated Circle
Use this to show the beginning and end of the process. Normally, the word "start" or "beginning," "stop" or "end" is included within the symbol.

FIGURE C-9. **Explanation of Flowchart Symbols**

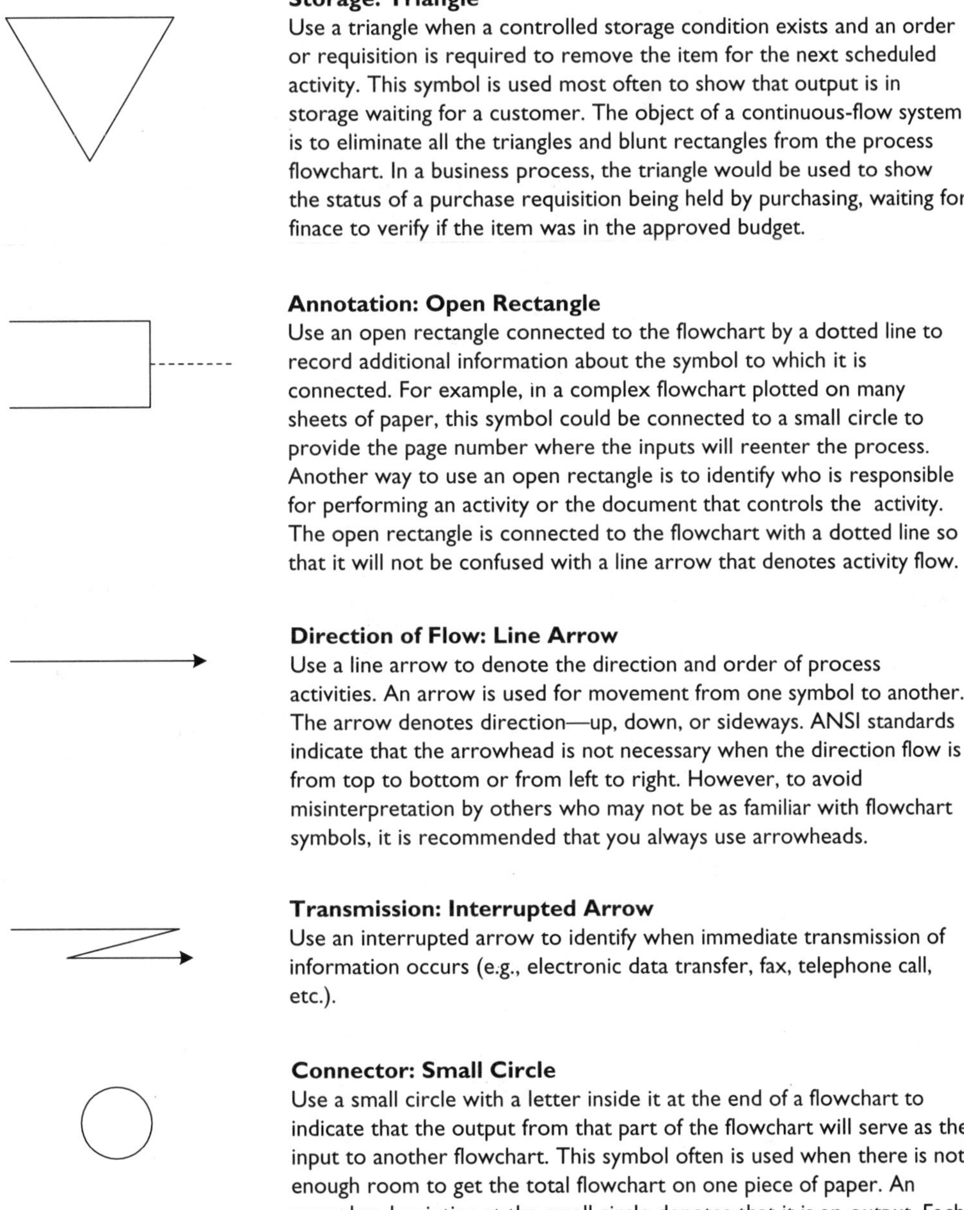

Storage: Triangle
Use a triangle when a controlled storage condition exists and an order or requisition is required to remove the item for the next scheduled activity. This symbol is used most often to show that output is in storage waiting for a customer. The object of a continuous-flow system is to eliminate all the triangles and blunt rectangles from the process flowchart. In a business process, the triangle would be used to show the status of a purchase requisition being held by purchasing, waiting for finace to verify if the item was in the approved budget.

Annotation: Open Rectangle
Use an open rectangle connected to the flowchart by a dotted line to record additional information about the symbol to which it is connected. For example, in a complex flowchart plotted on many sheets of paper, this symbol could be connected to a small circle to provide the page number where the inputs will reenter the process. Another way to use an open rectangle is to identify who is responsible for performing an activity or the document that controls the activity. The open rectangle is connected to the flowchart with a dotted line so that it will not be confused with a line arrow that denotes activity flow.

Direction of Flow: Line Arrow
Use a line arrow to denote the direction and order of process activities. An arrow is used for movement from one symbol to another. The arrow denotes direction—up, down, or sideways. ANSI standards indicate that the arrowhead is not necessary when the direction flow is from top to bottom or from left to right. However, to avoid misinterpretation by others who may not be as familiar with flowchart symbols, it is recommended that you always use arrowheads.

Transmission: Interrupted Arrow
Use an interrupted arrow to identify when immediate transmission of information occurs (e.g., electronic data transfer, fax, telephone call, etc.).

Connector: Small Circle
Use a small circle with a letter inside it at the end of a flowchart to indicate that the output from that part of the flowchart will serve as the input to another flowchart. This symbol often is used when there is not enough room to get the total flowchart on one piece of paper. An arrowhead pointing at the small circle denotes that it is an output. Each different output should have a different letter designation. Any output can reenter the process at a number of different points.

FIGURE C-9. (continued)

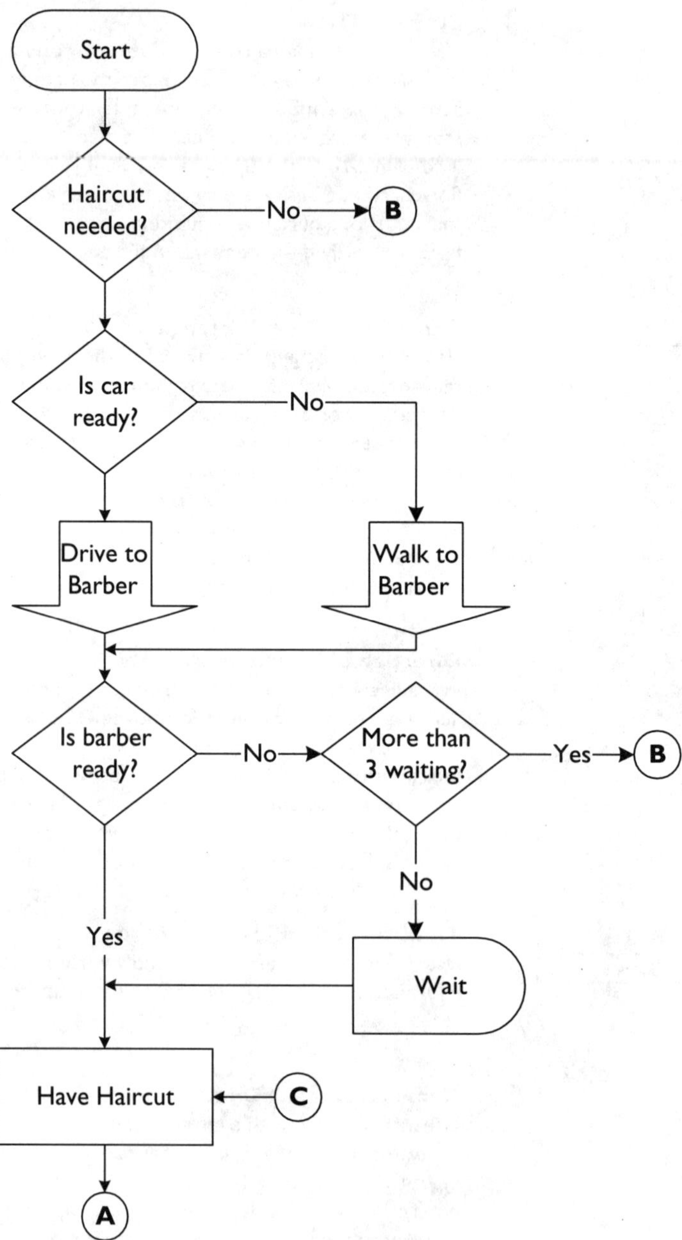

FIGURE C-10. Standard Flowchart of the First Process of Getting a Haircut and/or Going Fishing

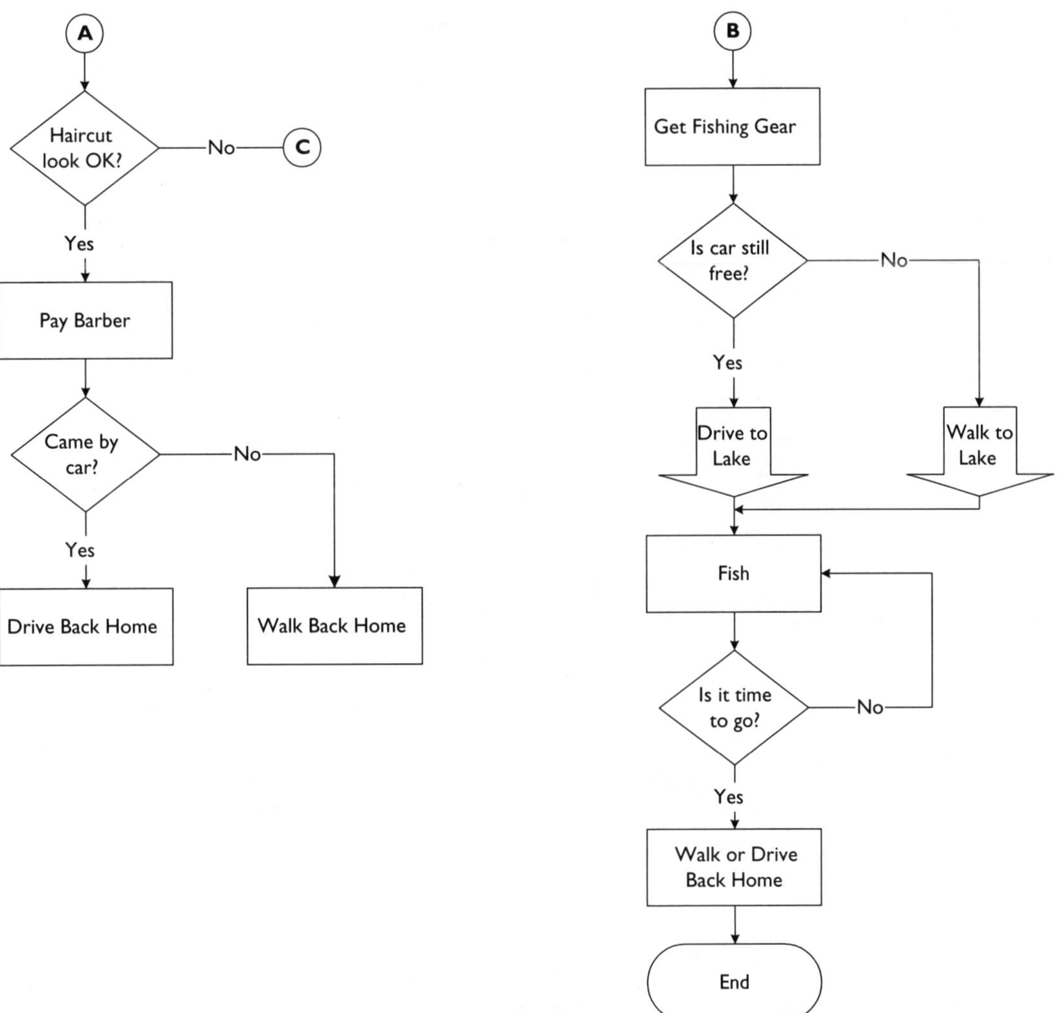

FIGURE C-11. Two Standard Flowcharts of Different Parts of the Process of Getting a Haircut and/or Going Fishing

quite involved. He or she may have a large staff, delegate authority, supervise various departments, and so on. Each supervisor has sales reports to complete and check against inventory changes. The manager must provide each supervisor with instructions to help ease the workload and promote uniformity among the different departments. This, in turn, helps the accounting department.

A typical procedure for a supervisor might include

1. Choosing the weekly sales total for an employee; reading the value of price items from column *X*, and the value of sales items from column *Y*.
2. Figuring out the *X* commission by multiplying the value in column *X* by 10%.
3. Figuring out the *Y* commission by multiplying the value in column *Y* by 5%.
4. Computing the total due: $50.00 + *X* commission + *Y* commission.
5. Entering the total pay opposite the employee's name in the payroll ledger.
6. Returning to activity 1, and repeating this for the other employees.

Figure C-12 flowcharts the procedure for calculating employees' weekly commissions. The activities in the procedure are listed beside each symbol in the flowchart to help people understand the details of the flowchart. Unfortunately, this is not usually practical on complex flowcharts.

The first five activities on the flowchart follow activities 1 through 5 of the written procedure above. Notice, however, that the flowchart allows for an activity not accounted for in the written procedure (i.e., eventually, the weekly sales totals for all employees will have been processed, and the procedure need not be repeated). Flowcharting the process, in this case, helps us to discover that activity 6 should be rewritten as follows:

6. If the weekly sales totals for more employees must be calculated, go to activity 1. Otherwise, stop.

This simple flowchart clearly and accurately depicts the activities involved in the procedure and the sequence in which they are to be carried out.

Functional Time-Line Flowchart

A functional time-line flowchart adds processing and cycle time to the standard functional flowchart. This flowchart offers some valuable insights when you are doing a poor-quality cost analysis to determine how much money the organization is losing because the process is not effective and efficient. Adding a time value to the already-defined functions interacting within the process makes it easy to identify areas of waste and delay.

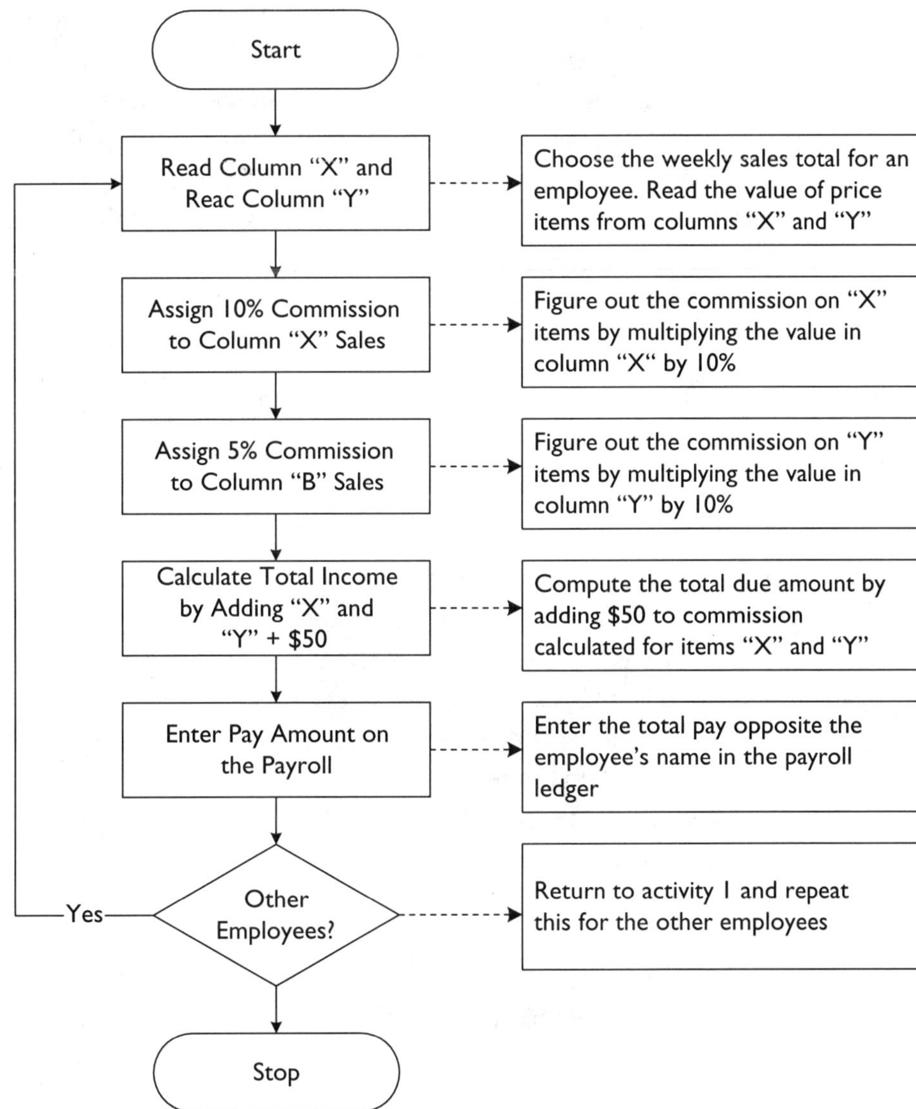

FIGURE C-12. **Paying commission flowchart and procedures**

Time is monitored in two ways. First, the time required to perform the activity is recorded in the column entitled "Processing Time (hours)." The column beside it is the cycle time (i.e., the time between when the last activity was completed and when this activity is completed). Usually, there is a major difference between the sum of the individual processing hours and the cycle time for the total process. This difference is due to waiting and transportation time.

One common error is to focus on reducing processing time and ignore cycle time. The result is focusing our activities on reducing costs, without considering the business from our customers' viewpoints. Customers do not see processing time; they see only cycle time (response time). To meet our needs, we work on reducing processing time. To have happy customers, we must reduce cycle time.

In one sales process, IBM was able to reduce processing time by 30%, thereby reducing costs by 25%. At the same time, it reduced cycle time by 75%. An unplanned-for side effect was a more than 300% increase in sales (65% sales closure). There is no doubt that there is a direct correlation between cycle time, customer satisfaction, and increased profits.

The time-line flow concept can be applied to all types of flowcharts. Often, elapsed time is recorded using the time that has elapsed from the time the first activity in the process started. When activities are flowcharted down to the task level, the functional name is substituted for the person's name doing the job.

1. New employee signs in at lobby and asks receptionist to call personnel.
2. Personnel placement representative greets new employee and takes him or her to personnel department to review pertinent procedures.
3. Placement representative takes new employee to medical department to fill out medical forms and make appointment with nurse for required tests.
4. New employee returns to personnel department to fill out payroll forms.
5. New employee and the placement representative go to security for pictures and temporary identification badge.

6. New employee returns to lobby to wait for appointment with nurse. He or she can go unescorted now that he or she has a temporary badge.
7. New employee goes to medical for blood tests and makes appointment for physical exam with doctor.
8. New employee returns to personnel department per instructions.
9. Placement representative takes new employee to lunch.
10. Placement representative takes new employee to meet his or her new manager and tour the department.
11. New employee goes to personnel so personnel can take him or her to benefits.
12. New employee reviews benefits package and selects benefits plan.
13. New employee goes to lobby to wait for the new employee orientation meeting.
14. New employee attends new employee orientation meeting.
15. New employee returns to lobby to wait for appointment with doctor.
16. New employee goes to medical for appointment with doctor and returns to personnel.
17. Personnel reviews new employee checklist and calls medical to find out if exam results are favorable.
18. New employee returns to lobby, turns in temporary badge, and signs out.

First impressions are key. How do you think the new employee feels about this company after a day of "hurry up and wait"? Probably, this person is questioning whether he or she made the right decision in joining the company.

Analyzing this flowchart quickly reveals wasted motion and time. For example, if the new employee reported to a special waiting room in personnel, the amount of time the employee and the personnel placement representative expended during the day would be greatly reduced. If personnel gave out the temporary badges, personnel would not have to escort the employee to other departments.

Let's think about what can be done to refine the flow, and make better use of the new employee's and the personnel placement representative's time.

1. Should the physical be conducted before the employee reports to work? Isn't it part of the search process, not the indoctrination process? If the new employee had left another job to join your firm and then failed the physical, what is your company's obligation to that person? How much would it slow down the process to get a new employee on board? Obviously, the physical should have been conducted before the new employee's first day.
2. Have the employee report first to a small waiting room in personnel. At that time, the personnel placement representative can provide a temporary badge.
3. From personnel, the new employee should go directly to benefits.
4. The employee indoctrination meeting should be held right after the meeting with the benefits department.
5. The new employee's manager should meet him or her at the end of the indoctrination meeting and proceed to security. A picture of the new employee should be taken for the permanent security badge.
6. The manager then should take the new employee to lunch.
7. The manager should escort the new employee to the work area and proceed with job training.
8. The new employee should keep the temporary badge until a permanent badge is available. This allows the employee to go directly home from work. When the employee's permanent badge is available, the manager should mail the temporary badge back to personnel.

In addition to simplifying the work flow, the new employee is now in his or her work area for the second half of the day. The result is a more efficient process that leaves the new employee with a much better impression of the company.

Geographic flowcharting is a useful tool for evaluating department layout and paperwork flow, and analyzing product flow, by identifying excessive travel and storage delays. In business processes, geographic flowcharting helps in analyzing traffic patterns around busy areas like file cabinets, computers, and copiers.

Taking an Information-Processing View

In addition to the four basic flowcharts we have covered already (block diagrams, ANSI standard flowcharts, functional flowcharts, and geographic flowcharts), there are information diagrams, often with their own set of symbols. As a rule, these are of more interest to computer programmers and automated systems analysts than to managers and employees charting business activities. The two books listed at the end of this report discuss some of these tools.

You can consider these types of flowcharts as diagrams that follow information through a process. As you and your colleagues prepare flowcharts, think of your organizational activities in terms of information processing. Begin with your organization's files. They are valuable because they contain information that is changed or used by your business processes.

Next, consider your employees. You and your coworkers have skills of various levels and types. Obviously, even a single worker's knowledge is substantially more sophisticated than the information in a file. But the principle still holds: An employee's value to an organization depends on his or her contributions of information. Whether it's how to load a pallet, introduce a new product, or resolve a conflict, information is a resource. This is particularly true in the service industries that, in 1989, employed more than 70% of workers in the United States. All of them can be considered information processors and providers.

Taking an information-processing view when preparing your flowcharts will create a common focus on getting and using quality input in order to produce quality output. At the same time, an information-processing view helps people decide how to draw flowcharts, and which elements to include. More specifically, you should

1. Feature the parts of the process for which information validity and reliability are most important.
2. Consider the three different information-processing dimensions of business processes: what information is processed, what activities are involved in processing the information, and which elements control other elements. If your flowchart doesn't have the impact you want, try drawing it to feature one of the other dimensions.

3. Remember that organizations consist of people, and whenever people are involved, information transmission and processing are complicated. Consequently, it is better to draw several easily understandable flowcharts than one comprehensive, but incomprehensible, master chart.

Data Dictionary

Many of you may never need to use a data dictionary because your flowcharts will be reasonably uncomplicated and straightforward. There will be some of you, though, who will need to go into considerable detail covering a broad range of activities. In this case, the use of a data dictionary becomes necessary in order to be sure all labels and definitions are clear and understood.

The most effective flowcharts use words and phrases that people will easily understand, and include only widely known, standard symbols. Often, an accompanying glossary of terms, known as a **data dictionary** by information-processing professionals, helps. Each entry in the dictionary refers to a label used in the flowcharts.

A data dictionary serves a number of reference purposes. For example, it alerts you to database homonyms. A database is a collection of information inside an organization's files. (Often these files are computerized.) Homonyms exist when the same label refers to different items. Consider, for example, the label "Enter Employee ID." On one flowchart, this might mean, "Record the employee's social security number on a form." On another flowchart it might mean, "Type the employee's name into a computer system and wait for the system to verify the entry." Because of their multiple meanings, database homonyms can cause confusion in a set of flowcharts.

Homonyms occur because flowchart labels must be brief. You don't have space for a detailed explanation on the chart itself, but you can include the definition in the data dictionary. Checking the dictionary before selecting a label will tell you if there are other ways in which your label is being used already. If this is so, you might select another label or take special measures to ensure that people using your flowchart know what you really mean.

You also can use the data dictionary for assistance with database synonyms—cases in which different labels have identical definitions. For example, "receivables" might refer to the same thing as "sales collectible."

As with homonyms, database synonyms may be necessary. People prefer to use familiar terms when constructing their flowcharts, and employees in different parts of the organization may have different words for an identical item. Recognizing the value of familiarity, information-processing professionals call database synonyms that are acceptable, "aliases."

Summary

Flowcharting is a key tool for understanding business processes and activities. Laying out a process or activity on a piece of paper in an easily understandable format often sets the stage for major process improvement. It is also an effective tool for analyzing the impact of proposed changes.

To improve the quality of their products and services, many businesspeople have used flowcharting techniques with enviable results. Others, however, have been less successful. Generally, this happens because they view their flowcharts as the end of, rather than the means to, what they are seeking. It is an easy mistake to make. Compared to some techniques for improving quality and productivity, flowcharting is easy to understand and use. Furthermore, in their enthusiasm for improvement, some people are tempted to flowchart in detail every process they can find. Fortunately, however, such diligence is rarely necessary.

Flowcharts serve one main purpose: to document a process or activity in order to identify areas in need of improvement. The "magic" doesn't come from documenting the process but from analyzing it—and that is where you should focus most of your efforts. Remember, the purpose of flowcharting and the following analysis is to gain enough knowledge to define and implement improvements. It should not become an end unto itself.

Flowcharts are tools. It is in the continuous improvement activities following flowcharting that their full value is realized. However, the flowcharting process itself prepares people for the productive changes ahead:

1. Those who participate in creating the flowcharts recognize their own competence and influence. They now know how their contributions serve to empower their coworkers. They are proud that their role is documented on a diagram that others will consult.

2. People see that the value of their performance affects how others use the output. This stimulates curiosity about customers' expectations and strengthens ties between employees and customers.
3. In creating flowcharts, people gain understanding of one another's jobs, resulting in increased cooperation in the work environment. Building flowcharts builds teamwork.
4. As the flowchart grows, participants are inspired by the available sources of assistance and support. The message of the flowchart is that there is power and companionship in the organization.
5. At the same time, individual accountability blooms. The flowchart triggers improvement efforts, adherence to standards of quality, and commitment to reduce process variations.
6. Objective setting is facilitated, even in those parts of the organization that have resisted performance measurement, or where people have argued about what are legitimate, realistic objectives.

Throughout all of this, flowcharts focus attention on opportunities for change. As business improvements occur, your team will recognize where the charts are no longer accurate, and where revisions are necessary. In addition, you'll create new versions of flowcharts as you and your coworkers become more skilled at constructing them. Some of this is growth in technical and artistic talents. But a much more important part is developing conceptual talents. The people in your organization will begin to view business activities more systematically, and more creatively. As you build flowcharts, and check their accuracy, you'll become more sensitive to ways in which you can make your business better.

Additional Reading

D. R. Jeffrey and M. J. Lawrence, *Systems Analysis & Design* (Prentice-Hall, 1984).

M. E. Modell, *A Professional's Guide to Systems Analysis,* (McGraw-Hill, 1988).

APPENDIX 

Tools

In this appendix we will give you a brief description of a number of tools that are very helpful throughout the seven phases of AAA. This manual is not designed to be a tool guide, since all of the tools will be explained in other books in this series. These guidelines are just designed to refresh your memory or give you a brief introduction to them.

We have also included blank copies of the four AAA forms we have described in the text.

We will begin with the two tools that we described in the text; the process model and the flow chart. The rest of the tools are listed in alphabetical order

Bar charts
Brainstorming
Cause and effect diagram
Check sheets
Dot plot
Force-field analysis
Gantt chart
Histogram
Line graph (run chart)
Measles charts
Nominal group technique
Operational definitions
Pareto diagram
Pie chart
Scatter diagram
Stem and leaf diagram
Subjective pareto

Process Model

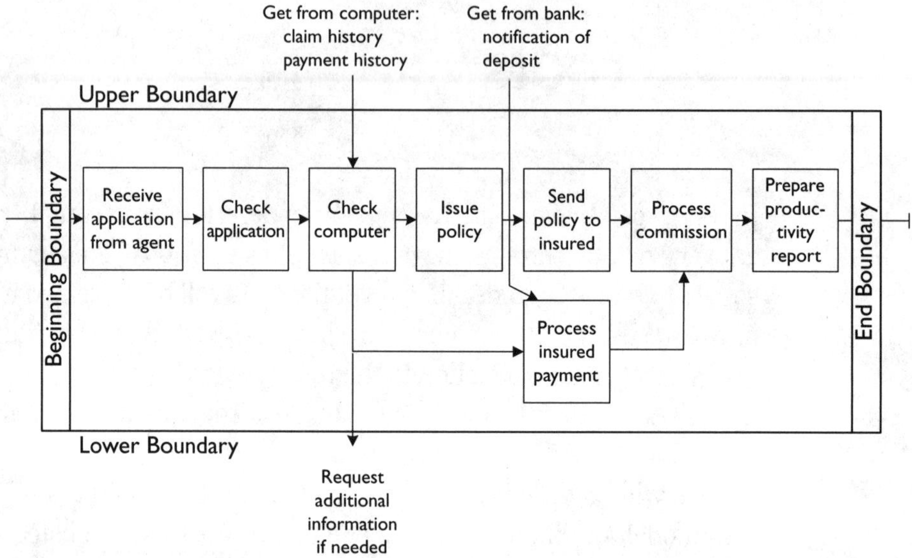

Why

A process model provides a global view of the entire process.

What

It does not break each process down to the task level, instead it provides a visual model of the boundaries of the process, the inputs to the process, and the output from the process. Any of the major blocks of the process model can be broken down further using the same technique until it gets to the task level.

How

1. Draw a box that represents the process.
2. Mark the upper, lower, beginning, and end boundaries.
3. List the activities to be completed (preferably in the order they are to be completed).
4. Add the inputs and outputs to each activity at the appropriate place on the model.

Tips

- Nest the major blocks to break them down and show the connections.
- Use this to provide a high level view and as the input for a flow chart when looking at tasks.

Flow Chart

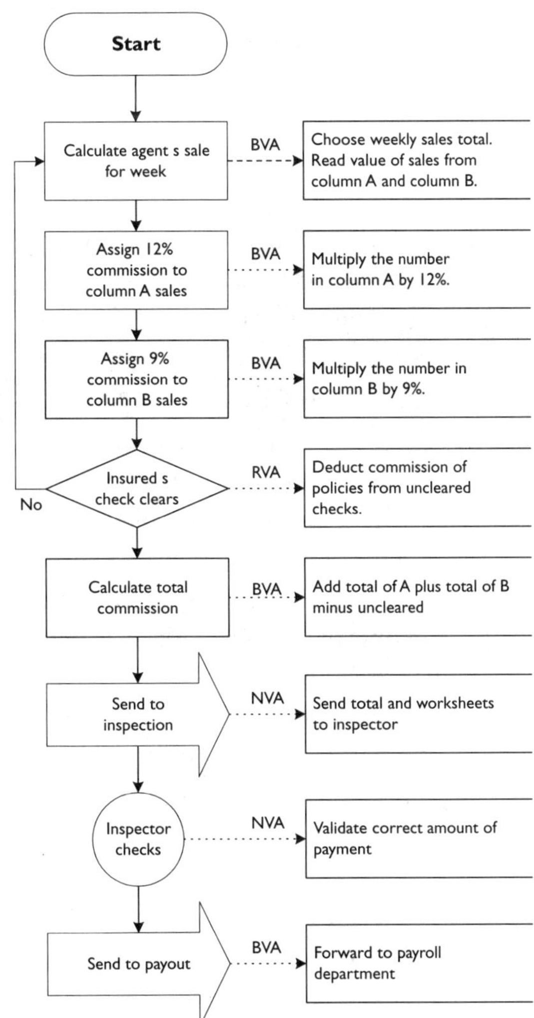

Why

Breaking process into a series of actions or decisions helps to uncover misconnects and potential causes of trouble.

What

A flow chart is a diagram detailing the actions and decisions of a process. The type of flow chart used depends on the complexity of the process and the amount of analysis needed. There are many types of flow charts. Refer to Appendix C for a full description of the common symbols used in a flow chart.

How

1. Choose a process to study.
2. Choose a flow chart type (top-down, matrix, integrated, workflow, or complexity/no complexity).
3. For a top-down flow chart, list the major steps across the top of the diagram. List the secondary steps under each major step.
4. For a matrix flow chart, list the people involved in the process along the top and the appropriate units of time along the left side. Flow chart the process according to who is responsible for each step and when each step is to be completed.
5. For an integrated flow chart, list the people involved in the process across the top and each process step below the person responsible.
6. For a workflow diagram, draw a floor plan of the area to be studied and use directional arrows to trace the flow of work through the area.
7. For a no complexity flow chart, trace the most common simple path process. For a complexity flow chart, add all the additional steps in the process.

Tips

- Check flow charts periodically and make the necessary changes.
- Don't make them any more detailed than you need to be able to make a decision or understand your process.

Bar Chart

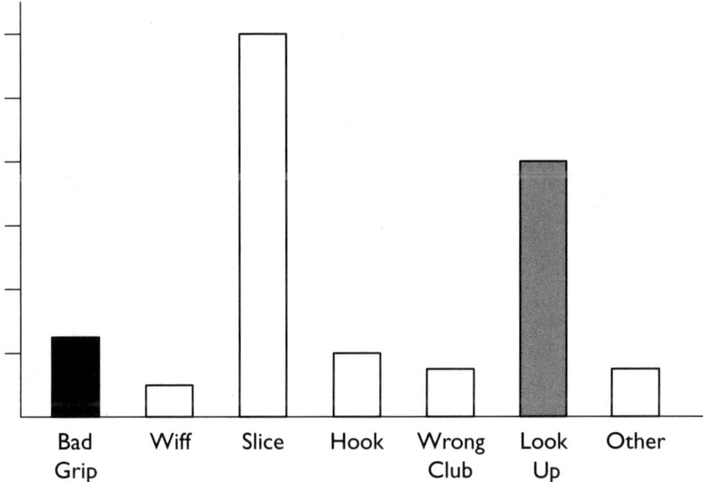

Why

A visual comparison of geometric figures is easier than comparing verbal descriptions.

What

A bar chart compares quantities according to the relative lengths of the corresponding rectangles or bars.

How

1. Collect data.
2. Label the horizontal axis with the items being compared.
3. Label the vertical axis with the quantities (units produced, cost per unit, etc.).
4. Above each item draw a rectangle whose height corresponds to the quantity at that point.

Tips

- All bars should be of equal width.
- Leave space between bars.
- Shade bars.
- A bar chart is appropriate for non-numerical data.

Brainstorming

Why

Often no one person has the solution.

What

Building on the principle "two heads are better than one," brainstorming is a group participation technique that taps the creative thinking abilities of group members.

How

1. Clearly define the problem that is to be brainstormed.
2. Going around the room, have each person give a possible solution to the problem. If unable to think of a new idea, a person may pass.
3. All ideas should be written down without discussion. The list should be kept in view of all group members.
4. Continue around the room until everyone has passed.

Tips

- ► Previously stated ideas may be built upon by other group members.
- ► Limit activity to a specific time frame.
- ► Accept all answers.

Cause and Effect Diagram (Fishbone)

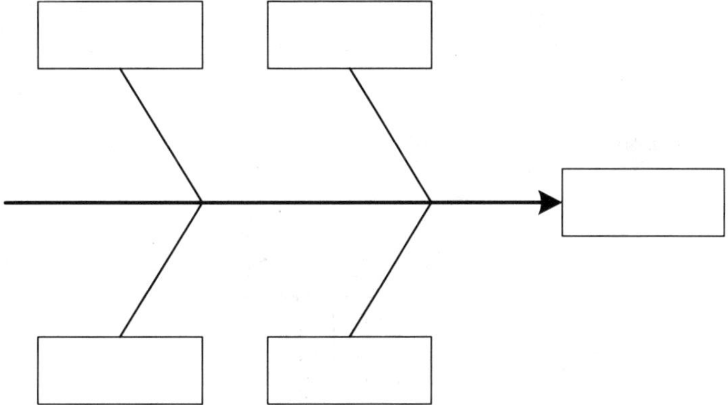

Why

Beginning problem solvers often focus on the effect, ignoring the root causes.

What

The cause and effect diagram identifies the relationships between a particular effect and its possible causes.

How

1. Clearly define the problem and state it on the right side of the diagram.
2. Decide on four or five major categories under which the causes will fall and list them on the left side of diagram. A popular choice is the 5 Ms:

Manpower, Machinery, Measurement, Methods, and Materials.

3. Brainstorm for possible causes. List each cause under its appropriate category.
4. Analyze causes and identify likely root causes.

Tips

- Do not limit categories to traditional choices.
- Causes can be listed in more than one category.
- Display diagram where others may see it; new ideas may be generated.

Check Sheets

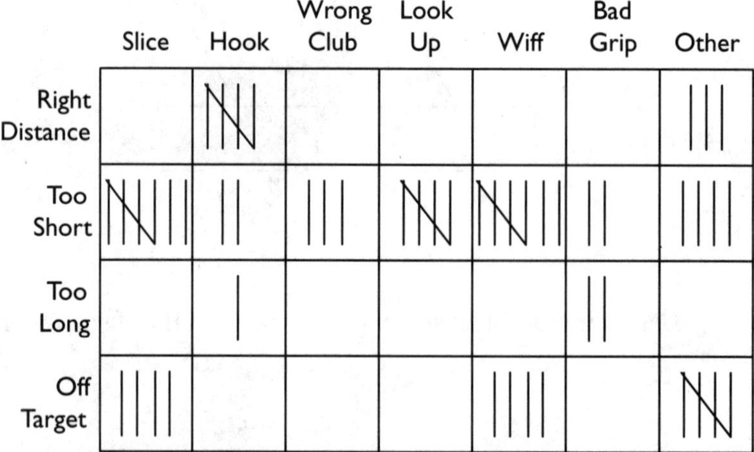

Why

Before you can analyze a process, you need to gather data about the process in an organized manner.

What

A check sheet is a structured form used to tally and analyze data.

How

1. Decide what process is to be studied and the time period in which data will be collected.
2. List the units of time across the top of the checklist and the problems down the left side.
3. Observe the process, making a check in the appropriate column each time a problem occurs.

Tips

- ▶ Observations should be as random as possible.
- ▶ A check list is a good starting point for most problem-solving cycles.

Dot Plot

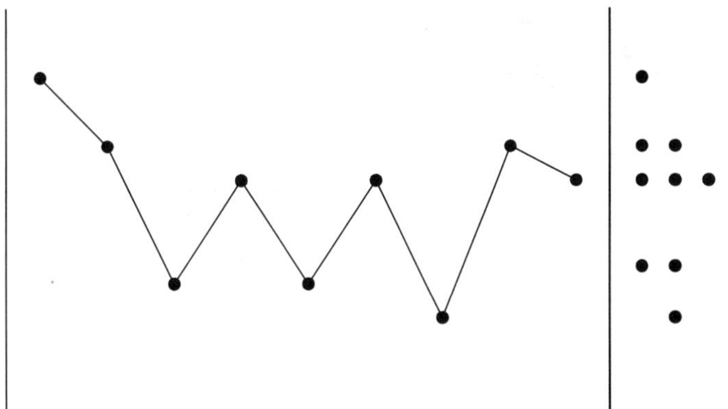

Why

A graphical representation of a distribution often reveals otherwise unnoticed abnormalities or patterns.

What

A dot plot is a graphical tool that allows the user to see two representations of the data at the same time.

How

1. Collect data over time.
2. Construct a line graph or run chart of the data.
3. Draw a vertical line to the right of the last data point of the line graph.
4. Place a dot to the right of the line for each data point. The vertical position of each dot should be the same as that of the corresponding data point.

Tips

- ▶ Create dot diagram off run charts or X & MR charts.
- ▶ Dot diagram presents information in a fashion similar to histogram or bar chart.
- ▶ The pattern of dots represents the distribution of the data.

Force Field Analysis

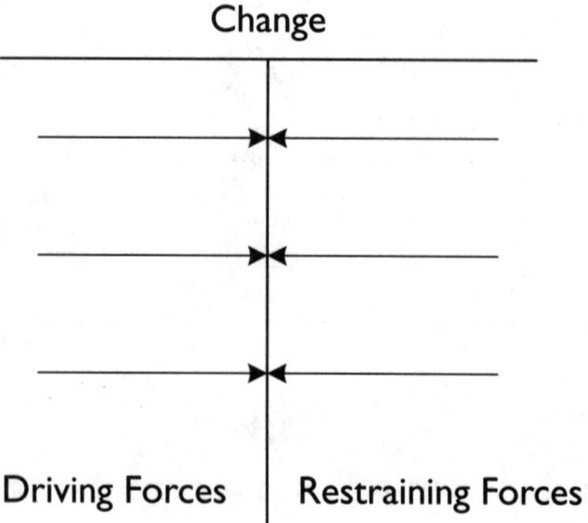

Why

When an organization is contemplating change, knowledge of facilitators and inhibitors can ease the transition.

What

In a table form, force-field analysis identifies the driving and restraining forces that affect a desired change.

How

1. Select a desired change to be analyzed.
2. Identify possible forces that restrain the change, or keep it from happening. These are listed on the right side of the table.
3. For each restraining force, identify a driving force that counters it. List these on the left side of the table.
4. The group should agree about the relative priority of each force.

Tips

- ▶ Strengthening driving forces often reinforces the negative.
- ▶ The change will occur only if driving forces are more powerful than restraining forces.

Gantt Chart

Activity \ Time	1	2	3	4	5	6	7	8	9
A									
B									
C									
D									

Why

To successfully complete a project, it is important to know how long each task will take and when it is to be completed.

What

A Gantt chart details the tasks in a process or project and outlines when each will be executed.

How

1. Choose a process or project to study.
2. List the activities involved in your process along the left side.
3. List appropriate units of time across the top.
4. Across from the activities, draw a horizontal rectangle whose length corresponds to the length of time the activity takes to complete.

Tips

- Have a complete list of the tasks before you put them into a Gantt Chart.
- A Gantt chart does not show what has to be done before another step can be started.

Histogram

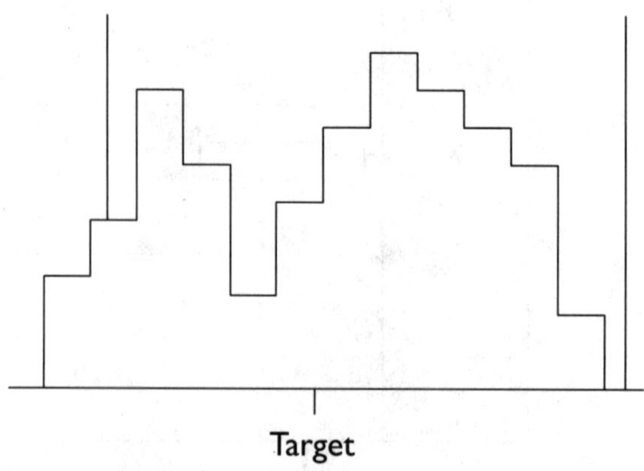

Why

Abnormal distributions are often indications that an assignable cause is present on the process.

What

By visually depicting the spread of distribution of data, histograms help you communicate information about a process and help you decide where to focus improvement efforts.

How

1. Collect data and arrange in ascending order.
2. Find the range of the data by subtracting the smallest data point from the largest.
3. Determine the number of columns. To determine column width, divide the range by the number of columns.
4. Scale horizontal axis according to the column width determined in Step 3.
5. Scale the vertical axis with the frequency of occurrence (number or percent of observations).
6. For each interval, draw a rectangle whose height corresponds to the frequency in that interval.

Tips

- Keep the number of rectangles between 6 and 12, so that the histogram is easy to interpret.
- All rectangles should be of equal width.
- Do not leave space between rectangles.

Line Graph (Run Chart)

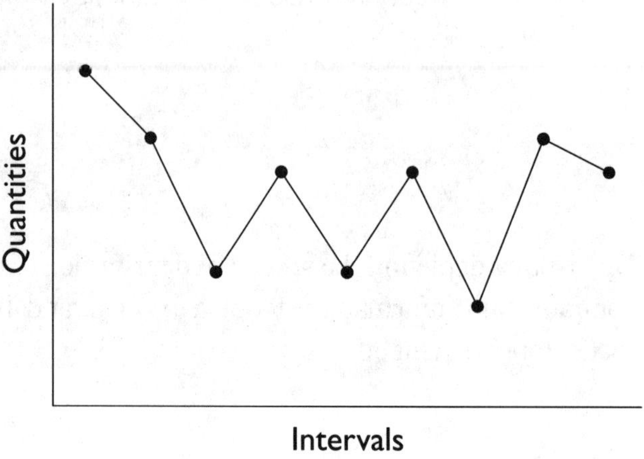

Why

Production processes exhibit variation over time; plotting process performance on a line graph or run chart enables you to analyze and communicate data in a graphical form that easily detects data trends.

What

A line graph illustrates data using line segments between data points.

How

1. Collect data (25–30 data points, minimum).
2. Label the horizontal axis with the intervals, usually of time (day, week, month, etc.), and the vertical axis with the quantities.
3. Above each interval, place a dot corresponding to the quantity observed at that time.
4. Draw line segments to connect the dots over each successive interval.

Tips

- ▶ More than one set of data can be displayed on the same graph.
- ▶ Collect new data; old data is suspect.
- ▶ Look for runs and trends.

Measles Charts

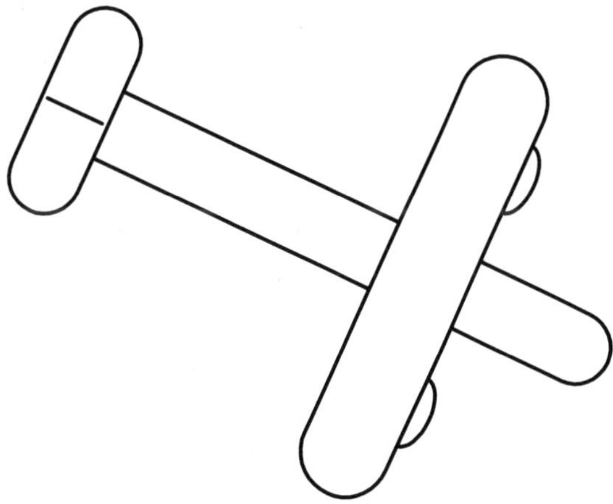

Why

Sometimes a breakthrough will occur when you know the location of defects, as well as their frequency.

What

A measles chart, sometimes called a plot, is a type of check sheet in which both the frequency and location of defects are recorded.

How

1. Determine what process or product is to be studied.
2. Draw a diagram of your process or product.
3. Mark the defects on the diagram where they occur in the process or product.

Tips

- The diagram of your process or product does not have to be in great detail.
- Use a different symbol for each type of defect.

Nominal Group Technique

Why

Often a team or group is controlled (dominated) by one outspoken individual, thus cutting off the good ideas of the rest of the group.

What

Nominal group technique is an idea-generating method similar to but more structured than brainstorming. It is used to arrive at possible solutions to a problem so that everyone has an equal say.

How

1. State the problem in question form and make sure it is understood by everyone.

2. All group members write down their ideas without discussion.
3. List all ideas on a flip chart without discussion. Combine similar ideas only with the permission of the contributors.
4. Clarify and discuss each idea.
5. The group should vote on each item with each person having a maximum number of votes.
6. Discuss and review results.

Tips

- The number of votes allotted to each group member should be less than the number of items.
- A second vote can be taken if an agreement is not reached after the first vote.

Operational Definitions

Why

Having common definitions for quality characters of products and services is essential for gathering meaningful data.

What

An operational definition is a precise description of what something is and how it is measured.

How

1. As a team, brainstorm to determine what aspects of your process are undefined.
2. Prioritize these items to determine what you will define first.
3. Compare and discuss the differences between results obtained from different data collectors.

4. Come to an agreement on the definition of the characteristics and measurement methods.

Tips

- ► Choose the definition that everyone agrees on, even if it does not seem clearly superior.
- ► If customers or suppliers are involved in data collection, they should also agree upon the characteristic's definition.

Pareto Diagram

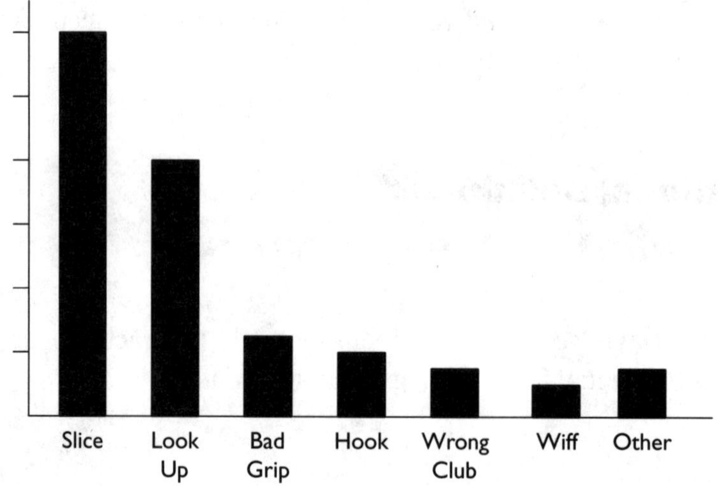

Why

Companies frequently have difficulty choosing the starting point for problem solving or identifying the basic cause of a problem.

What

The Pareto diagram is a specific form of a bar chart in which the items are ranked from left to right according to the comparison unit used (highest on the left): "The vital few versus the significant many."

How

1. Determine what items are to be compared and the unit for comparison (frequency, cost, etc.).
2. In a specific time period, collect data.
3. Compare the frequency or cost of each category.
4. List the categories along the horizontal axis from left to right in order of decreasing cost or frequency.
5. Draw a rectangle above each item whose height corresponds to the frequency or the cost of that item.

Tips

- ▶ Combine smallest categories in an "Others" category that is placed to the right of the last rectangle.
- ▶ Make sure graph is well labeled to show standard of measurement.
- ▶ Make a Pareto of a Pareto.

Pie Chart

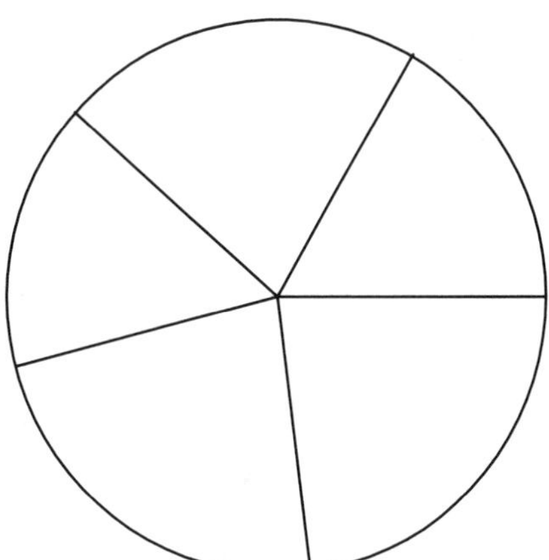

Why

A pie chart visually displays the size relationships among quantities of data.

What

A pie chart is a circle divided into wedges of proportionate size, one for each data category.

How

1. Collect data and arrange into categories.
2. Divide the number of data points in each category by the total amount of data to determine the size of each wedge.
3. Multiply that number by 360 to determine the number of degrees of each wedge.
4. Divide a circle into wedges, one of each desired size.
5. Label the wedges.

Tips

- ► If there are many categories with small amounts of data, they may be combined under the heading "Others"
- ► "Others" category should be the smallest wedge.

Scatter Diagram

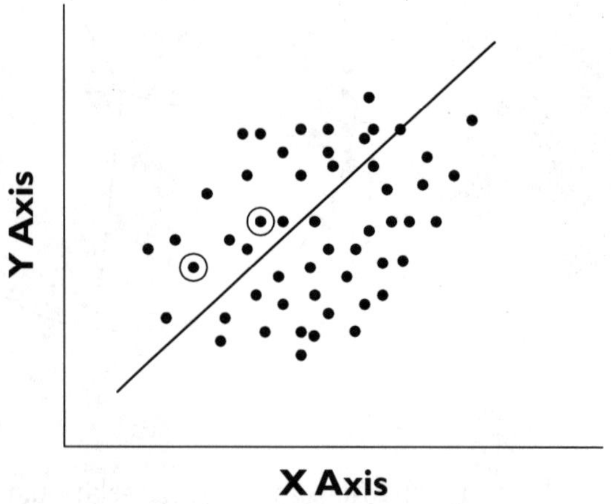

Why

A scatter diagram is used to determine the correlation between two variables.

What

A scatter diagram is a series of plotted points showing the relationship between two variables.

How

1. Collect data from the two variables to be studied. These are the data "pairs."
2. Scale and label the horizontal and vertical axes.
3. Plot the data using a dot for each data point.

Tips

- ▶ Include any additional information necessary for accurate interpretation of the data.
- ▶ Use at least 30 pairs of data for a more accurate representation of the relationship between the variables.

Stem and Leaf Diagram

Stem	Leaf
26	7
382	1
4	3

Why

The organization and summarization of large collections of data can become tedious and be subject to error.

What

By organizing multidigit numerals by their first (or first few) digits, data is easier to work with and the final digits can be used to construct bars showing the distribution of the data.

How

1. Collect data.
2. Note the range of values.
3. For two-digit observations, use the first digit for the category. For three-digit observations, use the first two digits, etc.
4. List the categories (the stems) in a vertical column to the left of a vertical line.
5. On the right of the vertical line, write the final digits of the data values (the leaves) adjacent to their appropriate initial digits.

Tips

- The digits on the right of any category fall into a rectangular shape, showing the spread of data without losing the specific numerical values.
- Stem and leaf diagrams should be used for multidigit data only where there is some variation in the first digits.
- The stem and leaf diagram is a convenient way to organize a large data collection quickly without losing accuracy.

Subjective Pareto

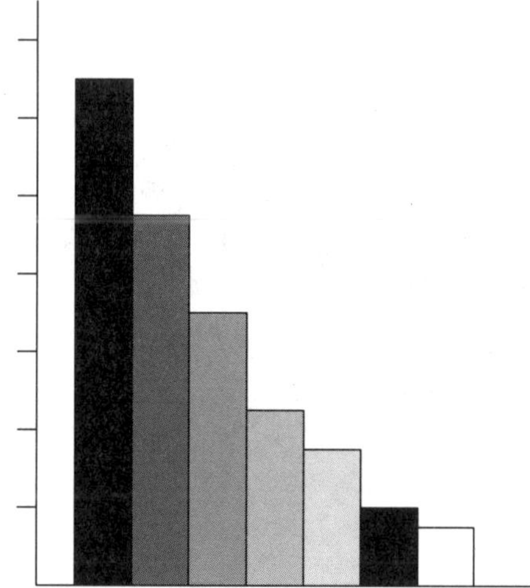

Why

Often people who work in the process will know which problem is most important and requires immediate attention.

What

A subjective Pareto is a Pareto diagram in which problems are ranked according to people's opinion of their importance.

How

1. Determine what items or problems are to be studied.
2. Allow each team member a certain number of votes (less than the number of items).
3. Work individually. Each person assigns points to the items according to how important they feel that item is.
4. For each item, total the team members' points.

5. Construct a Pareto diagram with number of votes as the unit of comparison (as opposed to cost or frequency).

Tips

- Instead of votes, try allotting each team member 10 dollars to "spend" on the items. The more money "spent," the greater the importance of the item.
- Subjective Paretos should not be used as substitutes for actual data collection.

APPENDIX 

Suggested Reading

Argyris, Chris, *Overcoming Organizational Defenses,* Allyn and Bacon, 1990.

Deming, W. E., *Out of the Crisis,* MIT Center for Advanced Engineering Study, 1986.

Harrington, H. James, *Business Process Improvement, The Breakthrough Strategy for Total Quality, Productivity, and Competitiveness,* McGraw-Hill, Inc. 1991.

Harrington, H. James, Hoffherr, Glen D., Reid, Robert P., *Having Fun with Numbers,* McGraw-Hill, Inc., 1997.

Harrington, H. James, Hoffherr, Glen D., Reid, Robert P., *Becoming More Creative,* McGraw-Hill, Inc., 1997.

Hoffherr, Glen D., *The Toolbook—Decision Making and Planning for Optimum Results,* Markon, Inc., 1993.

Hoffherr, Glen D., *Working Together for Optimum Results,* Markon, Inc. 1993.

Hoffherr, Glen D. *et al., Growing Teams—A Down-to-Earth Approach,* GOAL/QPC 1993.

Hoffherr, Glen D. *et al., Making Daily Management Work—A Perspective for Leaders and Managers,* GOAL/QPC 1992.

Imai, Masaaki, *Kaizen,* Random House Business Division, 1986.

Ishikawa, K., *Guide to Quality Control, 2nd ed.,* Asian Productivity Organization, 1982.

Moen, R. D., *et. al., Improving Quality through Planned Experimentation,* McGraw-Hill, 1991.

Moran, John W. *et al., A Guide to Graphical Problem-Solving Processes,* ASQC Quality Press, 1990.

Orr, Ellis R., *Process Quality Control: Trouble-shooting and Interpretation of Data,* McGraw-Hill Book Company, 1975.

Reid, Robert, and Howard Scott, *Change from Within; People Make the Difference,* CEEP Press, 1995.

Shewhart, W. A., *Economic Control of Quality Manufactured Product,* D. Van Nostrand Company, 1931, Reprinted by ASQC.

Taguchi, G., *Introduction to Quality Engineering: Designing Quality into Products and Processes.* Kraus International Publications, 1986.

Wadsworth, H. K. *et al., Modern Methods for Quality Control and Improvement,* John Wiley & Sons, Inc., 1986.

Western Electric Company, *Statistical Quality Control Handbook, 2nd ed.,* Western Electric Company, 1958.

Index

A

ERNST & YOUNG LLP/SYSTEMCORP INC.

GUIDED TOUR

Included with this book is Ernst & Young LLP's/SystemCorp Inc.'s Multimedia Guided Tour CD-ROM called "Area Activity Analysis: Aligning Work Activities and Measurements to Enhance Business Performance" and other related information.

System Requirements:
- Windows 3.1 or higher
- Sound Blaster or comparable sound card
- CD-ROM Drive
- 8MB RAM
- 4MB free disk space

Installation Instructions:
1. Start Windows.
2. Load Guided Tour CD into CD-ROM drive.
3. Select Run from the File or Start menu.
4. Type in **<drive>:\setup** where **<drive>** is the drive letter of your CD-ROM drive.
5. Follow instructions given in setup program.

CONTENTS OF CD-ROM GUIDED TOUR

1. **Multimedia overview of this book**
2. **Process Mapping Tool**
3. **Author's biographies**
4. **Other books in this series**
5. **High Tech Enablers Examples**
   To compete, today's organizations need to make effective use of technologies. Included are examples that we find helpful.
   - **ISO 9000 STEP-BY-STEP**
     An interactive multimedia application designed to help small, medium, or large companies attain ISO 9000 registration much faster and at an affordable cost.
   - **PMI's Managing Projects**
     An interactive multimedia application, based on PMI's latest version of A Guide to the PMBOK, that allows you to customize your organization's project management methodology and maximizes your ability to standardize, communicate, and control all aspects of your project through groupware task management.
   - **OFFICE CONTROL WEB**
     It is a browser-based document management solution for single or multi-site organizations. Integrate existing electronic documents or design powerful forms processing capabilities in full compliance with ISO or QS-9000.

ANY QUESTIONS?

If you need any technical assistance or for more detailed product information on any of the programs demonstrated, contact **SystemCorp** at (514) 339-1067. Fax in a copy of this page to get a 10% discount on any of our products.

SOFTWARE AND INFORMATION LICENSE

The software and information on this CD ROM (collectively referred to as the "Product") are the property of The McGraw-Hill Companies, Inc. ("McGraw-Hill") and are protected by both United States copyright law and international copyright treaty provision. You must treat this Product just like a book, except that you may copy it into a computer to be used and you may make archival copies of the Products for the sole purpose of backing up our software and protecting your investment from loss.

By saying "just like a book," McGraw-Hill means, for example, that the Product may be used by any number of people and may be freely moved from one computer location to another, so long as there is no possibility of the Product (or any part of the Product) being used at one location or on one computer while it is being used at another. Just as a book cannot be read by two different people in two different places at the same time (unless, of course, McGraw-Hill's rights are being violated).

McGraw-Hill reserves the right to alter or modify the contents of the Product at any time.

This agreement is effective until terminated. The Agreement will terminate automatically without notice if you fail to comply with any provision of this Agreement. In the event of termination by reason of your breach, you will destroy or erase all copies of the Product installed on any computer system or made for backup purposes and shall expunge the Product from your data storage facilities.

LIMITED WARRANTY

McGraw-Hill warrants the physical CD ROM(s) enclosed herein to be free of defects in materials and workmanship for a period of sixty days from the purchase date. If McGraw-Hill receives written notification within the warranty period of defects in materials or workmanship, and such notification is determined by McGraw-Hill to be correct, McGraw-Hill will replace the defective CD ROM(s). Send request to:

Customer Service
McGraw-Hill
Gahanna Industrial Park
860 Taylor Station Road
Blacklick, OH 43004-9615

The entire and exclusive liability and remedy for breach of this Limited Warranty shall be limited to replacement of defective CD ROM(s) and shall not include or extend to any claim for or right to cover any other damages, including but not limited to, loss of profit, data, or use of the software, or special, incidental, or consequential damages or other similar claims, even if McGraw-Hill has been specifically advised as to the possibility of such damages. In no event will McGraw-Hill's liability for any damages to you or any other person exceed the lower of suggested list price or actual price paid for the license to use the Product, regardless of any form of the claim.

THE McGRAW-HILL COMPANIES, INC. SPECIFICALLY DISCLAIMS ALL OTHER WARRANTIES, EXPRESS OR IMPLIED, INCLUDING BUT NOT LIMITED TO, ANY IMPLIED WARRANTY OF MERCHANTABILITY OR FITNESS FOR A PARTICULAR PURPOSE. Specifically, McGraw-Hill makes no representation or warranty that the Product is fit for any particular purpose and any implied warranty of merchantability is limited to the sixty day duration of the Limited Warranty covering the physical CD ROM(s) only (and not the software or information) and is otherwise expressly and specifically disclaimed.

This Limited Warranty gives you specific legal rights; you may have others which may vary from state to state. Some states do not allow the exclusion of incidental or consequential damages, or the limitation on how long an implied warranty lasts, so some of the above may not apply to you.

This Agreement constitutes the entire agreement between the parties related to use of the Product. The terms of any purchase order shall have no effect on the terms of this Agreement. Failure of McGraw-Hill to insist at any time on strict compliance with this Agreement shall not constitute a waiver of any rights under this Agreement. This Agreement shall be construed and governed in accordance with the laws of New York. If any provision of this Agreement is held to be contrary to law, that provision will be enforced to the maximum extent permissible and the remaining provisions will remain in force and effect.